Digital Dialogues and Community 2.0

CHANDOS
SOCIAL MEDIA SERIES

Series Editors: Geoff Walton and Woody Evans
(e-mails: g.l.walton@staffs.ac.uk and kdevans@gmail.com)

This series of books is aimed at practitioners and academics involved in using social media in all its forms and in any context. This includes information professionals, academics, librarians and managers, and leaders in business. Social media can enhance services, build communication channels, and create competitive advantage. The impact of these new media and decisions that surround their use in business can no longer be ignored. The delivery of education, privacy issues, logistics, political activism and research rounds out the series' coverage. As a resource to complement the understanding of issues relating to other areas of information science, teaching and related areas, books in this series respond with practical applications. If you would like a full listing of current and forthcoming titles, please visit our website www.chandospublishing.com or email wp@woodheadpublishing.com or telephone +44 (0) 1223 499140.

New authors: we are always pleased to receive ideas for new titles; if you would like to write a book for Chandos in the area of social media, please contact Jonathan Davis, Commissioning Editor, on jonathan.davis@chandospublishing.com or telephone +44 (0) 1993 848726.

Bulk orders: some organisations buy a number of copies of our books. If you are interested in doing this, we would be pleased to discuss a discount. Please email wp@woodheadpublishing.com or telephone +44 (0) 1223 499140.

Digital Dialogues and Community 2.0

After avatars, trolls and puppets

EDITED BY
TARA BRABAZON

Chandos Publishing
Hexagon House
Avenue 4
Station Lane
Witney
Oxford OX28 4BN
UK
Tel: +44 (0) 1993 848726
Email: info@chandospublishing.com
www.chandospublishing.com
www.chandospublishingonline.com

Chandos Publishing is an imprint of Woodhead Publishing Limited

Woodhead Publishing Limited
80 High Street
Sawston
Cambridge CB22 3HJ
UK
Tel: +44 (0) 1223 499140
Fax: +44 (0) 1223 832819
www.woodheadpublishing.com

First published in 2012

ISBN: 978-1-84334-695-1 (print)
ISBN: 978-1-78063-302-2 (online)

British Library Cataloguing-in-Publication Data.
A catalogue record for this book is available from the British Library.

Typeset by Domex, India.

Contents

List of tables and boxes

Tables

Boxes

List of abbreviations

BBS	Bulletin Board System
ccTLD	country code top-level domain
CDVEC	City of Dublin Vocational Education Committee
DRC	Disability Rights Commission
DSLR	Digital single lens reflex camera
EAFP	easier to ask for forgiveness
EDSA	Epifanio de los Santos Avenue
fps	frames per second
GATT	General Agreement on Tariffs and Trade
GB	Grameen Bank
g,d&ra	grin, duck and run away
GPS	global positioning system
gTLD	generic top-level domain
ICANN	Internet Corporation for Assigned Names and Numbers
ICT	information and communications technology
IM	instant messaging
IP	Internet Protocol
ISP	internet service provider
JISC	Joint Information Systems Committee
LGBT	lesbian, gay, bisexual and transgender
MIRAB	migration, remittance, aid and bureaucracy

MMOG	massive multiplayer online game
MMORPG	massive multiplayer online role playing game
MUD	Multi-User Domain, Multi-User Dungeon
NCAM	National Center for Accessible Media
QR	quick response
RIAA	Recording Industry Association of America
SL	Second Life
SMS	short message system
SNS	social networking site
TAME	Teachers Association for Media Education
TLD	top-level domain
TRIPS	Trade-Related Aspects of Intellectual Property Rights
WIPO	World Intellectual Property Organization

About the contributors

Nazlin Bhimani is the Research Support & Special Collections Librarian at the Institute of Education, University of London. Prior to this, Nazlin was the Librarian at Christ's College, Cambridge. She is interested in the information-seeking behaviour of users and has worked on JISC-funded research projects and has talked about the changing role of the information profession at several EU-funded training programmes. Nazlin is also a Fellow of the Higher Education Academy.

Tara Brabazon is a professor, teacher, writer and director of the Popular Culture Collective. She has published ten books including *The University of Google*, *Thinking Popular Culture*, *Tracking the Jack* and *Digital Hemlock*, along with over 150 refereed academic articles in the areas of media literacy, popular cultural studies and creative industries.

Alexander Cameron is a student at the University of Brighton, reading a BA (Hons) in Media Studies. Alex is interested in both advertising and popular culture and is hoping to continue in these areas upon his graduation.

Aziz Douai is an assistant professor of communication at the University of Ontario Institute of Technology, Canada. He received a PhD in Mass Communications from the Pennsylvania State University, Pennsylvania, in addition to a MSc in Advertising from Boston University, Massachusetts. His research interests include social media and social change, new media and activism, cyber-threats, Arab media and democracy, global media and international conflict, among other areas of international communications.

Katie Ellis is a lecturer in Media and Communications at Murdoch University in Western Australia. She is the author of two books on disability and media – *Disabling Diversity: The Social Construction of Disability in 1990s Australian National Cinema* (VDM-Verlag, 2008) and, with Mike Kent, *Disability and New Media* (Routledge, 2010). She is currently working on her third book, *Disability and the Media* (Palgrave), with Gerard Goggin.

Amanda Evans is a Unit Coordinator and Lecturer in Mass Communication at Curtin College, Western Australia. She has published in the areas of media studies, mass communication and cultural studies.

Faracy Grouse holds Bachelor Degrees in History and Anthropology and a Master's Degree in Creative Media. She is currently focusing on film projects and multi-media installations.

Matthew Ingram is a Senior Lecturer in Pharmaceutical Chemistry at the University of Brighton. In addition to scientific commitments he is also a researcher in new technologies and the impact they can have on the wider population.

Mike Kent is a lecturer in the Department of Internet Studies at Curtin University in Western Australia. His recent book, co-authored with Katie Ellis, *Disability and New Media*, was published in December 2010.

Laura Kinsella recently completed an MA in Creative Media at the University of Brighton. She has a background in documentary production and visual ethnography. Laura's key areas of interest lie in the field of media literacy and participatory culture.

Leanne McRae is a lecturer, course coordinator and curriculum designer of media, cultural studies, screen studies and mobility studies, in Perth, Western Australia. She specialises in international education and pursues research in popular cultural studies, creative industries, postwork, and the politics of intimacy.

Venessa Paech is an online community manager, strategist and researcher, interested in closing the collaborative gap between academia and practice in social media. Her work on virtual ethnography has been published in *Nebula* and she is regularly engaged as a lecturer on community technologies and behaviours.

Mick Winter was a member of the pioneering online community, The WELL, at its 1985 inception, and still hosts one of the first public pages on the world wide web. He is a graduate of the University of Brighton's MA Creative Media programme, and a freelance writer living in California.

Introduction: new imaginings

Tara Brabazon

Abstract: Technology redraws the boundaries between connection, consciousness and community. This introduction offers models and theories of community to provide new ways of thinking about how identity is enabled through the read write web.

Key words: community, social media, web 2.0, Benedict Anderson, imagined communities, minorities

> *I guess my question is are we playing to real fear or are we inventing fears ... that don't ultimately address what people are afraid of. Are we dealing with what is real, or what is expedient?*[1]
>
> Jon Stewart

Jon Stewart asks the key question of post-September 11 history. He pushes citizens and scholars to think about our lives and how we negotiate the spaces and places of identity and community.[2] This book takes his question as a propulsive intellectual engine. The pages that follow were forged between two moments of change. In March 2010 – and for the first time – Facebook attracted more visitors than Google.[3] This change in preferences signified a shift from searching to sharing. The second moment revealed another type of transformation. On 26 October 2010, Jon Stewart and Stephen Colbert organised a rally: the Rally to Restore Sanity and/or Fear. It was comedic, light, satirical, ironic and biting. It was also adversarial and operated against another event – the Restoring Honour Rally organised by Glen Beck and run on 28 August 2010. Promoted and fuelled by Fox News, Beck summoned the legacy of Martin Luther King Jr as he spoke from the Lincoln Memorial. But he was no King. He is no leader. Stewart and Colbert – in a potent inversion of the filmic cliché that 'I'm as mad as hell and I'm not going to take this anymore'[4] – decided to walk away from anger, revenge and fear and demand reason, rationality and argument. Their rally attracted nearly a quarter of a million people, four times greater than the attendance at Beck's gathering. While Colbert, Stewart and Beck gained fame on cable channels, it was Stewart and Colbert who used the online environment with greater boldness, insight, savvy and intelligence. Through Twitter, Foursquare and an array of smartphone applications, what began in television and ended in the National Mall gained profile, publicity and success through social media.

Digital Dialogues and Community 2.0: After avatars, trolls and puppets resonates with the consequences of these two moments. The writers in this collection track new modes and models of community and the building of connections, consciousness and social change. This is not a book of prediction, offering dreams, aspirations and a digi-topia. It is not a history of convergent media.[5] Instead, our study investigates how particular platforms, portals and applications hook into daily life and build relationships beyond geographical location or familial links.

It is timely for such a monograph. In August 2001, I published a small academic article entitled 'How Imagined are Virtual Communities?'[6] The date is important. This was a key period of transition between web 1.0 and web 2.0. Cutting through these clichéd descriptions, the piece emerged just as the read write web entered popular cultural currency. At that time, most consumers of websites were not producers. Most online activities were searching, reading and viewing, rather than commenting, writing and uploading. My article sketched provisional theoretical work on how Anderson's landmark monograph could be translated into the burgeoning web environment. I was – and remain – inspired by Benedict Anderson's *Imagined Communities*.[7] It is one of the great academic texts of the twentieth century. Anderson, in reviewing how formerly colonised people 'invented' nations to resist, reclaim and reinvigorate the languages, traditions and histories smashed by the colonisers, summoned the phrase 'imagined communities'. It was brilliant both in its provocation and currency. He showed how arbitrary – yet integral – these imaginings became in initiating and solidifying moments and monuments of resistance and challenge.

Anderson's arguments about language, power and colonisation can be migrated to the next century. Yet caution is still required.[8] Since my article was written, the web has matured. It is television with a cursor. It is a jukebox with a slot to swipe a credit card. It is a shop that delivers. It is a lover that texts commitment. But the web is also part of popular culture, weaving passion with interactivity. It has become embedded in the daily life of millions and added further layers of exclusion and disconnection for the already disempowered. Such exclusions are serious because as technology becomes part of popular culture, it disappears. Through everyday use, the toaster and microwave oven transformed from technology and into kitchen appliances. Similarly, Facebook is no longer a technological application but a community notice-board for the exchange of gossip, jokes and experiences. The exclusion of particular people becomes serious – more serious – when assumptions of connectivity and web literacy permeate. These exclusions are often forgotten when 'promoting' web 2.0.

> Eighty-eight percent of adults under age thirty are online ... The possibilities of using web 2.0 technologies to engage young people are endless, which is one of the reasons they can be so overwhelming. This book is a must-read for any organization, political campaign, or organizer that wants to engage new members, turn out voters, or educate the general public.[9]

The easy connection between 'young people' and 'new media' has consequences. The point is that 'read write web', 'web 2.0' or 'new media' are such disparate and complex phrases that it is detrimental intellectually, socially or economically to reify these platforms and phrases into the interests of a particular age group. Indeed, the book from which this extract is taken – Ben Rigby's *Mobilizing Generation 2.0* – collapses technology into a specific social group. This book does not replicate that strategy. Instead, *Digital Dialogues and Community 2.0* enters the rapidly maturing social media environment and documents the quest – if not the reality – for community. It also notes that alongside every engaged, connected and supportive group are those who are excluded, marginalised, ridiculed or forgotten. The quest for authenticity for some is the layering of injustice for others.

My short article published in 2001 expressed respect for Anderson and it migrated some preliminary configurations of his arguments to the online environment. Since that article was written, the read web has become the read write web, content is generated by users, and corporate media duels with social media. There is fascinating and productive research to be completed in this moment of transformation. Particularly,

I remain interested in the notion of community when it is imagined and imagining, disconnected from physical territory. Further, and building on the popularity of both Facebook and Jon Stewart and Stephen Colbert's rally, I want to know how social media creates political consciousness and how this consciousness manifests into social change both on and offline. Brian Eno offers some insight into the renewed complexity and interest encircling this project.

> I notice that as the Net provides free or cheap versions of things, the 'authentic experience' – the singular experience enjoyed without mediation, becomes more valuable. I notice that more attention is given by creators to the aspects of their work that can't be duplicated. The 'authentic' has replaced the reproducible.[10]

Following from Eno's realisation, the goal is not to segregate digital and analogue spaces and identities, but to look for productive, imaginative and creative relationships between these spheres.

That is the project of this book. New, emerging and established scholars have selected particular slices of social media to probe, test and question the movement between old and new ideas, ideologies and media. Topics vary from disability to Lady Gaga, mobile phones to the management of mobile online communities, individual production to collective consumption. *Digital Dialogues and Community 2.0* neither celebrates nor demonises social networking and the building of online identity and relationships. Instead, the contributors enter digital micro-environments to explore the desires for connection and communication. They explore the quest for authenticity. We activate and migrate Anderson's key debates from the analogue humanities.

However, there is also a considered dialogue with the important monographs from the present, including Sherry Turkle's *Alone Together*.[11] Her assumptions and arguments remain distinct yet relevant to this book. She probes the narcissism of technology and the blockage to human connection by digital communication. While welcoming her research, the scholars in this collection remain interested in social connections and consciousness and how identities can be shared and communities developed. Turkle argues that 'technology redraws the boundaries between intimacy and solitude'.[12] Our task is to explore how technology redraws the boundaries between connection, consciousness and community.

Communication and community

Put more clearly, and summoning one of the fathers of cultural studies, we test Raymond Williams' maxim that 'the process of communication is in fact the process of community'.[13] He suggests that a system of expression builds a group that expresses. We do not assume that community (inevitably) emerges from communication, just as we do not suggest that political change emerges from consciousness. However, the researchers in this collection open new spaces for thinking about language, identity and social connections. The goal is to move beyond Penenberg's somewhat sinister statement that

> these web lurkers, people who know you exclusively through your digital deeds, base their judgments on the ideas and observations you share with the world, the photos and videos you post, the widgets you employ on your personal web spaces, and the words others use to describe you.[14]

Such readings of the digital environment are the start of a study of online identity, not the end point. Reading the surfaces of the screen begins a dialogue. How this information is used and transformed into knowledge is a deeper, more complex and interesting project.

Particular words punctuate this book. Minority is one. Community is another. There are many attempts by empowered and dominant populations to transform 'minorities' into 'communities' and deny particular groups their right to a voice, a view and rights to full citizenship in nations. However, as communication technologies slice through national borders like a knife through butter, the undulating and permeable boundaries of community not only provide comfort and understanding, but fear, confusion and marginality. As Arjun Appadurai realised,

> we now live in a world, articulated differently by states and by media in different national and regional contexts, in which fear often appears to be the source and ground for intensive campaigns of group violence.[15]

Therefore, with so much vitriol, anger and hostility online, the writers in this collection summon a world after avatars, trolls and puppets (or projections, abuse and falsehoods) to assemble a case for innovation, passion, emotion, imagination, intelligence and wit.

From MySpace to OurSpace

These are politically divisive times. Arthur C. Brooks, in the profoundly disturbing book, *The Battle*, describes the debate of our age as split between the socialist, redistributionist minority and the free enterprise-enthused majority with a work ethic pumping through their veins.[16] *Digital Dialogues and Community 2.0* arches beyond extremism and separationist tactics that instil fear, blame and violence. We do not celebrate the Wisdom of Crowds. We do not chastise the electronic mob.[17] Instead, our task is to think about new forms of community, collectivity and communication.

This is not a book about technology. This is a book about identity that recognises Lee Siegel's concerns.

> We shop, play, work, love, search for information, seek to communicate with each other and sometimes with the world online. We spend more time alone than ever before. Yet people are not arguing about the effects of this startling new condition.[18]

The researchers in this collection are not startled by new media or treating engagements with online platforms as a form of 'condition' or illness. We investigate the strengths and problems activated through the quest for authenticity. In other words, during a period of hyper-mediation and multiple veils of screens that would shock Jean Baudrillard, there is a desire for connection. The reason and mechanisms for that connection are the foundation for this book.

Jon Stewart and Stephen Colbert ran a rally to restore sanity. This is a book that continues their impetus and restores the civility to social media, welcoming the strange, complex and ambivalent ideas that emerge when moving beyond abuse, ridicule and anonymous attacks on others. The question is one of consciousness. How do we understand our world beyond individual experience? How do we challenge and transform our common sense into a collective good sense?

This is the third book from the Popular Culture Collective.[19] The organisation and the publications that emerge from it have a particular style and imperative. The writers are active in the communities they write about and deploy research methods that capture that insider status. However, we maintain a desire for intervention and change. The last book from our Collective was titled *The Revolution will not be Downloaded*. While the read write web has expanded since the release of that book in 2008, it is clear that the revolution will also not be uploaded. Our imperative, however, is not only to democratise information – creating an information glut – but to enhance information and media literacy. This is not a book 'about' **You**Tube or **My**Space. Beyond you and me, this is a book about us.

Notes

1. 'The Daily Show featuring Jon Stewart', *Comedy Central*, 12 January 2011.
2. A discussion of the role of 'The Daily Show' in politics and the media is in Theodor Hamm's *The New Blue Media* (New York: New Press, 2008), pp. 155–90. An investigation of pre-Obama programmes is found in Jason Holt's edited collection, *The Daily Show and Philosophy* (Malden: Blackwell, 2007).
3. C. Chen, 'Facebook Got More Visitors than Google Search in 2010 – Yahoo! Finance', *TechNama*, 31 December 2010, *http://www.technama.com/2010/facebook-got-more-visitors-than-google-search-in-2010-yahoo-finance*
4. Network, 'I'm as Mad as Hell', *YouTube*, *http://www.youtube.com/watch?v=dib2-HBsF08*
5. A strong example of this project is Janet Staiger and Sabine Hake's edited collection, *Convergence Media Culture* (New York: Routledge, 2009).
6. T. Brabazon, 'How Imagined Are Virtual Communities?' *Mots Pluriels*, No. 18, August 2001, *http://www.arts.uwa.edu.au/MotsPluriels/MP1801tb2.html*
7. B. Anderson, *Imagined Communities: Reflections on the origin and spread of nationalism* (London: Verso, 2006).
8. I stated that '[m]y paper ... explores the appropriateness of Anderson's argument about the formation of the nation state to the communities triggered and moulded in cyberspace ... While there is a desire to unravel popular metaphors of the web, my project has a distinct imperative: to critique the easy application of *Imagined Communities* to the virtual environment': Brabazon, above note 6.
9. B. Rigby, *Mobilizing Generation 2.0: A practical guide to using web 2.0* (San Francisco: Jossey-Bass, 2008), p. xi.
10. B. Eno, 'What I Notice', in J. Brockman (ed.), *Is the Internet Changing the Way You Think?* (New York: Harper Perennial, 2011), p. 127.
11. S. Turkle, *Alone Together: Why we expect more from technology and less from each other* (New York: Basic Books, 2011).
12. *Ibid.*, p. 11.
13. R. Williams, *The Long Revolution* (London: Penguin 1965), p. 55.
14. A. Peneberg, *Viral Loop: The power of pass-it-on* (London: Hodder & Stoughton, 2009), p. 72.
15. A. Appadurai, *Fear of Small Numbers* (Durham: Duke University Press, 2006), p. 1.

16. A. Brooks, *The Battle: How the fight between free enterprise and big government will shape America's future* (New York: Basic Books, 2010).
17. L. Siegel, *Against the Machine: Being human in the age of the electronic mob* (New York: Random House, 2008).
18. *Ibid.*, p. 7.
19. T. Brabazon (ed.), *Liverpool of the South Seas* (Perth: University of Western Australia Press, 2005), and T. Brabazon (ed.), *The Revolution will not be Downloaded* (Oxford: Chandos, 2008).

Part 1
Communities, Exiles and Resistance

1

The inevitable exile: a missing link in online community discourse

Venessa Paech

Abstract: This chapter develops a new concept: 'the exile'. Within an online community, there is a range of characters and relationships. However, when a former member of the online community continues to return and harass members, a series of strategies is required from community managers to create unity against the chaos. This chapter reveals and assesses those options.

Key words: exile, community management, trolls, identity tourism

As more of us meet, work, shop, play and mate in virtually mediated zones, it follows that we will be concerned with obstacles that block the articulation and performance of these everyday activities. A typological family tree of mischief-makers and deviants has been mapped over decades of electronically mediated interaction between individuals, groups and communities.[1] Principal archetypes identified by scholars, criminologists and users are trolls, spammers, flamers, hackers, identity thieves, groomers, sock puppets, stalkers and pirates. But this bestiary of digital disruptors has a missing link – the community exile – who exists between the boundaries and borders of membership. A unique construct of authentic online community, the exile is empowered by a networked culture of identity recasting, out of touch policy-makers and technologists happy to fill the leadership gap.

Paul Levinson suggests that 'many of us are quick to laud nature as a model for technology. The truth is we prefer our devices to be unnaturally consistent'.[2] We expect the same of our online communities. The corporate world, in particular, would prefer the virtual consumer groups it hosts or supports to emotionally transact with a predictive, low-overhead, simplicity. The reality is that digital enclaves are created, powered and destroyed by messy, bloodied, unpredictable human animals. We cannot live in a world of networked tribes and not encounter warfare and expulsion. There are unmapped fault lines in our digital territories that compel and impugn certain people, spurring aftershocks that disrupt system levels, ebbs and flows. Community manager and author Patrick O'Keefe presents an uncomfortable truth: 'Creepy Banned User Guy (or Girl) is a Part of the Community Administrator's Life'.[3] Community territory is a contested zone, where differences and conflict are inevitable. A successful community is personal, but its consequences are social. They include the making – and monitoring – of exiles across these differences. If a community has form, meaning and context, then it will have lines that can be crossed.

The exile may adopt behaviours of other bad actors. They flame other community members with a vicious agenda. They deliberately post incendiary topics to incite heated responses, then sit back and watch the carnage. They attempt socially engineered hacks to identity and exchange. They stalk the collective. But although they can mimic a troll, sock-puppet or hacker, they are a different meta-type, absent from prevailing hierarchies. The exile is so innately defined by a singular community that revenge or re-entry becomes a consuming obsession.

Day, Farenden and Goss affirm that '[w]hatever social changes have occurred as a result of socio-economic policies, urban development and ICT infrastructure, community remains the building block of society'.[4] This continues to be borne out in the internet 'space', where the ascendancy of social networks is driving a prevailing discourse of relationships, reputation and influence. It is not just rhetoric. Online communities are a formative aspect of social living for many. In studying the vast online youth world of Habbo, Vili Lehdonvirta and Pekka Rasanen found that young people felt as close to their virtual friends as to offline family or peers.[5]

Buried underneath the popular discourse of social media revolution in the daily grind of online community is the hidden discursive of the exiles. They thrive in an environment with limited filters and unlimited lives. Community managers tell researchers that their resistance, often primitive and juvenile, is inexorable:

> Real, hands on community management requires the ruffling of feathers. Not on purpose, not intentionally – but naturally. It's just a fact of life... if no one hates you, you aren't doing everything you can.[6]

Part of belonging is unbelonging. Just as community custodians find themselves the target of users who do not wish to abide by community guidelines, so do those users find their place on a spectrum of 'otherness' To be an effective 'other', one must intimately understand its opposite – the familial.

Place is the thing

The most successful online communities enable a cogent sense of place. Social networks such as Facebook or Twitter may host a collection of smaller communities within their walls, but the platforms themselves are not a community. As online community researcher and designer Lizzie Jackson explains

> Online communities and social networks are very different, the first offers a sense of place, the other is not a place but a kind of group consciousness grown from comments, images, addresses, photos, and appointments to do something or be somewhere (whether real or virtual).[7]

While an online community possesses a group consciousness, a network does not necessarily coalesce around place and purpose. Howard Rheingold invokes the work of urban sociologist Ray Oldenburg to articulate the palpability of place for an online tribe:

> Although the casual conversation that takes place in cafes, beauty shops, pubs and town squares is universally considered to be trivial, idle talk, Oldenburg makes the case that such places are where communities can come into being and continue to hold together. They are the unacknowledged agorae of modern life.[8]

The online community exile is forged and distinguished by his or her one time active participation in community discourse. The rituals, practices and history that comprise this discourse depend on a socio-spatial consistency, the pull of the agorae. As Jan Fernback reminds us, within our cyberspaces '[t]here is a there there'.[9] Rules, conventions, habits, posting histories, avatars and blow ups provide layers of cultural wallpaper for residents of an authentic online community. These exiles are shaped by this motivated relationship to place and space, and they carry it beyond community boundaries when they are expunged. As Tara Brabazon suggests in the introduction to this collection, one way to frame this topology is a nation state model. Benedict Anderson's working theory of the nation as an 'imagined community', at once 'inherently limited and sovereign',[10] has long been a constitutional allegory for the virtual collective. Unified through remote interfaces, these digital citizens may never meet in the flesh. Yet, as Anderson writes, 'in the minds of each lives the image of their communion'.[11] In this fashion, the online community can become a nation state and body politic to citizens who have been exiled by their peers or leaders. Their existences and identities, included in their resistances, are calibrated against this state. Tara Brabazon explains how disembodied community can give rise to delinquent or subterranean expressions:

> When theorising virtual communities from the perspectives of national imaginings, it is clear that these social organisations are on the same discursive bandwidth. Both are disembodied modes of communication. The national body politic, like internet politics, is a metaphoric entity. While cyberspace grafts a keyboard prosthesis to the body, the nation state is a political prosthesis. Both result in deterritorialisation and disorientation. For a dispossessed population, the key is to use guerrilla tactics to create alternative spaces of meaning, memory and identity.[12]

The community body is a dense site for a member stripped of citizenship, a truth illuminated by Jones' early model of online community as a settlement of techno-social artefacts ripe for excavation.[13] While Jones is concerned with the empirical ebb and flow of social currents and stresses through a technical gaze, his invocation of bounded online community as a 'virtual tell' (a cyber-version of the mounds of human settlement debris in the Middle East) reveals the consequences of elective investment over time in a discrete environment. When members of online communities request the removal of all of their content, excavation is required. A post does not stand in isolation. It is nestled in a threaded public. It aggregates to shape status within that public. Even if the author is no longer invested in their content, others are tethered to their layers of meaning. Fellow participants in the discussion, community custodians and silent lurkers all have a social stake in community content. These artefacts of interaction are the bedrock of cyber-settlement and online community; critically constitutive of locatedness.

When asked for examples of the exile experience in her community, a community manager for a prominent youth virtual world described a moment in which disruption transformed into banishment. This community is a fully virtualised, multimedia zone, with mobile avatars, objects and multiple environments for member engagement and transition. There are over 100 million active members and countless bounded sub-communities within this critical mass.

> A member had turned sour and was getting in people's faces, constantly causing trouble. They were doing everything they could to interrupt routine; including harassing individuals, hacking member accounts and deleting rooms of furniture to confuse and distress regulars. Eventually the other members turned on this person and booted him out. They chased him all the way to his personal sites and warned him loudly to stay away from their community. He still comes up in conversation.[14]

We can presume that because this trouble-maker was identifiable to community members and the moderator (they knew his real name and where to find his personal websites), he chose not to evolve a serial pattern of assault after his banishment. However, the qualities of the exile exemplar are evident in this recount. A one time regular, this member shared a meaningful sense of place and locatedness with his peers. When he fractured into dissident behaviours, he went straight for the shared 'jugular,' even going so far as to literally disrupt socio-spatial norms by erasing rooms and the furniture contained therein. This is the virtual equivalent of burning down the house after a catastrophic domestic. The designated zone for conviviality has been forcibly removed and, along with it, shared memories and histories of community life. The actions of this user underscore that anonymity is a key driver in the transformation of the exile to serial pest. If the exile could continue to operate without the threat of discoverability and retaliation, the community manager believes he would have continued his assaults on the community zone.

The drive-by troll does not fuss over the scenery. While they may wish to undermine virtual community conventions and structures, they rarely mind which one. If they succeed with aplomb in a particular community, they may return to that zone for the promise of an easy mark. Whatever their preferred *baitus operandi,* it is considered a given that the more digital territories they cross, the merrier the 'lulz'. Community exiles, with their autochthonous history, understand their prey intimately.

There is no question of 'trolling' an unknown space. The community manager of an Australian online forum explains why the investment in a shared sense of place can lead to a 'sticky' exit strategy:

> Once users bond and are known among their peers – they've often formed an attachment that's hard to break and their status/reputation is not transferable to a new community. The importance of this aspect shouldn't be overlooked when examining the repetitious nature of their returns. Like all long-term or highly engaged members they've invested considerable time and effort into their online persona and they are not willing to 'retreat' and accept defeat by going elsewhere. Couple this with the fact that loyal and engaged members have a heightened sense of ownership pertaining to a community – these serial pests are indignant and refuse to accept that anyone has the power to exclude them.[15]

Once embedded within community boundaries, the exile knows where and how to strike the most resonant blow. This gives them intoxicating power over community members and leaders. The negotiation of that power reveals the online community as a highly political territory, riddled with as many agendas and tensions as offline analogue environments.

Panoptical temptation

When the analogue exile is cast out of his or her community, corporeality makes for conspicuous exclusion. The physical body is no longer present in social situations. Although they have had a flesh and blood relationship with their community, physical banishment robs them of embodied interaction and its visual and tactile social vernacular. The community cannot see, hear or touch the banished. The exile cannot laugh at, hug or punch those left behind. This inability to witness the community's life is the crucial aspect of penalty. Whether sent to another country or locked up behind bars, analogue-exile renders the subject invisible to the community and the community invisible to the subject. For the virtual exile, place persists and remains accessible through the visuality of the screen. When a member is purged from a digital tribe, technical barriers are put in place to prevent him or her from interacting with other members. However the (web)site that houses their online home is still active. The exile can surf there in an instant and witness life proceeding without him or her. Conviviality continues. There may even be discussion about the exile and the circumstances of the expulsion. If the exile believes he has been unjustly removed then it is galling to see the community going about its social business, unpunished, unaffected.

Although registration procedures (such as filling out a form or agreeing to terms of service) are part of a gate-keeping process, community life beyond the gate is often searchable to non-members. When accessibility is viewed as an essential ingredient for community sustainability and the preservation of social memory, our exiles are recast from somatic prisoners to panoptic, 'glocalised' guards. Community members are discarnate characters, mediated by the screens of our new media. The exile, once cast out, is in a sense more powerful than ever. Of course, there is nothing material ('real') preventing the virtual exile from switching off their computer and getting a flesh-bound life. But ask yourself, if you knew you could watch former friends (and enemies) live out their social lives, would you have the discipline to abstain completely? What if you felt you still had a score to settle? We watch (and bristle).

Reincarnation as networked norm

Early narratives of cyberspace were electrically utopic,[16] rendering a *noosphere*[17] the polymorphic properties of which could collapse corporeal constraints, promote camaraderie and help us move beyond the failings of our flesh.[18] The vision echoed Enlightenment ideals with its 'divine hyperpotency, a utopic Cartesian map sketched on a metaphoric "custom-made" canvas'.[19] The promise of rebooting humanity was existential cat-nip. Witness this testimony from programming pioneer Mark Pesce:

> Cyberspace is a mirror that gets held up to the third eye. And the third eye, ajna chakra, is the light that removes illusion. It shows things as they are. And so this removal of boundaries, or refiguring of boundaries, that we're seeing is showing the world perhaps more clearly. I think we're in a powerful state of coming together.[20]

The internet has always possessed a shameless and powerful adolescent energy manifesting in a culture of play, experimentation, resistance and reinvention that seems to perfectly complement the hyper-relativity of post-modernity. Sherry Turkle describes the sometimes 'stringent and chafing' world of identity prior to the plural lifestyling offered by electronically mediated communication:

> In the past such rapid-cycling through different identities was not an easy experience to come by. Earlier in this century we spoke of identity as 'forged'. The metaphor of iron-like solidarity captured the central value of a core identity.[21]

The online community exile leverages the gift of liquid identity to jockey repetitive attacks on the communities that have excluded them. Touching on this network normalcy, Andy Greenwald describes the web as 'the most teenage of media', where recasting the self in 'limitless hypertime' is not only enabled, but virtually mandated.[22] Angela Thomas-Jones' extensive case study of identity and the negotiated relationships by young people in online communities found a pervasive culture of identity iteration and role-playing to forge social competencies and arrive at a desirable self-definition.[23] In her ethnographic work with American teenagers, Danah Boyd encountered a similar result, finding young people attracted to an interactive commons where hierarchies and hegemonic structures of the physical world had limited or no sway. As she explains:

> Most teens I interviewed joined social network sites to interact with friends and peers, often to escape structural and social limitations they faced in other contexts. Many believed that MySpace and Facebook were effectively teen space. In a class assignment about the internet, one teen wrote that teens like the internet because 'it is under our control so we don't have to listen to anyone to tell us what to do or not to do'.[24]

The assumption – if not actuality – of inclusion and exclusion is significant. Moving beyond age and exploring the fascination with racially specific personas and their possibilities, Lisa Nakamura describes the protean capabilities of virtual actualisation as 'identity tourism'. She found that toggling through personality types was sometimes framed as an extreme sport, with a similar promise of freestyle buzz:

> The activity of 'surfing' the internet not only reinforces the idea that cyberspace is not only a place where travel and mobility are featured attractions, but it also figures as a form of travel which is inherently recreational, exotic and exciting, like surfing.[25]

Nakamura also reveals that the popular trope of border warfare in cyberspace – game changing battles over public versus private, creative versus commercial, liberty versus protection from excess or criminality – rarely includes discussion of the pervasive border patrol (and transgression) around identity. She notes that the 'figuration of cyberspace as the most recent representation of the frontier sets the stage for border skirmishes in the realm of cultural representations of the Other'.[26] Nakamura's point is critical in sketching the exile. The identity (re)play and our sense of entitlement to reinvent ourselves and our relations with others is a politically charged act. Diamandaki reminds us that 'by its very nature, *identity is political.* Identity creation is a process of negotiation, definition, and social battle. It involves political recognition, law and discourse, inclusion and exclusion'.[27] The exile composes and performs multifarious identities to warp and weave social boundaries. These personal proxies can help to retain anonymity and mitigate consequences. They are a risk-averse apparatus to recidivistic revenge on oppressors. In a mediascape where personae are reflexive and reputation is canonised by communities, identity can transform into a weapon.

Forgiveness not permission

There is a popular saying, often invoked in the business world: 'It is easier to ask for forgiveness than permission.' It acknowledges that playing by the rules is not always the route to a desired outcome. The motto has even found its way into programmatic lexicon. EAFP (Easier to Ask for Forgiveness than Permission) is a canonical concept used to manage exceptions in Python.[28] The socio-economic history of the internet is littered with prodigious *enfant entrepreneurs* who carry this axiom into boardroom battle. They include three figures who have shaped our modern telecommunications history: Microsoft chairman Bill Gates, Apple CEO Steve Jobs, and Facebook creator Mark Zuckerberg. These geeked up, cashed up warriors have each in turn been labelled *enfant terrible* – uncomfortably bowing to externalised power and hierarchies, compulsive and relentless in agitating transformative opportunity. They and their communities of devotees have been rendered legendary:

> From its beginning, the microcomputer was surrounded by an aura of vulgarity and radicalism that contrasted sharply with the mandarin pretension of the high tech mainstream. This is because so much of the new, smaller-scaled technology was left to be developed outside the corporate citadel by brash, young hackers – especially in California, where the socially divergent types had

> gathered along that strip of the San Francisco peninsula which was coming to be called Silicon Valley.[29]

The rule breaking was not merely at the fringe. It was a carefully calculated culture. Leading players in the computer industry realised that there was power in the PR of punk, presenting oneself as a voluntary exile from mainstream corporate dogma. At a company retreat for Apple Computer in 1983, Steve Jobs announced several 'sayings from Chairman Jobs' designed to inspire and perpetuate a culture of renegadism in his troops. One of those sayings was: 'It's better to be a pirate than join the Navy.'[30] The internet was seen by Jobs and fellow technologists as a boundless *tabula rasa* where risks could be taken with a virtual buffer. The speed of change meant that no one would be looking at mistakes, and if they were, their focus would quickly shift to the next big thing.

This was not a conspiracy, precisely. It was – and is – an incarnation of the economic phenomenon of lock-in, in which proprietary designs entrench consumer behaviours to the extent that alternatives are cost prohibitive or culturally unfathomable. Jaron Lanier identifies the lock-in as partially culpable in a trivialisation of ourselves and our interactions.

> Lock-in removes ideas that do not fit into the winning digital representation scheme, but it also reduces or narrows the ideas it immortalizes, but cutting away the unfathomable penumbra of meaning that distinguishes a word in natural language from a command in a computer program.[31]

Innovation is framed as impossible without risk-taking and resilience. Being first is the only way to win in a dynamic market of networked demand. The memory of the web's creation, and the laws of lock-in, continue to influence our social norms. When Zuckerberg declares the 'era of privacy is over',[32] such a slogan permits a social defence for an online community exile logging on under a proxy and outing private details of community members still active in the space. Digital disruptors and bad actors are locked into the reality of online communities. While few would defend the worst of their actions, most would concur they are a fact of virtual life. Lanier describes it thus:

> Just as the idea of a musical note was formalized and rigidified by MIDI, the idea of drive-by, trollish, pack-switch anonymity is being plucked from the platonic realm and made into immovable eternal architecture by software.[33]

Technology may be forensically neutral, but once deployed into the mess of humanity, it can grease behaviours that become habits. In their seminal research, MacKenzie and Wajcman showed how technological in(ter)ventions like automobiles and architecture are socially forged over time and across cultures.[34] Dutton reminds researchers that the computer industries (the explicit systems and outcomes it yields) are no different. Mapping the intersecting social movements of the internet over time, he offers an 'ecology of games' as a binding concept.[35] This process is at work in the explosive growth and popularity of shared gaming on social networking websites and mobile phones. The application-heavy environments of Facebook and mobile devices have renewed a primal enthusiasm for the 'g,d&ra' impulse (grin, duck and run away).[36] McClard and Anderson explain how the permission to be cheeky foments a social lightness of being.

> On Facebook life is a game. Although participants can open chat windows or belong to special interest groups of a more serious nature, the daily drivers of Facebook exchanges are games and quizzes. As technology mediates more and more of our daily social exchanges, the forms of our interaction change. Gaming – light, breezy and fun interactions with friends near and far – keeps ties alive without being burdensome.[37]

This culture of social gaming can be healthy and pleasurable. As McClard and Anderson argue, it 'keeps ties alive'. But gaming involves boundaries and rules, winners and losers, even in a casual form. Kirman, Linehan and Lawson explore how teasing at these boundaries can create sometimes volatile and disruptive social collisions, particularly in a virtual space where people from different cultures, with different mores and norms, engage.[38] They remind us that it is 'by pushing the boundaries of what can be considered good taste in social games, the mischievous players add serendipitous flavour to what may otherwise be a repetitive experience'.[39] The authors are careful to draw a distinction between in-game misconduct and truly anti-social behaviour or abuse, but point to the inevitability of anti-social play in a gaming eco-system. We should consider too that social gaming does not always mean casual. Players can become passionately invested in the tiny universes they are wielding. One of the most popular social games on Facebook is 'FarmVille', boasting over 80 million users.[40] A player told *The Independent* that 'FarmVille reminds me of the toy farm I had as a child ... We'd make our own buildings out of cardboard and spend our money on the animals'. Another reveals that she 'disapproves of some of her neighbours' approach to agriculture; particularly the factory-style farmers who sacrifice their integrity in favour of easy profits'.[41] What would happen if these virtual farmers had the plug pulled on their enterprise by the game creators, or another player? What if they could still witness the growth of others' farms on Facebook or another portal, but no longer reap what they had sewn with care? FarmVille and its peers could well be gateway drugs for anti-social online actors. When more intimate online connections are rebooted or terminated by virtual landlords, it is naïve to assume a tenant will uproot his or her crops and go quietly. If the gaming and the social are interchangeable, what happens when a player is forced to leave the game?

Looking to deepen my understanding of one of the community exiles I had encountered, I spoke to a psychiatrist. Reviewing that user's posting history and exchanges with other community members, he immediately detected a competitive timbre. 'Chess,' he said. 'This one is playing chess.'[42] The crowning of *enfant terribilism* and the culture of gamed sociability has helped to create a fertile environment for the bad boys (and girls) of online community to act out (of bounds). It is as if the internet itself is a Massive Multiplayer Online Game (MMOG) for the exile whose pathological attachment to their particular community 'game' is urgent and epic.

Culture jammer or parasite?

UK serial streaker, Mark Roberts, describes his disruptive antics as performance art,[43] but his legendary nude runs through sporting events are more akin to culture jamming. Roberts has made a name for himself by stripping down and slotting his naked form into hundreds of sporting events, often with thousands of eyes watching remotely via the media. Roberts' 'work' may well be performance art, but it is also performed resistance – a provocative remonstrance of sporting theatre and the communal rituals that surround it. Transgressing the literal and metaphoric bounds of the field, court or grounds, Roberts upends expectations of social experience and performs a systemic dissidence. Culture jamming has fascinated theorists of media and society for decades. Whether creating fake news stories, planting surreal messages in other people's products or overwriting billboards, jammers are dedicated to remixing and remaking the semiotics of the cultural systems that surround (and often circumscribe) them, treading 'a fine line between petty crime and conceptual art'.[44]

Critically engaged and connected to communities, culture jammers tend to view their engineered interventions as ennobling, guerrilla warfare. The online community exile is a digital culture jammer, 'anti-branding' the pleasures of community experience, obstructing exchanges that deliver value to those who dispatched him or her. They can become preoccupied with the disruption of social harmony and conviviality. An exile I was managing was surveying the community platform and noticed a supportive discussion between a member whose partner was seriously ill and their network of friends within the community. Identifying a chance to 'jam' an intimate social moment, the exile created a proxy account and launched a cruel interruption to the conversation. The daily business of community ground to an uncomfortable halt while members and management mopped up the damage.

For jammers like Roberts, capture is a tantalising prospect: 'The biggest thing with the crowd is to see how many policeman it takes to catch me. It's all about the chase'.[45] The online community exile shares this transgressive thrill. The following is a publicly posted message from one exile I encountered.

> Now the mods have to read each and every post of mine before they zap me. That's awesome. In the past they would simply zap me and wipe the slate clean of my posts, leaving no trace. Now, they zap me and only some of my posts. They leave the ones with the useful information. There are still a dozen up from previously banned handles. Is this place that desperate now that they're allowing me back in partial form!? That might turn me off altogether. I have to admit I enjoy the adversarial relationship we've honed over the last years. This will be zapped, but don't you worry, I'll be back in 2 minutes and 45 seconds (amount of time it takes to register a new handle).[46]

The exile relishes the friction between himself and his punishers. His claims are fallacy, dreamt up to brew contempt toward moderators and cast suspicion on protective figures and systems. Culture jammers disrupt dominant frequencies via popular transmitters. Exiles may hack at the social fabric of their former community to disrupt frequencies of belonging and trust. They may also try to subvert the technological architecture of an online community, thereby disrupting the infrastructure that supports social normalcy. The existence and prevalence of the exile phenomenon challenges utopian notions of virtual communities as an idyll detached from earthbound regressions. Their behaviours, already unsettling to community members and custodians, also disturb the rhetoric of online community and work to 'jam up' our post-millennial, socio-techno fetishism.

As our digital societies replicate eco-systems, with interconnected organic elements and inherent growth and decay, they become vulnerable to viruses and pests that throttle flow and function. The Red Queen Hypothesis, coined by biologist Leigh Van Valen in 1973, can be applied to the online community exile. Inspired by an exchange in Lewis Carroll's *Through the Looking Glass* where the Red Queen tells Alice, '[i]t takes all the running you can do to keep in the same place',[47] the hypothesis suggests that interaction is a more formative factor in driving evolution than environment alone. It argues that the interconnectedness of individuals and groups in nature is integral to the tactical behaviours of those entities, forcing a co-evolutionary symbiosis. An environment with amplified interaction – a bounded virtual community – is fertile ground for this symbiosis. The predator–prey arms race is the Red Queen Hypothesis in action. A predator invades an eco-system and that system evolves its defensive tactics in response to the attack. The predator then adapts its assaultive techniques to accommodate and override the system's latest defences, learning new ways to get at its prey.

The experience of a relentlessly assaultive exile is strikingly similar. If an online community does not capture and track the IP addresses of its registrants, an exile can safely create new identities from the same address. When the community management and technical personnel decide to up their defensive ante and prevent multiple accounts attached to one IP address, the exile will revert to the expansive network of IP proxies on the internet. Community custodians develop a suite of indicators they use to detect the presence of an exile turned serial pest. These include digital fingerprints like preferred email domains and linguistic tells. An exile I had been dealing with for over a year believed he had found a safe free email provider that community management had not yet detected. In truth, his full digital footprint was transparent with every new registration. The choice of email was an indicator, not an inconvenience. Blocking the email would prevent them from entering the site with this mail protocol, protecting other members from harassment. However, blocking also tips the hand of community custodians. The persistence of the resilient exile means they would quickly seek out an unknown alternative.

Meanwhile, staff have lost a valuable indicator of presence that helps swat the user when they return. John Gilmore famously said that '[t]he Net interprets censorship as damage and routes around it'.[48] The community exile turned serial pest interprets blocking as a challenge, and evolves around it. Douglas Rushkoff framed our contemporary media as a planetary level virus, replete with ideological codes and conceptual sequencing that can infect, mutate, vitalise or decay minds, moods and memory.[49] The banned user who persists in covert multi-handling is the active viral agent in the social stew of the macro online community ecosystem. Community management must balance infection and immunisation. They must accommodate indicators of toxicity, but not so many that an exile can irreparably poison the community.

I've got you under my skin

The cultures of our social lives instigate, support or repel our boundaries – be they firm[50] or fuzzy,[51] fixed or fluid.[52] Boundary narratives are what define and sustain a community, while our selves are constructed and bounded by our relations with others.[53] Grafted onto digitally networked containers and commons, our sociability is similarly bounded, policed and negotiated. Foster builds on this idea to demonstrate how online communities are a site of problematic interface between collective and individual socio-cultural impulse: *gemeinschaft* versus *gesellschaft*.[54] Leveraging an 'other' to constitute and define identity is a core sociological and psychological concept. Hegel,[55] Sartre[56] and de Beauvoir[57] are among the thinkers who have interrogated the role of 'the other' in the making of individuals, relationships and societies. Edward Said offered a politically charged investigation of this phenomenon in the context of colonised peoples, exploring Western casting of 'orientalism' in opposition to the qualities and characteristics it saw itself as possessing, or desired to possess.[58] Investigating community participation in South East England, Jewkes and Murcott found people 'constructed "communities" so that they encompass a relational notion of "not" something else'.[59]

The impulse to construe ourselves via imagined boundaries is deep and pervasive. Pioneering psychoanalyst Esther Bick demonstrated the role of our biological skin as a bounding and binding object through her work with infants.[60] This membrane contains our embodied and disembodied attributes (our physical components and our psychological universe) and our experience. Bick believed our relationship with the world is mediated via our skin, which takes on both primal and psychic meaning and function. Our egos are forged and performed via the conduit of this membrane. Without it, our core and imaginative selves are incapable of sustenance or sociability.

> In its most primitive form the parts of the personality are felt to have no binding force amongst themselves and must therefore be held together in a way that is experienced by them passively, by the skin functioning as a boundary. But this internal function of containing the parts of the self is dependent initially on the introjection of an external object, experienced as capable of fulfilling this function. Later, identification with this function of the object supersedes the unintegrated state and gives rise to the fantasy of internal and external spaces.[61]

Cataloguing our configuration of monstrous otherness, Richard Kearney deploys the work of Timothy Beal, who hints at why these shadows are uniquely resilient:

> No matter how many times we demonize, divinize or kill off our monsters, they keep returning for more. Not just Dracula. Not just the Devil. Nor the extraterrestrial of *Alien Resurrection*. All monsters are 'undead'. And maybe they come back because, as Beal suggests, 'they still have something to say or show us about ourselves'.[62]

Understanding the ties that bind prevent them unravelling.

The defining experience of making, implementing and resisting boundaries (and the identities and reputations they implicate) is potent in the disembodied world of cyberspace. Amy Kim explains that the sensorial deprivations of virtuality demand that identity be explicitly demarked and authenticated.[63] In the explicit construction of this identity, we cannot avoid the political. Torres' work with societies of Cuban exiles teaches us that

> social and political identity are closely linked precisely because of the coupling of nation and state – the nation being the soul, culture, history and social structures, and the state serving as regulator of these elements. Political identity is defined and regulated by the state.[64]

As the concept of ourselves gains greater complexity and nuance, our need for reflection and refraction increases. Miranda Mowbray reminds us that '[s]ince ethnicities are social identities, they require social recognition in order to exist'.[65] In this way, the virtual is always real to the user. Turkle assures us that, within our virtual interactions 'the notion of the real fights back. People who live parallel lives on the screen are nevertheless bound by the desires, pain, and mortality of their physical selves'.[66] Steve Jones describes our online personae as 'virtual bodies grounded in selves',[67] a network of aspects inscribing themselves upon environments and circumstances. Summoning William Gibson's iconic cyberpunk novel *Neuromancer*, Agre reminds us that 'Gibson famously defined cyberspace as a space apart from the corporeal world – a hallucination. But the internet is not growing apart from the world – to the contrary is increasingly embedded in it'.[68] Our real selves are embedded in the machine, even as we mask and augment them.

In a study of social networking website MySpace, Sessions discovered that the addition of visuality into online social exchanges, via a profile picture, altered user attitudes toward identity and trust.[69] She observed that 'theories of deception and authenticity are called into question as users are increasingly anchored to their bodies and expected to effortlessly present an online self mirroring the off-line self'.[70] This is important to consider in the context of the online community exile, as we conceive the flesh and blood needs that give way to resistant, even malicious, behaviour. Whether mirror or opposite to their analogue existences, the online lives of exiles tell us something about what online community is (and is not). As Turkle suggests, '[t]echnology is seductive when what it offers meets our human vulnerabilities. And as it turns out, we are very vulnerable indeed'.[71]

Permaban and punish

The exile is constituted when ejected from an established online community space as punishment for his or her transgressions. These transgressions will vary in severity but are likely to be deemed a gross violation of community principles or policies. While governance and enforcement mechanics vary from community to community, account termination, banning and the banishment that follows are usually at the upper end of the disciplinary spectrum. More minor infractions can invite warnings or denial of certain privileges, such as the ability to send private messages to other users, post images or post without prior vetting by a moderator. A ban usually involves the technical blocking of a user's account name and details (such as email and IP address). For some online trouble-makers, a ban is sufficient deterrent. Their return on time and energy invested has been diminished and, if they do return, they will behave. However, when the actor is emotionally invested in the community, a ban is unlikely to dissuade. If he or she has pathologically embedded needs within that community, expulsion (however necessary), may trigger a return and retaliation cycle that lasts indefinitely. It is easier to take away the virtual toy rather than slam the door on the flesh and blood predator.

Yet it is simpler for the virtual actor to sneak back in than the real world outcast to reappear. If a disruptor is ejected from a gathering, repeated attempts at re-entry could be addressed by a call to the police, the possible laying of charges or the imposition of restraining orders. No such regulatory protections exist online for the disruptor whose only 'crime' is malicious, serial annoyance. Instead, the 'Streisand effect' is in play. Coined by technology blogger Mike Masnick in 2005, the term refers to attempts by Barbra Streisand to have an aerial photograph of her home removed from public online collection, citing privacy concerns.[72] The more Streisand attempted to control the circulation of images, the more people learned about the photograph and proactively distributed it. The viral gestation rendered her goal moot, leaving the Streisand effect to be coined in any instance where there is an effort to clamp the flow of information.[73]

The phenomenon proves that siloing actors and content is difficult in a networked culture. However, it risks reification through hive justice and the creation of a conducive environment for the resilient exile, whose defensive (now defendable) response to exclusion is to fight back against 'censorship'. Community custodians form part of the 'totalitarian' clampdown and the exile proliferates, rerouting around community governance. A permaban (internet terminology for a permanent ban) is anything but permanent for an exile.

If reincarnation is a networked norm, then so too is the virtual death or 'frag'[74] that triggers the rebirth. Community moderators are executioners as well as governors, calling 'game over' for members who are addicted to the community experience. The work of Klastrup exposes the different levels of game-world death experiences, including the literalised event and its larger symbolism in-game.[75] Gaming death is a culturally dense occurrence, with implications for players, programmers, designers and spectators. However, despite this complexity, it remains relatively easy to overcome, perpetuating resurrection.

> Fragging and murder in a virtual world differ from murder in real life because the dead can come back to active life. Virtual death is a temporary, albeit complete, interruption of one's virtual experience. The duration of virtual death varies from seconds to rounds of a game to the next log in. In some virtual worlds, death requires creation of a new avatar and possibly acquisition of a new network address.[76]

Klastrup identifies two key issues that impact on the exile experience: virtual death must be a luminal experience to ensure that players are wary of it, and death can make a hero of the dedicated player.[77] When the online community member in exile decides to protest against that banishment, he is banking on the multiple lives the virtual universe affords him.

It is helpful to consider Michel Foucault's interrogation of penal practice here. Foucault invites researchers to consider the social and political power at play in disciplinary relationships and systems. Applying his ideas to an online community paradigm offers a pathway to understanding the virtual dissenter and his or her subsequent expulsion as social acts with real consequence. As Brabazon reminds us, social intercourse of identities within online communities are 'a performance of both digital and analogue power'.[78] Community administrators hold the power to grant or withdraw access to the community space. Each bounded online community is unique and this network of gatekeepers will be different in every instance. Sometimes it may be a single individual. Other times, it may be a small team of professionals, or a large unit of volunteer moderators. Working as a community manager, I have experienced this power. I have the ability to sever individuals from their virtual bodies and disengage them from their self-selected community. In a technically simple move, we terminate an account and ban its owner from re-entry. In this sense, the permaban is a form of public torture: an execution of status and presence that confers the implied imprint of guilt on the virtual body. Foucault describes the social impact of the criminally marked body:

> The body, several times tortured, provides the synthesis of the reality of the deeds and truth of the investigation, of the documents of the case and the statements of the criminal, of the crime and the punishment.[79]

Branded by community members and management (proxy governors and executioners), the exile's attempts to re-enter the community behind their sentencing only 'reiterates the reality' of his or her state. With each new virtual body and return to their heterotopic home, the exiled and their executioners replay the theatre of the original crime. Reincarnations of the exile form part of their federated meta-identity, which has been de-normalised by their transgressions, expulsion and compulsive attempts at regeneration. They signify a socially conferred stigma that sets them apart from other members. They have been fragged, teetering on the brink of divinisation and vilification.

Erving Goffman's work on spoiled identity and stigma resonates here. The remaining community members are 'normals' who perceive the exile as a spoiled abstraction of their 'stable' social selves. Assumptions and discrimination are impossible to avoid as each new bit of exile mischief appears to justify the decision to expel, and conflates Goffman's 'virtual social identity' with 'actual social identity'.[80] Community members have the foundation of a formidable 'other'.

This exiled 'other' is not merely a figure of stigma and disdain. Foucault suggests that an unintended outcome of perpetually (or repetitively) inscribing crime and punishment upon a convict's body is that the tainted form can become a site of social empathy. This effect has a dual manifestation with the online community exile. With each penetration of the community space, the exile becomes more deeply embedded in the genetic memory of the community. Just as each appearance by the exile is an opportunity to overwrite his inscription by defending against the banishment or avenging his persecutors, the repetitious relationship of exile to community (and members) is a chance for the community to recalibrate themselves against the exile. We know that a bounded, cohesive online community experiences life-cycles, and new members drop in at various stages of those cycles. An exile returning to a community over a sufficient period of time will encounter newcomers unfamiliar with his or her history within the space. Having not been personally wronged by the exile, these uninitiated may support a second chance for the residual 'body' of the banished. The romance of the outlaw extends to cyberspace. These exiles can develop allies and fans in absentia, which further entrenches their role in community lore.

Legibility and responsibility

Anonymity is presented as an alchemic event of the internet age. It can be a transformative, disembodied state offering unprecedented freedoms for marginalised and dissenting voices. It can also shelter malicious operators from discovery and consequence. Suler has documented the psychological mechanics of these benign and toxic variations of the online disinhibition effect.[81] Both are evident in bounded online communities, where individuals can safely indulge passions and express opinions that they are discouraged or denied in their offline everyday lives, no matter how hateful or offensive these may be to their virtual peers.

Recognising the challenge of sustaining mature sociability in an environment where identity can warp and weave from the illegible to the immersive, Erickson and Kellogg propose a paradigm of 'social translucence' that many social networks and online communities have adopted.[82] Features such as avatars, presence indicators and visual boundaries aid the emergence of place, the zone where cultural expectations and predictors develop and exert themselves over time. Here Erickson and Kellogg illustrate how a 'translucent' approach can lead the members of an online community to a sense of place:

> Collective awareness of who is present, what people are doing, and the state of those activities, shared artifacts, and a shared understanding of mutual capabilities and constraints, are the basic building blocks of social interaction that will inevitably give rise to convention and shared practices, and thus the emergence of cultural expectations.[83]

However, when place and its social makeup is a motive, mandating interactive 'translucency' via visual indicators and cues does not necessarily offer a solution to the exile problem. Encouraging transparency and personability can deepen the community experience for members, but is unlikely to dissuade an agent dedicated to dissembling that very experience. The visibility and awareness that Erickson and Kellogg commend may give the exile more concrete sticks and stones to throw at the remaining members. In my experience, communities that have moved to introduce greater measures of transparency around identity (such as the addition of personal profile pictures) have found these features and functionalities to be both leveraged by exile elements as a means of creating further chaos, and rejected by other members out of fear that trouble-makers would use any additional personal information (such as physical appearance) against them. Tensions are emerging between those who believe technologically mediated living in public can generate a mature civic sensibility, and those who believe that the transparency of our networked publics make protecting privacy more urgent than ever. These tensions are played out each day on a smaller scale within bounded online communities, whose citizens want and need to share and belong, but are often reminded by interlopers and bad seeds that they inhabit a privacy purgatory.

Social responsibility is a problematic concept in an online environment. The internet is a pervasive and transformative force, with the potential to create lasting social change and improve the lives of global citizens. Yet, despite John Perry Barlow's iconic declaration of cyber independence,[84] the internet is not a single country and lacks unilateral oversight. 'Governed' in practice by corporations, popular discourses of digital responsibility have emphasised the *pas de deux* between commercial interests and personal benefit. What are we content to surrender online to make transacting and interacting less arduous? Other debates about responsibility centre on democratisation of access and the relationship between technology and personal responsibility (exemplified by online gambling, identity theft, bullying and stalking). Intoxicated by our own reflections and unseen bogeymen, we are overlooking the question of online community ethics. How should we handle members who cannot – or *will not* – fit in? It can be challenging to compel people to share the burden of care or rehabilitation for troubled actors in an analogue society. The disinhibitive culture of the internet makes that effort impossible. Charity, benevolence and social justice have flourished across histories and geographies when tethered to ubiquitous institutions or ideologies, such as religion and capitalism. Even the most sizable and densely networked online community exists outside these embodied structures, leaving its members unable, and often unwilling, to help those with problematic personalities to assimilate harmoniously. As Cova, Kozinets and Shankar observe, '[i]n an online environment characterized by low entry and exit barriers, virtual communities lack sufficient means to oblige their members to integrate in the system, and be loyal to it'.[85]

The social contract is awkward to prosecute amidst what N. Katherine Hayles dubs 'flickering connectivities'.[86] This leaves members and exiles to social self-policing. In the case of resilient exiles, each interaction with their virtual familiars helps to (re)constitute their outcast identity and demark sub-groupings of allies, neutrals (collateral membership) and executioners. They are accountable to these boundaries, not to externalised justice apparatus.

Banning and banishment are usually the result of some conflict, and this conflict is part of the emotional topology of a community. Lukasiak's interrogation of the cyclic nature of behavioural warfare within online communities, via René Girard's theories of mimetic conflict,[87] offers a productive lens through which to examine the pathway to social annexing in the virtual world.[88] As Girard confirms,

> [w]hether the violence is physical or verbal, an interval of time passes between each blow. And each blow is delivered in the hope that it will bring the duel or dialogue to an end, constitute the coup de grace or final word. The recipient of the blow is thrown momentarily off balance and needs time to pull himself together, to prepare a suitable reply. During this interval his adversary may well believe that the decisive blow has indeed been struck. Victory – or rather, the act of violence that permits no response – thus oscillates between the combatants, without either managing to lay final claim to it. Only an act of collective expulsion can bring this oscillation to a halt and cast violence outside the community.[89]

Lukasiak believes the communal gaze is integral in the performance of online conflict, suggesting that 'watching' is complicit in the fracture(s) taking place. The inevitable outcome of this conflict cycle is framed as expulsion, but casting out is far from the end of the journey.

Just as stable community members embed their online engagements into everyday practices and patterns, so does the community turncoat require shared ritual. The flowering of identity and narrative in rich, bounded, virtual community is an optimised target for an exile. The actions of a single malicious user can provoke personal and social distress that rapidly permeates the community eco-system, undermining trust and diminishing cooperative achievement. Interconnectedness enables this fallout. A casual troll with limited access to shared secrets and vulnerabilities will not succeed in compromising long-term community wellbeing if ties are robust. Exiles actively perform their otherness, understanding precisely what the monstrous 'other' means for those members. In doing so, they can create maximum social carnage. Community management steps in to expel the user and the content, feeding the exile ego and sense of purpose. Critical community tethers – such as emotional security, affiliation and a familiar symbolic system that lets members comfortably negotiate community expectations and boundaries – all become levers to such actors. When pulled, they can create genuinely distressing consequences for members, who experience their natural order in disarray.

Meanwhile, the toxic user is looking for consistency; he or she seeks validation and attention from the group that once offered exactly that. The reinforcement and need fulfillment identified by McMillan and Chavis in their formative work to define community[90] is still present; however, it has become perverted. The relationship is no longer one of affinity, and the shared value system has collapsed. Believing themselves aggrieved, the serial pest exploits known emotional vulnerabilities and learned culture, using the intelligence he or she has about members to unsettle them and induce a sensation of instability and risk. Barbs from a former cohort engineered to cut as deeply as possible require both delicate counsel and zealous mop-up.

Practitioners I have surveyed described similar observations. Respondents indicated favoured tactics of returning exiles are those that benefit from their knowledge of the community.[91] By far the most common is what I call Big-Brotherism: making other members feel unsafe and unsettled about their everyday interactions. By suggesting, as one of my exiles does, that 'the mods gave me all your personal details,' trust in peers and authority is destabilised. Other popular techniques reported by managers, moderators and members include targeting vulnerable members and the stockpiling of other accounts to enable uninterrupted warfare.

Community is contingent upon interpretation. Its daily business is the transaction of meanings. With each appearance of an exile and his or her recognisable closet of masks, the community itself performs this witness and interpretation. Becoming ritual over time, seeing, outing and reacting to exile antagonism in fact contributes to exile rectivism: a variation of not feeding the troll, more difficult to defend against, as silent witness can be as powerful as engaging in conversation (feeding).

The engagement and witness of the 'other' becomes essential to 'us' and 'them' alike, allowing both parties to feel powerful. Gazing from the 'inside', current members experience theirs as the dominant social narrative. Thumping at the gates, exiles understand that their otherness creates a powerful mystique. They are woven into community myths and, if they choose, can cast a glowering shadow on the cave walls. This power dialectic is defining for exile and tribe. As Nicholson Baker tells it, '[w]hacking trolls is, for some Wikipedia editors, a big part of why they keep coming back'.[92] The power of a shared enemy reaffirms one's sense of belonging and justifies the time, energy and emotion invested in the community to date. Members cluster in solidarity, shelter in shared practices, norms and rituals that the invading iconoclast threatens to diminish.

While the exile may target individual members of the community in his or her actions, it is the presence of an established, cohesive, heterogenic community that has enabled and contextualised their engagements. They implicitly acknowledge community boundaries and semiotic vocabularies by repetitively penetrating, obstructing, unpacking and subverting them. Their psychic and material investment in fusing the community circuit board is not a casual act. It has emerged from their stock in the systems of community. Paradoxically, once ejected, the exiled member may be closer to the community than ever. This dependency is reflected in the gaze of the politically annexed. Writing about Latin American exiles, Sznajder and Roniger observe that

> [o]nce a person is pushed into exile, she or he may lose the entitlements attached to citizenship but, at the same time, he or she may become even more attached than before to what is perceived as the 'national soul'.[93]

Every tool is a weapon if you hold it right[94]

The online community exile, the bad seed of the virtual neighbourhood, wreaks a distinct, disembodied mayhem beyond the privilege of analogue physicality. This social vandalism is inexorably bound to the virtual tribe from which they have been banished. They are not concerned with indiscriminate 'lulz', nor the denigration of a brand or product. Their actions are deliberatively designed to cleave and rupture explicit social tethers within the departed community. To achieve this they may exorcise an endless array of aliases for re-entry and burn up, fire taunting salvos in orbital reach along the external digital footpaths that community members traipse, or construct a rival community. We cannot neutralise them with the same techniques that may apply to the curmudgeons or drive-by pests of a customer tribe. The average guides to managing communities across social media may assist with 'challenging members', but rarely accommodate the exiled member who cannot let go. We should consider them in our playbooks, and should not confuse their existence with failure. Their 'otherness' is *fait accompli*; it is an inevitability of the community organism. Without the community, there would be no relationship to begin with; no exile when tribal governance exerts itself; no desire for return engagement, vengeance or entertainment at the expense of their former peers. Exile and members develop a symbiosis that recalls parasite and host in natural eco-systems. Their intersection is the site of an energising friction that reveals an unwritten politics of the digital age, and it is this we are obliged to de-cloak. This meta-troll is the product of a thriving online community system that delivers them motivation, context and opportunity.

Rather than revealing a structural fatigue or Achilles heel, the contrivance of the exile that will not vanish quietly into the digital night corroborates a vibrant tribalism – precisely the quality that digital evangelists insist is essential and transformative. When creating an authentic micro-society, managers encounter the banished, agitating from the social fringe. For non-exiled residents and guardians of virtual community, policing these actors and their transgressions is becoming an anticipated, defining aspect of community experience. As our social selves move and port across dynamic new channels, the socially annexed will proliferate. Negotiating accepted practices and evolving coping tactics to accommodate exile intrusion will be required to sustain community life cycles over time.

We know the online community exile exists. Testimony from practitioners and personal experiences on the web underscore the validity of their presence and the lucidity of their borderlands. Exiles are part of our human eco-system and any micro-systems we architect or spawn. They can be mitigated and must be accommodated but, critically, they cannot be designed 'out' of community. They reveal a politically charged landscape of online community, rife with complex social theatre and paradoxes of governance. Observation exiles suggest that their repeated attempts to re-enter their former community become ritualised and self-defining. They need the collective to witness their insurgent presence to actualise their social selves. Denying them this witness may remove their disruptive power, but also risks inflaming their anger against their removal and those who instigated it. The exile is sensitive to this witness, like certain breeds of attention-hungry social actors. In outing and unpacking their existence and behaviours, scholars risk this inflammation of ego and antagonism. Future research into our virtual exiles should take the appropriate methodological measures to ensure that open discourse around this important issue does not reward or spur toxic behaviour within communities.

As we homestead into a new century of digital tribes with nuanced social codes, systems, regulations and landlords, we should not ignore our exiles. Theirs is an experience that teaches us about the world we are making and will resist expectations we impose. We should ask who are we leaving behind and what those individuals can – and will – do to prolong their relationship with a community that has excommunicated them. The otherness of the virtual 'undead' is coded into our social DNA, and it matters.

Notes

1. This work includes that from S. Golder and J. Donath, 'Social Roles in Electronic Communities', Association of Internet Researchers (AoIR) Conference 'Internet Research 5.0', 19–22 September 2004, Brighton, England; J. Suler, 'The Bad Boys of Cyberspace: Deviant behavior in online multimedia communities and strategies for managing it', in *The Psychology of Cyberspace* (1997), *http://www-usr.rider.edu/~suler/psycyber/badboys.html*; M. Williams, 'Virtually Criminal: Discourse, deviance and anxiety within virtual communities', *International Review of Law, Computers & Technology*, 14(1), 2000, pp. 95–104; J. Denegri-Knott, 'Sinking the Online "Music Pirates": Foucault, power and deviance on the web', *Journal of Computer Mediated Communication*, 9(4), 2004.
2. P. Levinson, 'Web of Weeds,' *Wired Magazine*, Issue 3.11, November 1995, p. 1, *http://www.wired.com/wired/archive/3.11/levinson.if.html*
3. P. O'Keefe, 'Creepy Banned User Guy (or Girl) is a Part of the Community Administrator's Life', *ManagingCommunities.com*, 29 March 2009, *http://www.managingcommunities.com/2009/03/29/creepy-banned-user-guy-or-girl-is-a-part-of-the-community-administrators-life*
4. P. Day, C. Farenden and H. Goss, 'Maps, Networks and Stories: A Community Profiling Methodology', *Constructing and Sharing Memory: Community informatics, identity and empowerment.* Proceedings of the 3rd Prato International Community Informatics Conference; CIRN, 9–11 October 2006, p. 5.
5. V. Lehdonvirta and P. Rasanen, 'How do Young People Identify with Online and Offline Peer Groups? A comparison between UK, Spain and Japan', *Journal of Youth Studies*, 14(1), February 2011, pp. 91–108.
6. P. O'Keefe, 'Has Anyone Called You Hitler, Stalin or Gestapo? (or How I Know I'm Doing My Job)', *ManagingCommunities.com*, 5 August 2008, *http://www.managingcommunities.com/2008/08/05/has-anyone-called-you-hitler-stalin-or-gestapo-or-how-i-know-im-doing-my-job*
7. L. Jackson, 'Moderation vs. Facilitation,' *Lizzie Jackson.com*, 2007, *http://lizziejackson.com/2007/08/08/moderation-vs-facilitation*
8. H. Rheingold, *The Virtual Community: Homesteading on the electronic frontier* (revised edn), (Cambridge, MA: MIT Press, 2000), p. 9.
9. J. Fernback, 'There is a There There: Notes toward a definition of cybercommunity', in S. Jones (ed.), *Doing Internet Research: Critical issues and methods for examining the net* (London: Sage Publications, 2009), p. 203.
10. B. Anderson, *Imagined Communities: Reflections on the origin and spread of nationalism* (New York: Verso, 1983).
11. *Ibid.*, p. 6.
12. T. Brabazon, 'How Imagined are Virtual Communities?', *Mots Pluriels*, No 18. August 2001, *http://www.arts.uwa.edu.au/MotsPluriels/MP1801tb2.html*
13. Q. Jones, 'Virtual-communities, Virtual Settlements and Cyber-archaeology: A theoretical outline', *Journal of Computer Supported Cooperative Work*, 3(3), December 1997.

14. V. Paech, 'Dark Matters: The inevitability of the online community exile', Dissertation, University of Brighton, 2010, p. 34.
15. Paech, *ibid.*, p. 96.
16. S. Hiltz, *Online Communities: A case study of the office of the future* (Norwood: Ablex Publishing, 1985); H. Rheingold, *The Virtual Community: Homesteading on the electronic frontier* (Reading: MIT Press, 1993); N. Negroponte, *Being Digital* (New York: Knopf, 1995).
17. E. Raymond, 'Homesteading the Noosphere', April 1998, *The Cathedral and the Baazar*, *http://www.catb.org/~esr/writings/cathedral-bazaarhome steading*
18. A. Stone, *The War of Desire and Technology at the Close of the Mechanical Age* (Cambridge, MA: MIT Press, 1996); S. Turkle, *Life on the Screen: Identity in the age of the internet* (New York: Simon & Schuster, 1995); J. Barlow, 'A Declaration of Independence of Cyberspace', 1996, *http://homes.eff.org/~barlow/Declaration-Final.html*
19. B. Ajana, 'Disembodiment and Cyberspace: A phenomenological approach', *Electronic Journal of Sociology*, 7, 2005.
20. M. Pesce, 'Mark Pesce interviewed by Gordy Slack', Center for Theology and the Natural Sciences, 28 October 1997, *http://hyperreal.org/~mpesce/ctnsinterview.html*
21. Turkle, above note 18, p. 179.
22. A. Greenwald, *Nothing Feels Good: Punk rock, teenagers and Emo* (New York: St. Martin's Press, 2003), p. 277.
23. A. Thomas, *Youth Online: Identity and literacy in the digital age* (New York: Peter Lang, 2007).
24. D. Boyd, 'Taken Out of Context, American Teen Sociality in Networked Publics', 2008, p. 290, *http://www.danah.org/papers/TakenOutOfContext.pdf*
25. L. Nakamura, 'Race In/For Cyberspace: Identity tourism and racial passing on the internet', in D. Bell and B. Kennedy (eds), *Cybercultures Reader* (London: Routledge, 2000), pp. 712–20.
26 L. Nakamura, *Cybertypes: Race, ethnicity, and identity on the internet* (London: Routledge, 2002), p. 45.
27. K. Diamandaki, 'Virtual Ethnicity and Digital Diasporas: Identity construction in cyberspace', *Global Media Journal*, 2(2), Spring 2003, *http://lass.calumet.purdue.edu/cca/gmj/OldSiteBackup/SubmittedDocuments/archivedpapers/Spring2003/diamondaki.htm*
28. Python Software Foundation, Python Glossary (last updated March 2011), *http://docs.python.org/glossary.html*
29. T. Roszak, *The Cult of Information: The folklore of computers and the true art of thinking* (New York: Pantheon Books 1986), p. 141.
30. F. Rose, *West of Eden: The end of innocence at Apple Computer* (London: Arrow Books, 1989), p. 56.
31. J. Lanier, *You Are Not a Gadget: A manifesto* (New York: Knopf, 2010), p. 10.
32. M. Kirkpatrick, 'Facebook's Zuckerberg Says the Age of Privacy is Over', 9 January 2010, *Read Write web*, *http://www.readwriteweb.com/archives/facebooks_zuckerberg_says_the_age_of_privacy_is_ov.php*
33. Lanier, above note 31, p. 67.

34. D. MacKenzie and J. Wajcman (eds), *The Social Shaping of Technology* (London: Open University Press, 1985).
35. W. Dutton, 'The Social Informatics of the Internet: An ecology of games', in J. Berleur, M. Numinen and J. Impagliazzo (eds), *Social Informatics: An information society for all? In remembrance of Rob Kling*, IFIP International Federation for Information Processing, vol. 223 (Boston, MA: Springer, 2006), pp. 243–53.
36. UFList, FAQ, UFlist.org, 2001, *http://uflist.org/why/#q47*
37. A. McClard and K. Anderson, 'Focus on Facebook: Who are we anyway?', *Anthropology News*, 2008, p. 10, *http://www.aaanet.org/issues/anthronews/upload/49-3-McClard-and-Anderson-In-Focus.pdf*
38. B. Kirman, C. Linehan and S. Lawson, 'Exploring the Edge of Good Taste: Playful misconduct in social games', in 3rd Vienna Games Conference Future and Reality of Gaming (FROG), 25–27 September 2009, Vienna.
39. *Ibid.*, p. 2.
40. A. Hartley, 'FarmVille now has 80 million Facebook users,' *TechRadar*, 2010, *http://www.techradar.com/news/gaming/farmville-now-has-80-million-facebook-users-671731*
41. T. Walker, 'Welcome to FarmVille: Population 80 million', *The Independent*, 22 February 2010, *http://www.independent.co.uk/life-style/gadgets-and-tech/features/welcome-to-farmville-population-80-million-1906260.html*
42. Paech, above note 14.
43. B. Wheeler, 'Serial Streakers, Uncovered', *Globe and Mail*, 4 July 2009, *http://artoftheprank.com/2009/07/04/jump-the-worlds-greatest-streakers*
44. M. Dery, 'The Merry Pranksters and the Art of the Hoax', *New York Times*, 23 December 1990, *http://www.nytimes.com/1990/12/23/arts/the-merry-pranksters-and-the-art-of-the-hoax.html*
45. Wheeler, above note 43.
46. Paech, above note 14.
47. L. Carroll, *Through the Looking Glass, and What Alice Found There*, 1871 (Milan: Taylor & Francis, 2002), p. 161.
48. P. Elmer-Dewitt, 'First Nation in Cyberspace', *TIME International*, 6 December 1993, No. 49, *http://www.chemie.fu-berlin.de/outerspace/internet-article.html*
49. D. Rushkoff, *Media Virus!* (New York: Ballantine Books, 1996).
50. A. Lareau, *Unequal Childhoods: Class, race, and family life* (Berkeley: University of California Press, 2003).
51. L. Efimova and S. Hendrick, 'In Search for a Virtual Settlement: An exploration of weblog community boundaries', 2005, *https://doc.novay.nl/dsweb/Get/Document-46041/weblog-community-boundaries.pdf*; P. Bartle, 'What is Community? A Sociological Perspective', 2003, *http://www.scn.org/cmp/whatcom.txt*
52. Anderson, above note 10.
53. S.B. Sarason, *The Psychological Sense of Community: Prospects for a community psychology* (San Francisco: Jossey-Bass, 1974); D. McMillan and D. Chavis, 'Sense of Community: A definition and theory', *Journal of Community Psychology*, 14, 1986.

54. D. Foster, 'Community and Identity in the Electronic Village', in David Porter (ed.), *Internet Culture* (New York: Routledge, 1996), p. 3.
55. G. Hegel, *Phenomenology of Spirit*, A. Miller (trans) (Oxford: Clarendon Press, 1807: 1977).
56. J. Sartre, *Being and Nothingness*, H. Barnes (trans) (London: Routledge, 1943: 1996).
57. S. de Beauvoir, *The Second Sex* (New York: Knopf, 1953).
58. E. Said, *Orientalism* (London: Vintage Books, 1978).
59. R. Jewkes and A. Murcott, 'Meanings of Community', *Social Science and Medicine*, 43(4), 1996, pp. 555–63.
60. E. Bick, 'The Experience of the Skin in Early Object Relations', *International Journal of Psycho-Analysis*, 49, 1968, pp. 558–66.
61. *Ibid.*, p. 1.
62. R. Kearney, *Strangers, Gods, and Monsters: Interpreting otherness* (London: Routledge, 2003), p. 34.
63. A. Kim, *Community Building on the Web: Secret strategies for successful online communities* (Boston: Addison-Wesley Longman Publishing Co. Inc., 2000).
64. M. Torres, *In the Land of Mirrors: Cuban exile politics in the United States* (Ann Arbor: University of Michigan Press, 1999), p. 23.
65. M. Mowbray, *Virtual Ethnicities*, 2002, p. 2, *http://www.hpl.hp.com/techreports/2002/HPL-2002-217.pdf*
66. Turkle, above note 18, p. 267.
67. S. Jones, *Virtual Culture: Identity and communication in cybersociety* (London: SAGE, 1997).
68. P. Agre, 'Life after Cyberspace', EASST, 18(3), 1990, p. 3.
69. L. Sessions, 'You Looked Better on MySpace: Deception and identity on web 2.0', *First Monday*, 14(7), 2009, *http://firstmonday.org/htbin/cgiwrap/bin/ojs/index.php/fm/article/view/2539/2242*
70. *Ibid.*, p. 1.
71. S. Turkle, *Alone Together: Why we expect more from technology and less from each other* (New York, Basic Books, 2011), p. 1.
72. M. Masnick, '"Streisand Effect" Snags Effort to Hide Documents, All Things Considered', NPR Podcast, 2008, *http://www.npr.org/templates/story/story.php?storyId=87809195*
73. A. Chakrabortty, 'Brain Food: Internet censorship and the Barbra Streisand effect', *The Guardian*, 20 October 2009, *http://www.guardian.co.uk/uk/2009/oct/20/brain-food-internet-censorship-barbra-streisand*
74. S. Conger, 'Web 2.0, Virtual Worlds and Real Ethical Issues', in P. Candace Deans (ed.), *Social Software and Web 2.0 Technology Trends* (University of Richmond, USA: Idea Group Inc., 2009).
75. L. Klastrup, 'Why Death Matters: Understanding gameworld experience', *Journal of Virtual Reality and Broadcasting*, 4(3), 2007.
76. Conger, above note 74, p. 111.
77. Klastrup, above note 75.
78. Brabazon, above note 12.
79. M. Foucault, *Discipline and Punish: The birth of the prison* (New York: Random House, 1975), p. 47.

80. E. Goffman, *Stigma: Notes on the management of spoiled identity* (New York: Prentice-Hall, 1963).
81. J. Suler, 'The Online Disinhibition Effect' *CyberPsychology and Behavior*, 7, 2004, pp. 321–26.
82. T. Erickson and W. Kellogg, 'Social Translucence: Using minimalist visualizations of social activity to support collective interaction', in A.J. Gersie, D. Benyon, A. Munro and K. Hook (eds), *Designing Information Spaces: The social navigation approach* (London: Springer-Verlag, 2002).
83. *Ibid.*, p. 6.
84. Barlow, above note 18.
85. B. Cova, R. Kozinets and A. Shankar, *Consumer Tribes* (London: Elsevier/ Butterworth-Heinemann, 2007), p. 261.
86. N. Hayles, *My Mother was a Computer: Digital subjects and literary texts* (Chicago: University of Chicago Press, 2005).
87. R. Girard, *Violence and the Sacred,* Patrick Gregory (trans) (Baltimore: Johns Hopkins University Press, 1977).
88. Z. Lukasiak, *Online Conflict in the Light of Mimetic Theory*, 2009, *http://blog.p2pfoundation.net/online-conflict-in-the-light-of-mimetic-theory/2009/11/25*
89. Girard, above note 87, p. 151.
90. McMillan and Chavis, above note 53.
91. Paech, above note 14.
92. N. Baker, 'The Charms of Wikipedia', *New York Review of Books*, 55(4), 2008, *http://www.nybooks.com/articles/21131*
93. M. Sznajder and L. Roniger, *The Politics of Exile in Latin America* (Cambridge: Cambridge University Press, 2009), p. 4.
94. A. DiFranco, 'My IQ', *Puddle Dive*, 1993.

2

Call it hyper activism: politicising the online Arab public sphere and the quest for authenticity and relevance

Aziz Douai

Abstract: There has been much talk, inside and outside universities, about the role of the read write web in either facilitating or creating political resistance, consciousness, activism and social change. This chapter explores the deployment of web 2.0 in Arab societies, and how it transforms information flows between citizens. An under-researched field, the aim is not to offer generalisations, but to study specific examples and nodes of change and challenge.

Key words: Arab Spring, resistance, activism, social media, user-generated culture, participatory culture

This chapter examines the claim that web 2.0 offers a new platform for political dissent and activism in allowing web users to act, react, and effectively construct alternative narratives about political life.[1] Nowhere can such a claim be viewed, monitored and studied than in 'closed' societies where authoritarian governments have heavy-handedly managed the flow of information in the public sphere for generations. The case of Arab societies offers mixed support to those claims, nourishing the hopes of internet evangelicals while interjecting a dose of reality. The user generated and interactive interface of the modern web has facilitated new forms of mediated political dissent, shaking up the strong grip of Arab governments over the information landscape in their societies.[2] Conversely, these web-mediated forms of dissent have often been unable to translate their promise into offline movements capable of shaking up the political status quo.[3] Even in the case of Egypt, substantial research is required to understand the role of Facebook, Twitter and YouTube in assisting, framing or encouraging political change.

Beyond the dualities and the tension created by online promise and offline limitations, the online Arab public sphere increasingly exhibits specific traits, particularly its overtly political nature and alternative spaces for genuine, bottom-up dialogue. In addition, as Nathaniel Poor stipulated in his definition of the online public sphere, those two preceding characteristics facilitate the entry of new members whose 'ideas are judged by their merit, not by the standing of the speaker'.[4] In this chapter, I examine the political and participatory bent of the online Arab public sphere and the creation of a genuine, authentic discursive space.[5]

From blogging to YouTube: politicising the internet

The proliferation and diversity of a politicised blogosphere is one of the tangible ways in which the online Arab public sphere demonstrates its vitality and vibrancy. This vibrant blogosphere privileges discussion of local concerns, featuring issues pertinent to local readers, unlike the pan-Arab discursive space that satellite television has created.[6] Arab bloggers vent their outrage and frustrations about the lack of genuine political reforms and human rights infringements current within their societies. This outrage has not gone unnoticed by the state. According to Reporters without Borders, an alarmingly high number of bloggers are harassed, incarcerated, physically abused and mistreated in Egypt, Bahrain, and Jordan, among other countries in the region.[7] The case of Egyptian blogger Kareem Amer illustrates how serious and threatening Arab governments perceive the power these bloggers have wielded in Arab politics. Arrested in 2006, this blogger was sentenced on 22 February 2007 to three years in prison for 'inciting hatred of Islam' and one year for 'insulting' the Egyptian president.[8]

While activists may have realised that 'the revolution will not be tweeted' – as a sceptical Malcolm Gladwell put it – a politically driven zeal suffuses their use of the internet.[9] The Initiative for an Open Arab internet encapsulates this vision in its introduction:

> The internet in the Arab world has a snowball effect; now that the snowball is rolling, it can no longer be stopped. Getting bigger and stronger, it is bound to crush down all obstacles.[10]

While government censorship figures prominently among the litany of obstacles, these online activists are increasingly joining global networks of activists such as Global Voices Online. They constitute about 40 per cent of the overall digital audience in the Arab world, according to an estimate by Harvard's Berkman Center for Internet and Society.[11] Yet, their influence casts an oversized hue on political discourse. Mostly young and internet savvy, these 'digital natives' – to use Prensky's description – have established transnational networks, such as Mideast Youth, that smartly galvanise global support for the causes of political reform, peace, and religious tolerance in the region.[12] With a multinational volunteer staff, Mideast Youth, for instance, lists among its successful past projects the establishment of the Middle East Interfaith Blogger Network, the Afghan Press (in both English and Dari), and the Free Kareem Campaign – winning accolades and recognition from many international organisations.[13]

The participatory nature of web 2.0, as exemplified by YouTube, fosters the politicisation of the online Arab public sphere. As Green and Burgess argue, YouTube signals a larger societal shift in attitudes toward the structure of authority and power demonstrably evident in how activists and citizens have harnessed this new platform for political dissent.[14] YouTube's video exchange capabilities have made it easy for activists to use videos to name and shame tyrants and human rights predators. A cursory search on YouTube yields plenty of videos showing actual cases of political corruption, police abuse, and other infringements perpetrated by Arab security forces. For instance, in a case that captivated the global community's attention, an unidentified YouTube user posted a video of Egyptian police officers abusing and sodomising a prisoner inside a police station. The secret video gained wide global media coverage, and galvanised an international outcry against human rights violations by the Egyptian police. The Middle East Director for Human Rights Watch publicly rebuked the Egyptian government and called for accountability, demanding that the perpetrators be brought to justice: 'The people responsible for this disgusting crime must face justice. The government should send the message that it won't tolerate torture by police or any other officials.'[15] In countries as far from Egypt as Canada and the United States, this YouTube video was discussed as a flagrant case of Egyptian police brutality.[16] Not coincidentally, its unprecedented reach and influence explain why YouTube has been labelled 'the most blocked website' in the Arab world.

Arab online activists have also been effective in shaming the state apparatus and focusing public and global attention on Morocco. In 2007, for instance, YouTube videos showed gendarme/police officers taking bribes from motorists on Moroccan highways. The 'Targuist Sniper', as the person (or people) who shot and posted the incriminating videos on YouTube, became a web sensation. The videos led to a national discussion about police corruption and bribery among security forces. As a citizen reporter, the 'Targuist Sniper' became a modern Robin Hood to be emulated by other activists in Morocco and elsewhere.[17] In fact, when violence erupted in the aftermath of a police confrontation with demonstrators in a southern Moroccan city in 2008, YouTube videos became the medium of choice for citizens wishing to document police abuse and violent intervention.

Corrupt local political officials have realised that they are not immune from the power of YouTube. A YouTube video led to the downfall of a Moroccan town mayor, and a member of the Islamist Justice and Development Party, after being implicated in a political corruption scandal. The video captured the mayor and a city council treasurer allegedly negotiating a bribe with a local businessman. At the national level, the Islamist party first supported the mayor's denials, then shifted its position and expelled him from the party's ranks. From YouTube, the details of the scandal captivated the Moroccan public's attention.

Perhaps a better measure of success is how these YouTube videos forced traditional mass media outlets to cover and investigate corruption and human rights abuse claims circulating among YouTube videos. Al Jazeera Television devoted hours of programming to debating and investigating political and prisoner abuse and torture in Egyptian jails. Among Moroccan newspapers, the 'Targuist Sniper' became almost a heroic figure, with newspapers following his latest video posts. Moroccan reporters would vie to obtain an interview with him, and then publish it as a cover page story. In these instances, YouTube videos played the role of a taboo breaker, making it possible for traditional mass media to touch on risky topics.

From call-in programs to online comments: participatory culture

The new architecture of web 2.0 is based on user generated content, relying on high levels of interactivity and participation in shaping public opinion online. Less studied is the role that satellite television channels play in offering new spaces for mediated debate through the interactive features of their websites. Some scholars have credited satellite television channels with invigorating the Arab public sphere, publicising political arguments and involving audiences via call-in programs in which viewers share their views and ask questions on the air.[18] Al Jazeera Television and Al Arabiya Television have offered up their web pages as platforms for online public debate. They attract a large number of visitors who vigorously debate political events and news covered by the channels.

Research findings on the nature of online comments illuminate the significant contribution made by users to the online Arab public sphere. In an ethnographic study of the online public debate about the war on Iraq, Al-Saggaf discovered that the comments of Al Arabiya readers provided an alternative narrative that constructed the war on Iraq in a fashion radically different from articles on the Al Arabiya website. Al Arabiya.net is the website of Al Arabiya Television, a Dubai based pan-Arab television news channel and Al Jazeera Television's main competitor in the Arab world. The website receives an estimated 26,000 unique visitors per month, according to web-tracking data.[19] Al-Saggaf observed[20] that interaction and opinionated contributions remained the hallmark features in these comments:

> Debate among readers or respondents was minimal in the Al Arabiya data analyzed in these studies. Views were not rationally criticized or evaluated; rather they were asserted. Two readers do not respond to each other's comments on the same issue more than twice in the present sample.

Yet the diversity and rich range of opinions turn out to be the main strengths that lure readers to the site.[21] These ethnographic studies conclude that Al Arabiya.net provides

> a public space for political discourse that is mediated online. It includes previously excluded individuals such as Arabs abroad and makes it possible for comments posted to it to be judged by their merit, not by the status of those who made them.[22]

Bringing marginalised voices to public debate is a prerequisite to the democratic, participatory public sphere, be it online or offline.

Comments from Arab web surfers on message boards offer further evidence as to how the previously excluded voices can provide counter-narratives to international media. In the aftermath of the 9/11 terrorist attacks, making sense of the role of Islam and its use to justify terrorist acts is a hot and emotional issue in online discussions. While western media may generalise the extremist tendencies and drifts in Arab public opinion, an empirical examination of online discussions regarding the events of 9/11 reveals these generalisations to be deeply flawed and misleading. Some evidence can be gleaned from Abdulla's descriptive content analysis of message boards on three popular Arab portals: Masrawy (*http://www.masrawy.com*), Islam Online (*http://islamonline.net*), and Arabia (*http://www.arabia.com*).[23] Her analysis of hundreds of comments discussing the 9/11 terrorist attacks reveal that a majority of comments perceived the terrorist attacks as political, rather than religious, and clearly opposed such indiscriminate destruction. Indeed, Osama Bin Laden received insults and critical invective. Among the comments Abdulla cites, a male poster's message regarding Al Qaeda's leader represented the sentiments of many: 'By God Bin Laden is the worst terrorist. He is using our great religion to kill people in its name. He is taking people backwards to pre-Islamic times.'[24]

Online responses to recent media controversies support the contention that these readers' comments counter the narratives promoted by traditional mass media. The independent streak of this alternative space that the internet has fostered is evident in another extended analysis of the online Arab public sphere that this author has recently undertaken. The research study examines more than 4,000 online comments on global political events relevant to Muslims. Specifically, the research compares the responses of the online Arab public sphere to Switzerland's ban on the construction of minarets in 2006, and to the tensions in 2010 surrounding a proposed Islamic Center and Mosque two blocks from the site of the 9/11 attacks in New York City. The findings suggest that readers' comments significantly differ between the two websites. While the comments of Al Arabiya readers strongly repudiated the Swiss minaret ban, those of Al Jazeera readers were less outspoken in their opposition to the ban. Conversely, regarding the so-called 'Ground Zero' mosque project, Al Arabiya readers were less outspoken compared to Al Jazeera readers in supporting the planned Islamic Center. Among other things, these findings suggest that there is some self-selection concerning exposure and reaction to political news. Further, some comments related the issues of freedom of religion raised by these issues to the lack of freedom in the Arab world.

The online Arab public sphere's near 'obsession' with the political is materially embedded with attempts by digital natives to carve out a space unconstrained by the power of authoritarian states. They tirelessly lead permanent campaigns to improve the tenor and quality of the political discourse in Arab societies. Their achievements notably include forcing and encouraging mainstream media to engage with politically risky issues. They are also building alliances with global activist communities, similar to the transnational advocacy networks that predate the rise of the internet.[25] For instance, Mideast Youth strategically activated these nodes of the global activist community during its campaign to demand the release of the Egyptian blogger, Kareem Amer. However, as Bennett observes regarding 'networked politics' and global activism, these online political activists must be reminded of their vulnerability to hubris, particularly exaggerating their capability to achieve a radical, immediate transformation of Arab politics.[26]

Notes

1. Similar claims are embedded in works such as H. Rheingold, *Smart Mobs: The next social revolution* (Cambridge, MA: Perseus Books, 2002); H. Jenkins, *Convergence Culture: Where old and new media collide* (New York: New York University Press, 2006); and G. Lovink, *Zero Comments: Blogging and critical internet culture* (London, New York: Routledge, 2008).
2. N. Sakr, *Satellite Realms: Transnational television, globalization and the Middle East* (London: I.B. Tauris & Co Ltd, 2002).
3. For examples, see M. Engler, 'The Limits of Internet Organizing', *Dissent Magazine*, 5 October 2010, retrieved 15 October 2010 from *http://www.dissentmagazine.org/atw.php?id=278*; M. Gladwell, 'Small Change: Why the revolution will not be tweeted', *The New Yorker*, 4 October 2010, *http://www.newyorker.com/reporting/2010/10/04/101004fa_fact_gladwell*
4. N. Poor, 'Mechanisms of an Online Public Sphere: The website slashdot', *Journal of Computer-Mediated Communication*, 10(2), 2005, retrieved 15 April 2010 from *http://jcmc.indiana.edu/vol10/issue2/poor.html*
5. This analysis of the politicisation of the online Arab public was written a few months prior to the so called 'Arab Spring' revolutions and the political turmoil enveloping many countries in the Middle East and North Africa in 2011. Driven by young and technologically savvy crowds, the massive street protests in Egypt, Tunisia, and elsewhere in the region have toppled two authoritarian regimes, and created what may in future be considered the constitution of a wide-ranging Arab democratic movement.
6. A. Douai, 'Offline Politics in the Arab Blogosphere: Trends and prospects in Morocco', in A. Russell and N. Echaibi (eds), *International Blogging: Identity, politics, and networked publics* (New York: Peter Lang, 2009), pp. 133–51.
7. RSF (Reporters without Borders), 'Blogger Abdul-Moneim Mahmud Freed, but Kareem Amer Still Held', 4 June 2007, retrieved 25 October 2010 from *http://en.rsf.org/egypt-blogger-abdul-moneim-mahmud-freed-04-06-2007,21995.html*

8. RSF, 'Detained Human Rights Activists Allege Mistreatment at Opening of Trial', Reporters without Borders Middle East and North Africa Update, 2 November 2010, retrieved 5 November 2010 from *http://en.rsf.org/bahrain-detained-human-rights-activists-02-11-2010,38730.html*
9. Gladwell, above note 3.
10. OpenArabNet, 'About Us', The Initiative for an Open Arab internet, retrieved 5 October 2010 from *http://openarab.net/en/?page_id=2*
11. L. Setrakian, 'The Arab Digital Vanguard: Cyber activists reshaping the Middle East, *ABC News*, 22 September 2010, *http://blogs.abcnews.com/mideastmemo/2010/09/the-arab-digital-vanguard-cyber-activists-remaking-the-middle-east-billion-dollar-bullets-why-americ.html*
12. M. Prensky, 'Digital Natives, Digital Immigrants', *On the Horizon*, 9(5), 2001, 1–2, *http://www.marcprensky.com/writing/Prensky%20-%20Digital%20Natives,%20Digital%20Immigrants%20-%20Part1.pdf*
13. Mideast Youth, 'What We're All About', 2010, *http://www.mideastyouth.com/about-us*
14. J. Burgess and J. Green, *YouTube: Online video and participatory culture* (Cambridge, UK: Polity Press, 2009).
15. Human Rights Watch, 'Egypt: Hold police accountable for torture', 22 December 2006, *http://www.hrw.org/english/docs/2006/12/23/egypt14924.htm*
16. C. Urquhart, 'Why Torture is Routine in Egypt', *The Toronto Star*, 4 March 2007, *http://www.thestar.com/news/article/188036*
17. OpenNetInitiative, 'Policing Content in the Quasi-Public Sphere', *http://opennet.net/sites/opennet.net/files/PolicingContent.pdf*
18. M. Lynch, *Voices of the New Arab Public: Iraq, Al-Jazeera and Middle East politics today* (New York, Columbia University Press, 2006).
19. WebBoar, 'Alarabiya.net', *WebBoar Website Analysis*, *http://www.webboar.com/www/alarabiya.net*
20. Y. Al-Saggaf, 'The Online Public Sphere in the Arab World: The war in Iraq on the Al Arabiya website', *Journal of Computer-Mediated Communication*, 12(1), 2006, p. 328.
21. *Ibid.*
22. *Ibid.*, p. 329.
23. R. Abdulla, 'Islam, Jihad, and Terrorism in Post-9/11 Arabic Discussion Boards', *Journal of Computer-Mediated Communication*, 12(3), 2007, pp. 1063–81.
24. *Ibid.*, p. 1077.
25. M.E. Keck and K. Sikkink, *Activists beyond Borders: Advocacy networks in international politics* (Ithaca and London: Cornell University Press, 1998).
26. W.L. Bennett, 'Communicating Global Activism: Strengths and vulnerabilities of networked politics', *Information, Communication and Society*, 6(2), 2003, pp. 143–68.

3

What's in a name? Digital resources and resistance at the global periphery

Mike Kent

Abstract: Postcolonial theory was transformative of both the humanities and social sciences after the Second World War. However its power and influence is even more startling and unpredictable when applied to 'virtual' geographies and nations. This chapter examines questions of ownership and rights over 'virtual nations' via their domain names. The right to own, buy and sell virtual real estate has proved one of the most challenging and fascinating applications of postcolonial theory in the twenty-first century.

Key words: postcolonialism, colonisation, digital postcolonialism, virtual geography, ccTLDs, domain names

> *Postcolonialism is an inadequate, and at times, a dangerous term. It does suggest that colonial relationships and institutions have been replaced – that colonialism is over.*[1]
>
> Tara Brabazon

Postcolonial theory critiques the structure and processes of colonisation, imperialism, neo-colonialism, neo-imperialism and, indeed, the configuration of the postcolonial. The field of study traces its immediate origins back to the work of Edward Said, and more directly to his book, *Orientalism*, that was first published in 1978.[2] Said's work developed the idea that colonialism was a discourse of domination, as well as a form of military domination.[3]

Postcolonial theory seeks to examine the condition of the colonised and the formerly colonised, the ongoing relationships between the coloniser and the colonised, and the mechanism through which control is maintained and resistance to that control is activated. In this context, the end of the formal control of many former colonial possessions following the Second World War, while significant, did not signal the end of colonial relations and imperial oppression at both the periphery and core respectively. The complex social and economic consequences of former colonial relationships now stretch from the peripheral former colonies through to the households of metropolis Los Angeles, from child labour manufacturing soccer balls in India to imported domestic help in the United States.

Once these postcolonial relationships move online, they are dispersed, fragmented, ambivalent and harder to track. They disconnect from geography, although they are more connected to space and place than would be expected. However, they become intimately linked to virtual geography – how virtual space is named and controlled.

This chapter explores the implications of digital postcolonialism and how formerly colonised countries have sought to renegotiate their digital postcolonial relations. In doing so, it focuses on five case studies, all of which have their origins in the dot com bubble at the turn of the last century. South Africa and New Zealand both wished to reclaim what they viewed as digital property that belonged to the nation from corporations that were able to claim it before the nations were aware of its value. Tuvalu, Moldova and East Timor, in contrast, have made novel use of their respective country code top-level domains (ccTLDs) to both exploit and activate their digital sovereignty. As with most postcolonial relations, the actions and negotiations of participants in these disputes are not clear cut. My research moves along the shadowy contours of digital sovereignty and how this interfaces with its analogue foundations. My goal is to cast a more focused gaze on colonial configurations in the digital realm.

Resistance and the nation state

The modern nation state was founded with the Peace of Westphalia in 1648. This mode of boundary construction was then 'exported' to the rest of the world through European colonial expansion. In this context it became, rather than a political mechanism to prevent religious war, a form of colonial domination. The nation state as a structure, having been determined as static and unchanging by the Peace of Westphalia, once applied to the periphery became transient and fluid. The borders at the periphery were reshaped by the ebb and tide of different actors at the core. Colonial maps were redrawn after wars between European empires, and the absent sovereign was replaced as structures of domination remained in place. The aftermath of the fall of the Ottoman Empire and the Austro-Hungarian Empire remain potent examples of the seemingly transient nature of the nation state at the periphery, despite its inception as an unchanging territory.

The core is reinterpreted at the periphery. The nation state, while installed as a vehicle for the administration of domination from the core, was also subject to reinterpretation at the periphery and became a vehicle for resistance to that domination. Control of the land was vital to the project of (analogue) colonisation. Regaining control of the land and its resources was a central element of the struggle for liberation from colonial control. The people of India were able to use the formation of the nation state as a vehicle for crossing through ethnic and religious lines that might otherwise divide them. While the European empires rapidly retreated following the Second World War, the nation states they had put in place remained, as a residue of their presence as a potentially enabling formation to resistance to those empires' influence.

The nation state as a site of resistance can similarly be activated in negotiating digital postcolonial relations. The internet is often seen as being a global phenomenon that, by transcending the borders that surround the territory of a single nation state, is beyond regulation. While the level to which this is true is continually tested, the internet also generates its own form of digital or virtual territory. While this can take the form of literal virtual worlds such as Second Life and World of Warcraft, digital space is also generated across the internet and world wide web by its addressing system. Each address is uniquely allocated for the whole network; unlike the analogue side of the screen where there might be use of the same name or trade mark in different jurisdictions, the world wide web has only one space for each unique address. Partly as an attempt to mitigate this, the world wide web has a number of top-level domains (TLDs), the most common of which are the familiar generic TLDs (gTLDs) such as .org and .edu. These are designed to signify a particular type of place, such as an organisation or educational institution. A far larger number of TLDs are allocated to particular nation states and their territories as a country code TLDs (ccTLDs), although this has not reduced the perception of the ubiquitous .com as the most valuable of the TLD spaces to occupy.

SouthAfrica.com

In 1995, a Seattle based company, Virtual Countries Inc., registered the internet domain name Southafrica.com, as it did for the domain names of 30 other countries,[4] including Newzealand.com, Russia.com and Korea.com. The latter was later sold to the South Korean government for US$5 million.[5] On 30 October 2000, at the height of the dot com bubble, the South African Department of Communications issued a press release stating its intention to take Virtual Countries to the World Intellectual Property Organization (WIPO), which acts as a domain name dispute body. It was reported that Virtual Countries had asked for between five and ten million dollars to allocate the domain name to the South African government.[6]

In response, Virtual Countries, on 3 November 2000, filed a law suit with a United States District Court in New York claiming that both the Republic of South Africa and the South African Tourist Board should be barred from taking any action to reallocate control of the domain name, and that the court recognise Virtual Countries as the legitimate owner of the domain name. South Africa successfully argued in this case that it was beyond the jurisdiction of the court to make any such judgment, based on the legal immunity enjoyed by the Republic of South Africa as a sovereign nation. The exceptions to this immunity under United States law (as outlined in the Foreign Sovereign Immunities Act 1976) were deemed to be not applicable and the case was thrown out in a ruling on 18 June 2001.[7] South Africa also indicated that it would not pursue the case through WIPO at that stage.[8]

However South Africa then, in 2002, went on to lobby for greater recognition of national and place names under the ICANN dispute resolution procedures through the Second WIPO Internet Domain Name Process. Michael Froomkin, Professor of Law at the University of Miami, commented on the South African submission for changes to the WIPO dispute resolution procedure:[9]

> The South African ambassador, whose nation is involved in litigation in the US over its attempt to hijack the southafrica.com domain from a non-resident company, argued passionately that country names on the internet (by which it turned out she meant mainly .com) are the property – yes, property, just like natural resources! – of the nation and should not be subject to colonialist expropriation by non-resident foreigners. The argument makes

> almost no sense to me, since I think language is our common property, but I could not help but be struck by the passion with which it was delivered.

South Africa argued in its submission to the process that many companies had been able to register domain names associated with different developing nations before those nations were aware of those activities, or how they would later impact on the nation's control over what South Africa views as its national resources.[10] As Matthew Rimmer from the Faculty of Law at the Australian National University notes:[11]

> The Republic of South Africa read the dispute in terms of post-colonialism. The appropriation of identity, place and language remain important matters in the context of developing nations.

While for the South African government this was seen in the context of postcolonial struggle, much of the broader domain name ownership debate is more closely linked to intellectual property laws associated with trade marks. Important transformations occur as an analogue legal foundation is digitised. Off screen, it is possible for more than one holder of a trade mark legally to coexist. Once on the internet, however, there can be only one unique domain name for each of these trade marks to use throughout the ex-nominated designation of the .com. While countries' names do not constitute a trade mark, South Africa argued that its national symbols, including its national domain name, were protected under the Paris Convention of 1883[12] – a treaty that is administered by WIPO and provides for the protection of such symbols, not as trade marks, but to prevent unauthorised exploitation of those symbols. While this argument was not without merit, the treaty, while protecting the official names of countries, does not protect their common name.

The law specifically pertaining to domain name registrations within the United States, and thus applicable to Virtual Countries through the sovereign territory it inhabits, is the Anti Cybersquatting Consumer Protection Act 1999.[13] Once again, this law was designed to support the owners of commercial trade marks, rather than nation states. As with much internet regulation in the United States, this legislation supports the generation of private, as opposed to public capital.[14] While the government of South Africa structured the conflict through the prism of postcolonialism, Virtual Countries took the position that it was a case of 'reverse hijacking', where a more powerful organisation tries to usurp control of a web address from a less powerful, but legitimate owner of that address.

By the end of 2002, the dispute remained unresolved in Virtual Countries' favour. In October 2002 WIPO submitted to ICANN its Report of the Second WIPO Internet Domain Name Process.[15] Amongst the recommendations was that country names be afforded special protection as domain names. These recommendations were adopted at the ICANN board meeting on 15 July 2005.[16] However, the protection was not retrospective and South Africa was not able to gain access to this domain name through this mechanism. Following the unsuccessful appeal by New Zealand to WIPO over Virtual Countries' ownership of Newzealand.com, the South African government began negotiations with Virtual Countries in May 2003,[17] although as at the time of writing the site is controlled by Virtual Countries' successor company, NewMedia Holdings.

Throughout this dispute, both sides sought to maximise their chance of success by choice of jurisdiction and adjudicator in the dispute. Both sought to make the best utilisation of their differing assets and abilities. Greg Paley, the American owner of Virtual Countries, tried to position the dispute in terms of free speech.[18]

> They want to stop free speech. They want to stop a US business from allowing people in SA to congregate on a site and discuss issues close to their hearts in a forum not controlled by them.

This was an interesting position given that Virtual Countries is a commercial site that promotes tourism, rather than a place for political discussion and debate. However, by trying to mask consumption with the pretence of democracy, Virtual Countries was hoping to receive protection under the United States constitutional guarantees of free speech. For its part, the South African government was able to avoid the judgment of the US courts through its sovereign immunity, and instead tried to have the dispute resolved through WIPO where, as a nation state, it had more influence.

NewZealand.com

The context in which these struggles for control of both virtual resources and sovereignty take place is important in determining the outcome.

In 2003, the New Zealand government bought newzealand.com from Virtual Countries for a figure reported to be near NZ$1 million.[19] Prior to this, New Zealand had appealed to WIPO over ownership of the domain name, which had ruled against the country to the point where Queen Elizabeth II, in her capacity as head of state for New Zealand, was found guilty of reverse domain name hijacking.

WIPO found, in a questionnaire response to the Second WIPO Internet Domain Name Process in 2002, that New Zealand law did not 'in any circumstances' preclude the use of country names as part of any special protection for the domain name system.[20] As a result, WIPO ruled that the dispute over newzealand.com had been brought before it in bad faith. However, the government of New Zealand may well have felt aggrieved at this as it had successfully used the same appeal process to gain control of newzealand.biz in October 2002. In this earlier case, the London based company concerned, iSMER – perhaps influenced by sharing the same sovereign in whose name the dispute was brought – had agreed to relinquish the domain name and explicitly acknowledged that it was 'in the wrong' in this case, having registered the name in bad faith.[21] It seems that this type of resolution process is more arbitrary, or is perhaps subject more to the rules based on the jurisdiction of the litigants.

Hrynyshyn notes that different locations within the structure of social power held by different agents will influence their ability to engage in the process of social shaping, the ability to influence decisions and exercise power.[22] The above two examples illustrate how different actors leveraged their relative positions to influence the outcome. Ultimately it seems that nations do not have automatic control of their own 'dot com' domains. While this may be the case, nations and regions are explicitly granted their own exclusive online space as part of the internet addressing system. These ccTLDs place the various actors in quite different positions.

Tuvalu and .tv

The former British colony of Tuvalu was granted independence in 1978. Tuvalu means 'eight standing together' – a reference to the eight traditionally inhabited atolls of the group of nine that make up the nation. It is a small nation (26 sq km), where the highest point rises only five metres above sea level. It is the world's fourth smallest nation by landmass, and one of the most isolated. Among the 50 least developed countries in the world, Tuvalu is situated last in the United Nations Economic Vulnerability Index.[23] There are 832 telephone lines listed in the current telephone directory, along with 20 email addresses.[24] Contact with the outer islands is through radiophone. There is only one internet service provider.

The Tuvalu economy consists primarily of subsistence fishing and farming. The American Central Intelligence Agency lists the islands as having no arable land, and no naturally occurring fresh drinking water. The average income per capita is around US$1,600 for each of the approximately 10,472 inhabitants.[25] Much of the government's income is derived from foreign aid, largely from Australia, New Zealand, the United Kingdom, Japan and South Korea. This is supplemented by the sale of stamps and coins, and from money returned to the Islands by citizens working overseas. There are no known mineral deposits or other significant natural resources on Tuvalu. The economy has been classed as a MIRAB economy, one that is based primarily on 'migration, remittance, aid and bureaucracy'.[26] While there is a Tuvalu currency, the Australian dollar is the most common legal tender in circulation. Rising sea levels as a result of global warming are of sufficient threat that the country's government has been actively courting countries that would be willing to resettle the entire population in the event that the nation is submerged beneath the sea.[27]

By any measure, Tuvalu is at the periphery of the world both economically and spatially.[28] The nation was formerly part of the British Empire as a colony until the late 1970s. Queen Elizabeth II, as the United Kingdom monarch, is still the head of state. The islands were also occupied by United States forces in 1942 as part of the war in the Pacific. Having arguably moved from being a part of the British Empire to the American Empire, Tuvalu has proved to be one of the most innovative states in the way in which it negotiates its relationship with the threats of digital colonisation.

The Tuvalu nation is one of the foremost examples of the nation state serving as a site of resistance to the type of digital colonial exploitation alluded to by South Africa – or, more accurately, being able to take advantage of the changing nature of sovereignty in an increasingly digitised and online world. Access to the internet and telephone system in Tuvalu is severely limited, both by infrastructure and literacy with technology. The rate of penetration of the internet is a low 34.8 per cent, in a region where the average internet penetration is 61.3 per cent.[29]

There is only one website hosted from the country and the one satellite link used for internet communication for the nation has a bandwidth capacity similar to the broadband capacity of a single home in more developed economies.[30]

This does not mean, however, that Tuvalu is without national assets or resources in this area, and the government there has chosen to exploit them more effectively than any other. At the start of the dot com bubble in 1998, the government of Tuvalu leased control of the .tv top level domain to a Canadian company, Information.ca. This was to be for an initial payment of US$50 million and ongoing royalty payments.[31] While this transaction did not progress, Tuvalu did secure a deal with a Californian based company – the .tv Corporation – in 2000. This provided Tuvalu with a one-off payment of US$12.5 million and the promise of guaranteed revenue of US$50 million over the subsequent twelve and a half years, along with a 20 per cent stake in the company.[32] The subsequent collapse of the dot com bubble led to the sale of the company to Verisign in 2002.[33] This resulted in another US$10 million windfall for the Tuvalu government in exchange for the 20 per cent ownership in the previous company. The arrangement with Verisign continues to generate approximately US$2 million annually for the country.[34] The impact of this money on the government was significant. The United States' Central Intelligence Agency estimates the GDP of Tuvalu in 2002 to have been US$14.94 million.[35] It allowed Tuvalu to pay to become a member of the United Nations, pave the capital's main road and install street lighting.[36]

To nominate a sign is to mark it, or render it special. Those in power rarely require special status, legislative rights or lobby groups to defend and define their interests. In such an environment, women, black and gay communities are marked signs, 'othered' by ex-nominated cultural forces. Those commonly seen as unmarked or ex-nominated are colonising, white-dominated citizens and nations, men and heterosexuals. Such semiotic systems also operate digitally. Within the internet, the ubiquitous .com is unmarked. Other domain name suffixes are nominated, first, in terms of position and organisation such as .org, .gov or .edu and, secondly, by where they originate. For example, .au indicates from Australia, .uk from the United Kingdom, and .dz from Algeria. These national suffixes are like flags on ships. They mark a virtual space's country of origin. As Hrynyshyn has noted, these designations are semantic, not technical. Computers do not need them to address data. These designations do not only mark the country of origin; in doing so, they also mark a particular address in relationship to its core-peripheral positioning within the analogue world. However, by their semantic nature, these symbols can also carry other meanings. They have potential value beyond being signifiers of national identity.[37] In Tuvalu's case the .tv represents one of the most easily recognised two letter words in the Latin script.

Tuvalu, formally a colonised nation, has at first sight done something extraordinary. It has transformed itself, or at least its internet domain, from a nominated to an ex-nominated sign, utilising capitalism as the method for revisioning and reclamation. Tuvalu's .tv has been transformed from the marked status of a formally colonised nation state, via American capital, into an ex-nominated sign for a globalised media. Almost a boutique ex-nominated sign, it has moved from a minority to elite signification. While this has also involved ceding its digital sovereignty to that domain, this was a loss of governance that the country could not use. The people of Tuvalu are a long way from crossing the digital divide from periphery to core. They are not in a position to experience the assets that they have sold.

The colonised have to understand the language of the coloniser to enable an effective resistance. This was true for traditional colonisation, but it is doubly true for digital postcolonial relations. The lease of these assets that Tuvalu's citizens could not access can potentially provide resources that one day might enable a level of economic development where this access will be possible. The realisation of these 'resources of sovereignty' is in part because of the nature of the country's 'sovereign territory' on the internet. They are unlike traditional assets of sovereignty, such as a nation's embassy, which actually impinge on the sovereign territories of other nations. Had Tuvalu sold these assets to a hotel chain to create that chain's hotels outside the jurisdiction of the nation in which they reside, it no doubt would have caused some level of resistance within the international community. As no nation states have as yet exercised their own sovereignty over their designated internet domain, the decision of one country to grant a private company exclusive use of this area of its sovereignty has gone largely without comment.[38]

The nation state is significant in negotiating with the interface of digital colonisation and acting as the agency for the activation of resistance to digital colonisation. The traditional paths of resistance to colonisation are transformed by the unique requirements of the digital environment. Whereas, in the traditional colonial struggle, the control of the land and the removal of control from colonising forces are paramount, digital colonisation requires different strategies. Rather than control of land being central, this struggle is centred on access, and rather than trying to expel the centre, access is used to negotiate the colonised away from the periphery towards the digital core.

.md: who represents Moldova?

In 1999, at the ICANN general meeting in Berlin, the government Advisory Council addressed a proposal that would have restricted the rights of nations to assign their ccTLD. This position was supported by a number of large industrialised nations, including the United Kingdom, France and the United States, as well as the Australian delegate who was chairing the meeting. However, it was opposed by representatives of Moldova, a country that in 2000 had only 25,000 people online or 0.6 per cent of the global population.[39] The .md national domain suffix of that country – like .tv – had the potential to be reinscribed and provide a source of national revenue, and on behalf of similar small countries the representatives objected to this potential loss of sovereignty. The representatives were then asked to remove themselves from the discussion. Before they left they argued that ccTLDs should be treated like gTLDs and that the 'wealth should be spread' by allowing countries to enjoy the profit that could be generated by sales of their domains.[40] As word of the proposed restriction and the exclusion of the Moldovan delegation reached the rest of the ICANN delegates, there was enough resistance voiced at the proposal for the item to be removed from the agenda.[41]

While at first glance it seems that this was a straightforward win for the rights of small states against the interest of larger powers, the nature of the Moldovan delegation generates an added complexity to the negotiation. On closer examination, these events illustrate the complex and opaque nature of digital postcolonial relations. Moldova originally had not planned to attend the meeting, citing financial constraints. However, at this time it had just finalised an agreement for the commercial resale of the .md ccTLD to an American company called DNT. At the suggestion of DNT, it had designated the company's two principle operators as its delegates to the ICANN conference. It was one of these, Dana Gallup, who had been the representative at the government Advisory Meeting, and had been asked to leave as a result of not being an accredited official of the Moldovan government[42] and because of a perceived conflict of interest on the issue.[43] While they made the argument for fewer restrictions on national governments over how they chose to exploit their online resources through the use of their ccTLD, it was these very delegates who were actively exploiting this resource.

What's in a domain (name)?

Internet addresses can provide different signifiers at different levels of their domains. Each of these domains is provided with its signified content by separate dialogues. My personal email address is mikekent@iinet.net.au, from the domain name of my internet service provider (ISP) – iinet.net.au. This address can be broken into its component levels. The .au at the end signifies and marks that this address is specifically from Australia.[44] It is signified by the fact that it will have been issued by an Australian organisation, and more than likely represents interests or entities within Australia. In the case of my professional email address, mike.kent@cultware.com, this sign is left deliberately unmarked, indicating on one level that there is no particular national affiliation,[45] and no need for any such affiliation.

The next level of the domain represents the broad type of address that is represented. While initially there were only a few of these designators available – such as .com, .net, .org and .edu – subsequently many more have become available (the .biz from the New Zealand case study being a good example of this new wave).

The next level of the domain name is the proper name of the domain itself, and is determined at the time of registration. The signified nature of this component is closely linked to the law of trade marks off screen. Yet the southafrica.com and newzealand.com examples show that this is clearly removed from the national designations such as .au and .tv. Finally, when the domain is part of an email address, the signifier of an individual before the @ sign is the signified representation of either an individual, such as mike.kent, or a position, such as admin or info.

Wass has noted that different countries adopt different positions on how their ccTLD is utilised.[46] In countries such as the United Kingdom and Australia that embrace the use of the domain to mark national identity, the domain is subdivided with its own general domains – hence an address that can end .com.au or .co.uk. Other countries seek to act as their own general domains. Thus .tv and .md act in the same way as an address with a .com or .org with no sub-national designations in place.

These examples of nation states attempting to project their sovereignty and possessions into the digitised internet environment need to be understood in that new context. Thus, in the case of Tuvalu, the country was able to lease out some of its digitised national territory in the form of the .tv domain name. This domain was specifically set aside for that nation state, and needed Tuvalu to act before it could become active. Within the .au domain of Australia, it is under Australian law that disputes are resolved over ownership and, as such, the domain can be seen to be subject to Australian sovereignty. However, once outside that sovereign territory when New Zealand and South Africa tried to assert their respective national ownership of the unmarked .com domain names, they were no longer within that national territory, and the private company resident under the sovereignty of the United States was found to have the superior position by virtue of having been the first to register these addresses.

These are both examples of different, and rival, digital agents negotiating their relationships with each other. However, there is something that sets the nation state apart as a subset of these rival agents. The two key differences between the nation state and the large corporation are, first, the exercise of the monopoly of legitimate violence by the nation state within its territory (the dominion of the East India company over India notwithstanding), and, secondly, that the nation state comprises a population of citizens who live within this jurisdiction (as opposed to shareholders). Once digitised on the internet, these distinctions become less relevant, as digital citizens are highly independent of their national territory of residence, and violence – legitimate or otherwise – becomes more complicated to exercise. The nation state, however, maintains the residue of the space where it is the dominant political division within the world, and the ability of sovereign nations to influence the digital colonial administration through this residue sets them apart from other competing digital actors in this respect. This is obviously further complicated when nations delegate not only their domain names, but also their political representation to outside agents such as DNT.

Edward Said claimed that '[o]ne of the first tasks of the culture of resistance was to reclaim, rename and reinhabit the land'.[47] In the digital environment, this traditional mode and site of resistance is transformed. Rather than control of the land and a spatial understanding of what separates the coloniser from the colonised, in this new environment the line between the digital citizen and the digital underclass is determined by access. While Tuvalu and other nations in the global periphery have managed to transform their internet signifiers to generate income, this digital space now no longer represents them. Said called on the Oriental to be given its own voice, rather than to be described from a distance by scholars in the west.[48] Tuvalu may well have abandoned its digital voice; however, in the context of a small underdeveloped country in danger of slipping beneath the waves as the world warms, perhaps this, sadly, is the only value that realistically can be gained.

Cautions and conflicts: .tp and Timorese independence

Once a nation's domain name is reinscribed, it loses its affiliation with that nation. The .tv no longer represents Tuvalu's internet space in the way the .nz still does for New Zealand and .za does for South Africa. These ccTLDs can represent different levels of significance for different nations. In 2003, when the Afghanistan ccTLD was reactivated after years of inactivity, the communications minister noted '[f]or Afghanistan, this is like reclaiming part of our sovereignty'.[49]

Traditional resistance to the process of colonisation involved the restoration of history, and integration and community building, to form an independent nation. Within the digital context, this type of resistance is illustrated by individual nation states enacting policies to promote and project their unique culture and language into the digital environment. Prominent examples of this can be seen in France and Canada, which both share a concern for the French language. Particularly in Canada, cultural difference from the United States plays an important role in the shaping of the nation's identity. In some cases it is not just language and culture, but also political conflict that enters this digital environment.

Douglas Rushkoff observed: 'By getting online each culture spreads its own iconography back to the rest of the world.'[50] East Timor had been a colony of Portugal since the sixteenth century. In 1974 this status resulted in it qualifying for a place in the ISO 3166-1 directory of two-letter suffixes for nations and territories as .tp for Timor Portugal. This was a significant event as this was the list from which ccTLDs are drawn. Following the Portuguese revolution that same year, East Timor unilaterally declared its independence in 1975. Later that year Indonesia invaded the newly independent East Timor, leading to a 22-year insurgency against the Indonesian occupation until the country voted for independence in a referendum in 1999. During this occupation, it is estimated that 102,800 people in East Timor were killed by the occupying Indonesian forces from a population of just 1.2 million, with many more displaced and injured.[51] The .tp domain remained unused, as Indonesia did not recognise East Timor as an independent territory. However, in 1997 Martin Maguire – who operated a small internet service provider in Dublin – after consulting with the East Timor's resistance leaders in exile, registered the domain on behalf of East Timor.[52] He registered the domain by giving the name of independence leader, Xanana Gusmao, who was in gaol at the time, and giving his address as that of the Indonesian Military commander in East Timor.

The website, www.freedom.tp, was established and launched in 1998 to correspond with the anniversary of the Santa Cruz massacre.[53] In January 1999 the site was subject to an internet based denial of service attack that shut down the whole ISP.[54] This attack was well coordinated with 18 separate simultaneous attacks from different locations.[55] While Maguire believes it was the work of the Indonesian government, others have cast doubt on the ability of Indonesia to mount such a sophisticated attack.[56] Ultimately those responsible have never been identified.

While the site may not have generated a huge amount of media attention prior to this event, it did subsequently. Maguire received a message soon after the attack from an internet enthusiast in the United States: 'Hi Guys, You've probably been too busy to realise this, but your attack is now the biggest item on the web. You guys are the first internet war!'[57] This event occurred at the start of a period of intense world media attention focused on the East Timorese occupation that eventually led to President Habibie of Indonesia agreeing to a referendum on independence for East Timor, and the bloody activity of the pro-Indonesian militias leading up to that referendum.

How much this act of virtual independence can be linked to the subsequent analogue independence for East Timor is hard to determine with any precision. It is, however, a potent example of the virtual and analogue struggle against colonialism working in tandem. Following independence, Maguire suggested commercialising the use of the domain by marketing .tp as an abbreviation for 'telephone.' However, there was resistance from the East Timorese government who were uncomfortable with the .tp domain's link to the previous colonial occupation by Portugal. The domain is currently being transferred to .tl, standing for Timor Leste.

As Brabazon cautioned at the start of this chapter, postcolonialism does 'suggest that colonial relationships and institutions have been replaced – that colonialism is over'. As these illustrations have shown, postcolonial relationships have leaked into the digital realm. How possession of digital space is negotiated becomes a complex and, at times, contradictory process. The .md domain was eventually reclaimed by the Moldovan government to represent that nation online.[58] Niue, like Tuvalu, actively moved its ccTLD to an ex-nominated status as .nu, which means 'now' in Swedish. The funds generated were used to provide free internet access to everyone on that island.[59] Tuvalu is certainly better off financially and only notionally disadvantaged by selling its domain.

The sale of these virtual assets of sovereignty was able to provide direct, concrete benefit to the communities of both Tuvalu and Niue, although others question the longer term implications and broader questions of social justice that are raised by the sale of these virtual assets. Derek Hrynyshyn cautions that these sales of online identity are driven by global inequalities of wealth. Norway holds territory with the domain suffix .bv, which in Dutch signifies a company (the equivalent of Ltd in English). However, Norway as a wealthy western country has no need or desire to cede its virtual sovereignty.[60] It is unlikely that Australia would give up its .au domain to gold companies or Canada its .ca to California. These countries start with ex-nominated domains by virtue of their wealth and core periphery status and different locations in the structure of social power.

Notes

1. T. Brabazon, *Tracking the Jack: A retracing of the Antipodes* (Sydney: UNSW Press, 2000), p. 47.
2. E. Said, *Orientalism* (London: Routledge & Kegan Paul Ltd, 1978).
3. R.J.C. Young, *Postcolonialism: An historical introduction* (Oxford: Blackwell, 2001), p. 383.
4. 'The Right to Southafrica.com', *Sedo.com*, 13 March 2001, *http://www.sedo.com/links/showhtml.php3?Id=140&language=us*
5. M. Rimmer, 'Virtual Countries: Internet domain names and geographical terms', *Media International Australia Incorporating Culture and Policy.* No. 106, February 2003.
6. 'The Right to Southafrica.com', above note 4.
7. 'US Court Declines Jurisdiction Over Southafrica.com Dispute', *ICANN Watch*, 25 June 2001, *http://www.icannwatch.org/article.pl?sid=01/06/25/092829&mode=thread*
8. L. Harrison, 'US Dotcom Keeps Ownership of SouthAfrica.com', *The Register*, 12 July 2001, *http://www.theregister.co.uk/2001/07/12/us_dotcom_keeps_ownership*

9. Rimmer, above note 5, p. 133.
10. *Ibid.*
11. *Ibid.*, p. 133.
12. Paris Convention for the Protection of Industrial Property, 20 March 1883, *http://www.wipo.int/treaties/en/ip/paris/trtdocs_wo020.html*
13. S.1948, Intellectual Property and Communications Omnibus Reform Act of 1999 (Introduced in the Senate), enacted as P.L. 106-113, 19 November 1999, *http://thomas.loc.gov/cgi-bin/query/z?c106:S.1948*
14. Rimmer, above note 5, p. 127.
15. World Intellectual Property Organization, 'The Recognition of Rights and the Use of Names in the Internet Domain Name System: Report of the Second WIPO Internet Domain Name Process', 3 September 2001, *http://www.wipo.int/amc/en/processes/process2/report/html/report.html*
16. ICANN Board Meeting, Luxembourg Approved Resolutions, *http://www.icann.org/minutes/resolutions-15jul05.htm#p2*
17. S. Whitford, 'SA Negotiates for Southafrica.com', *IT Web: The Technology News Site*, 6 May 2003, *http://www.itweb.co.za/sections/internet/2003/0305061036.asp?O=S&cirestriction=southafrica.com*
18. P. de Wit, 'Government wants Southafrica.com', 1 August 2001, *http://www.itweb.co.za*, as cited in Rimmer, above note 5, p. 127.
19. 'SouthAfrica.com Petition Launched', *Demys News Service*, 28 May 2003, *http://www.demys.net/news/2003/05/28_za.htm* (last accessed in 2005).
20. 'HM The Queen Found Guilty of Reverse Domain Name Hijacking', *Demys News Service*, 20 December 2002, *http://www.demys.net/news/2002/12/02_dec_20_queen.htm* (last accessed in 2005).
21. 'HM The Queen Wins Domain Name Dispute', *Demys News Service*, 8 October 2002, *http://www.demys.net/news/2002/10/02_oct_08_zealand.htm* (last accessed in 2005).
22. D. Hrynyshyn, 'Globalization, Nationality and Commodification: The politics of the social construction of the internet', *New Media & Society*, 10(5), 2008, pp. 751–70.
23. B.C. Parks and R.J. Timmons, 'Globalization, Vulnerability to Climate Change and Perceived Injustice', *Society and Natural Resources*, 19(4), April 2006, pp. 337–55.
24. Tuvalu Telephone Directory, *http://www.tuvaluislands.com/telecom/telecom-index.htm*
25. World Fact Book, Central Intelligence Agency, 2011, *https://www.cia.gov/library/publications/the-world-factbook/geos/tv.html*
26. S. Boland and B. Dollery, 'The Value of Sovereignty-Conferred Rights in MIRAB Economies: The case of Tuvalu', Working Paper Series in Economics No. 2005-9, University of New England, School of Economics, 2005, *http://www.une.edu.au/bepp/working-papers/economics/1999-2007/econ-2005-9.pdf*
27. Parks and Timmons, above note 23.
28. In digital discourse, Tuvalu, like much of the Pacific, is spoken about, not too. See T. Wesley-Smith, 'Net Gains? Pacific Studies in Cyberspace', *The Contemporary Pacific*, 15(1), Spring 2003, *http://muse.jhu.edu/journals/contemporary_pacific/v015/15.1wesley-smith.html*

29. Internet World Stats, September 2010, *http://www.internetworldstats.com/stats6.htm#oceania*
30. L.R. Duffield, M.D. Hayes and A. Watson, 'Media and Communications Capacities in the Pacific Region', *eJournalist*, 8(1), 2008, pp. 21–34, *http://ejournalist.com.au/v8n1/Duffield.pdf*
31. Boland and Dollery, above note 26.
32. *Ibid.*
33. M. Kane, 'VeriSign buys .tv web domain', *CNET News*, 7 January 2002, *http://news.cnet.com/VeriSign-buys-.tv-web-domain/2100-1023_3-802156.html*
34. Duffield, Hayes and Watson, above note 30.
35. World Fact Book, above note 25.
36. C.H. Hanley 'Two Little Letters Bring Riches, and Questions, to Tiny, Trusting Nations', *AP Worldstream*, 7 April 2004.
37. Hrynyshyn, above note 22.
38. Tuvalu has, in the past, made a point of 'renting' different aspects of its sovereignty including its fishing rights, telephone codes, passports, and sales of stamps and coins: Boland and Dollery, above note 26.
39. Internet World Stats: Usage and population statistics, *http://www.internetworldstats.com/euro/md.htm*
40. ICANN, Minutes of Government Advisory Council Meeting, 25 May 1999, *https://gacweb.icann.org/download/attachments/1540204/GAC_02_Berlin_Communique.pdf?version=1&modificationDate=1312231401000*
41. D.M. Gallup, 'Moldova's .MD: The little domain that roared', in E.S. Wass (ed.), *Addressing the World: National identity and country code domain names* (Latham, MD: Rowman and Littlefield, 2003), pp. 120–36.
42. ICANN, above note 40.
43. Gallup, above note 41.
44. .au has been available since March 1986, having been allocated to Robert Elz of Melbourne University to manage soon after the domain name system was implemented.
45. Although this default affiliation is often seen as coming from the US, for whom the marking of .us is virtually never used having only been released to the general public in 2002, until that time it was reserved for non-federal governments in the US and educational institutions offering less than four-year university degrees. P.E. Steinberg and S.D. McDowell, 'Mutiny on the Bandwidth: The semiotics of statehood in the internet domain name registries of Pitcairn and Niue', *New Media & Society*, 5(1), March 2003.
46. E.S. Wass, 'Conclusion: Only time will tell', in Wass (ed.), above note 41, pp. 147–50.
47. E. Said, *Culture and Imperialism* (London: Chatto & Windus, 1993).
48. Said, above note 2.
49. Wass, above note 46.
50. D. Rushkoff, 'Americaphobia and the Engineered Fear of Progress', paper presented at the Conference on the Internet and Society, Harvard University, 28–31 May 1996.

51. P. Hainsworth, 'Reconstruction in East Timor', *Political Insight*, 1(3), December 2010, 96–97, *http://onlinelibrary.wiley.com/doi/10.1111/j.2041-9066.2010.00041.x/full*
52. S. Taggart 'Irish Eyes Smile on Dot-TP', *Wired Magazine*, 8 March 2002, *http://www.wired.com/politics/law/news/2002/03/50659*
53. M. Maguire, 'East Timor's .tp', in Wass (ed.), above note 41, pp. 17–30.
54. C. Nuttall, 'Virtual Country "nuked" on Net', *BBC News*, 26 January 1999, *http://news.bbc.co.uk/2/hi/science/nature/263169.stm*
55. *Ibid.*
56. Taggart, above note 52.
57. Maguire, above note 53.
58. Gallup, above note 41.
59. R. St. Clair, 'Niue's .nu: Providing a free internet to an isolated nation', in Wass (ed.), above note 41, pp. 77–86.
60. Hrynyshyn, above note 22.

4

I have seen the future, and it rings

Mick Winter

Abstract: This chapter investigates the mobile phone as a mobile computing service that is ideal and appropriate for developing nations. The potential of the smartphone for commerce and social connectivity is emerging with startling opportunities for women and disempowered communities.

Key words: mobility, mobile phone, mobile computing, e-commerce, QR codes, Google Goggles

I have seen the future, and it rings.

As a matter of fact, the damn thing won't stop ringing.

The most important media communication tool of the future is in the hands of the idiot at the next table who is shouting while you are trying to read the newspaper. This disruptive use of technology is (sadly) our present. Will the future be any better, or will this pattern of disruption, abuse and sonic invasion continue?

Your coffee shop neighbour is particularly annoying because of what researchers at Cornell University are referring to as 'halfalogues'.[1]

> Why are people more irritated by nearby cell-phone conversations than by conversations between two people who are physically present? Overhearing someone on a cell phone means hearing only half of a conversation – a 'halfalogue.' We show that merely overhearing a halfalogue results in decreased performance on cognitive tasks designed to reflect the attentional demands of daily activities ... This may be because the content of a halfalogue is less predictable than both sides of a conversation ... Less predictable speech results in more distraction for a listener engaged in other tasks.[2]

Despite frequent annoyances, few people are ready to forsake their mobile phones. Currently there are approximately 6.8 billion human inhabitants of this planet, and it was estimated that they would collectively have owned more than 5 billion mobile telephones by the end of 2010.[3] There are currently only 1.3 billion personal computers worldwide.[4] Therefore, in moving beyond avatars, trolls and puppets, mobile phones are an integral part of the story.

In developing countries the mobile phone is, and will remain, the only computing device that the vast majority of the people will ever own. According to an UNCTAD report in 2010, use of mobile phones in the Least Developed Countries went from two mobile subscriptions per 100 people in 2003 to 25 per 100 in 2009.[5] In one striking example the country of Bhutan went from zero mobile subscriptions per 100 people to 50 subscriptions per 100 people in just six years.[6]

It is not only in developing countries that mobile phone usage is dramatically increasing. In fully industrialised countries, mobile phone usage is also rising, particularly when compared to the percentage of people using landlines. In the developed world, there are *more* than 100 mobile subscriptions per 100 people.[7] Worldwide, over the period 2007 to 2009, the number of mobile cellular subscriptions increased by 1.9 billion while the number of fixed telephone lines decreased by 57 million.[8]

Mobile phones are also likely to be the primary real-time news source for much of the global population. Ninety per cent of the world's population is now covered by a mobile cellular network, and in China and India more than 90 per cent of villages are now connected through mobile.[9] Although radios are common and televisions increasingly so, mobile phones are bidirectional and can provide not only news and information selected by the user, but location-targeted news and information as well. Smart mobile phones possess a number of features that make them flexible, diverse and resilient suppliers of content. Their satellite based global positioning system (GPS) allows the phone to 'know' where it is at all times. The phone can tell its owner how to navigate between locations, notify the presence of friends in the immediate area, inform the owner about sales at geoproximate stores or of restaurants in which he or she might be interested, warn of possible high-crime activities in the area, take photographs for analysis by programs such as Google Goggles,[10] and scan posted QR (Quick Response) codes for information that is relevant to the current location.

In communities confronting economic challenges, there may be only one or two mobile phones per village, but they are used by many people. In Uganda, for example, friends will combine to buy shared airtime, independently operated phone kiosks allow people to pay by call, and 'step messaging' involves phone messages being delivered the 'last mile' by foot.[11] In fact, being the village 'phone lady' in Bangladesh and several African countries has created a dramatically increased income for women, and in turn increased economic possibilities for all members of their village.[12] In Gambia, former street beggars, many blind or legless, are now working as sales representatives for one of the country's largest mobile phone carriers. The people, who had already staked out good 'sales' locations for contact with tourists when begging, now have renewed dignity, much greater safety (assured by the police after being prodded by the mobile phone carrier) and an income higher than the national average.[13]

Mobile phones and social change

Mobile phones, used by nearly five billion people, are transformative. Some change is unintentional. Other shifts and movements are intended. As Twitter co-founder Biz Stone has stated, '[h]umanity is the agent of change, and we're here to foster it'.[14] Some examples of change are quite dramatic, such as those connected with political or social upheaval and natural disasters. There are some key moments to track when considering the relationship between mobility and telephony.

Iran – 1979 Islamic Revolution

Prior to the current use of mobile phones, one of the earliest examples of using electronic mobile devices for change was in 1979 in Iran. Audio cassette tapes smuggled into Iran carried the sermons of the Ayatollah Ruhollah Khomeini, who was in exile in France and Iraq. These cassettes were listened to in the home or via portable Walkman-style players. The recordings helped to support the revolution in which Iranians overthrew the government of Shah Mohammad Reza Pahlavi, who had ruled since 1941.[15]

Philippines – People Power II

In the Philippines, during 2001, the trial to impeach President Joseph Estrada for corruption was set back by an 11:10 vote of the Senate which disallowed evidence of corruption on the part of Estrada.[16] Citizens and the opposition were incensed. Within minutes of the Senate's dismissal of the evidence, text messages went out to people throughout Manila – a typical one being 'Go 2 EDSA. Wear black.'[17] Hundreds of thousands of people wearing black showed up at Epifanio de los Santos Avenue (EDSA). It was the site of the shrine where praying nuns faced down tanks during the 1986 revolution – the *first* People Power movement that forced the removal of Ferdinand Marcos as president. Eighty-eight hours after the Senate vote, Estrada left the palace and Vice-President Gloria Macapagal-Arroyo assumed office as President of the Philippines.

Spain – 2004 election

In 2004, President Jose Maria Aznar blamed Basque separatists for the Madrid train bombings. Citizens who were convinced that those responsible were actually Al Qaeda sent out the text 'Who did it?' to notify people about anti-government rallies on the day prior to the election. Aznar's party lost.[18]

United States – World Trade Organization protest

The 1999 protest against the World Trade Organization's (WTO) conference in Seattle has been called by communications professor, William Briggs, 'the first wired mass demonstration'.[19] Briggs, in his article, stated that

> the internet and e-mail allowed small groups to coordinate a mass protest, not just in Seattle but across the U.S. and in other countries. Cell phones and pagers helped organizers move demonstrators, block streets and coordinate protests. Video cameras and digital cameras documented police tactics and streamed the pictures onto the web and to the world.[20]

The use of this digital activism was so effective that the next WTO conference in 2001 was held in Qatar, in the knowledge that its location far from the United States and Europe would keep the number of protestors to a minimum.

United States – sex information

In San Francisco, the Department of Public Health created SexInfoSF.org to provide young people with sex information via their mobile phones. For example: 'Txt "sexinfo" to 61827', 'Txt "5" for STD info', 'Txt "1" if ur condom broke', 'Txt "5" if s/he's cheating on u', 'Txt "6" if ur not sure u want 2 have sex'.[21] In the first 25 weeks the service received more than 4,500 inquiries of which 2,500 led to further information and referrals. The campaign was modelled after a similar program in the UK, and has since been replicated in Washington, DC.[22]

Haiti – 2010 earthquake

The digital reaction to the earthquake demonstrates an effort to deal with a social change caused by nature. Within an hour after the disastrous magnitude 7 earthquake in Port-au-Prince, Haiti on 13 January 2010, the non-profit Yéle Haiti, founded by Haitian hip-hop singer Wyclef Jean, was receiving $5 donations via text messaging.[23] The American Red Cross (supported by the US State Department) followed shortly afterwards, and was quickly receiving $10 contributions through the same method.[24] Mobile phone owners would text the word 'Haiti' to an SMS address, and the money donated would be added to their phone bill.[25] Facebook and Twitter messages circulated throughout the US, notifying people of the donation procedure.

The results were dramatic: 'Within 48 hours the Red Cross had received $5 million in donations through mobile texting.'[26] Several hours after the disaster, before and after photographs of the destruction could be seen on the web, thanks to satellite images and Google Earth.[27] This enabled the world – and particularly relief workers and rescue teams – to see exactly where the worst destroyed areas were located in the city. Real-time news about Haiti continued to be circulated throughout the internet, with text messaging from people on the ground in Haiti being recirculated across the net.

Power and telephone landlines were down throughout the country, but many mobile phone towers remained functional enabling Haitians, foreigners and arriving support teams to provide real-time eyewitness reports via text to the internet. As Lauren Maynard confirmed at the social media agency Room 14's blog, capturetheconversation.com, 'Twitter has essentially become the communication hub for all live information out of Haiti'.[28] Google also set up a website where those with friends and relatives in Haiti could find out the probable intensity of the earthquake at specific street addresses.[29] Another Google site, developed in conjunction with the US State Department, was a 'Person Finder',[30] helping viewers find, or providing information on, people in Haiti. Both of the Google websites were accessible by computer and mobile.

Bangladesh – Grameenphone

The Nobel Peace Prize-winning Grameen Bank (GB)

> has reversed conventional banking practice by removing the need for collateral and created a banking system based on mutual trust, accountability, participation and creativity. GB provides credit to the poorest of the poor in rural Bangladesh, without any collateral.[31]

Grameenphone is a joint venture created by the bank's non-profit Grameen Telecom company. With Grameen Bank financing, a Grameenphone borrower buys a mobile phone to become the 'telephone lady' of the village. She provides the telecommunication services to the village while earning profits for herself. Today there are 210,000 telephone ladies in Bangladesh earning good income for their families.[32] As Grameenphone states on its website:

> Grameenphone is now the leading telecommunications service provider in the country with more than 23 million subscribers as of December 2009. Presently, there are about 60 million telephone users in the country, of which a little over one million are fixed-phone users and the rest mobile phone subscribers.[33]

In addition, Grameenphone has more than 4,500 full- and part-time employees and indirectly supports more than 150,000 vendors, retailers and others who are essential to the functioning of the company.

Worldwide – Carrotmobs

Based on the examples of what author Howard Rheingold has called 'smart mobs'[34] (groups mobilised by mobile phone messages and flash mobs (people who appear out of nowhere, do something playful for a few minutes and then disappear), a San Francisco movement called 'Carrotmob' now has more than 90 campaigns in North America, South America, Europe, Southeast Asia and Africa. Carrotmob's mobile phone based consumer activism encourages businesses to be socially responsible and rewards them with consumers purchasing their products or services. Carrot comes from the phrase 'carrot or stick', based on Carrotmob's belief that rewarding responsible businesses with customers is more effective than punishing them with boycotts. As Carrotmob says on its website:[35]

> It's easier to understand if you look at an example. In the first ever Carrotmob event, a liquor store agreed to invest in upgrades that made their store more energy-efficient. In exchange, hundreds of Carrotmobbers showed up at once to support the winning liquor store.

Through supportive actions such as this, Carrotmob has helped small businesses throughout the world afford to become more sustainable, socially responsible, and energy-efficient – from a restaurant in Finland to a convenience store in Berlin to a bubble tea shop in Singapore.

Day-to-day use of mobile phones

While individual phone users are involved in – and are critical to – all of these examples, there are other less dramatic but still significant examples taking place worldwide, particularly in developing countries. In Kenya, watchdog groups are reporting cases of land grabbing to the authorities. Doctors are using automatic texting to remind patients to take their medication. Regional organisations are providing information to buyers looking for low prices, and sellers looking for high prices – for example, farmers and fishermen can text to find the best place to sell their produce or catch.[36]

Telephone carriers in many countries, increasingly in conjunction with regular banks, offer 'mobile banking'. Customers purchase vouchers for a certain amount from local agents and text a code number to a distant relative who can then take the code number to an agent and collect cash. With a number of systems, customers can text the money directly to the other person's mobile phone, or even keep the cash on account as a basic, non-interest form of savings account.[37]

Throughout the world, witnesses are videoing acts of police brutality and government oppression. Farmers obtain weather forecasts, agricultural advice and information needed for the irrigation of crops.[38] Villagers use texting to confirm that a doctor will be available in a distant town, ensuring that their long journey on foot will not be in vain.[39] Health experts in cities give medical and first aid advice to residents of rural villages.[40] Women selling crafts and food discover which markets and buyers will offer the best prices for their products. Women weavers in Nigeria have been able to reduce transaction costs by using mobile phones.[41] Youths and adults in Kenya obtain information about sexually transmitted diseases, particularly HIV/AIDS, make medical appointments and receive test results.[42] In Uganda, Google offers Google Trader – a free Craigslist-type exchange, accessible via SMS – that lets people buy and sell goods and services.[43] In Nigeria and Ghana, in order to combat counterfeit drugs, drug packaging that contains a code is being used; sending a text to a special number can confirm if the drug is legitimate.[44]

All of these activities may be mundane tasks for people in urban areas, particularly in industrialised countries, but for residents of rural areas with no landline telephones these capabilities are life-changing and empowering. While much of the telephone usage in poorer regions of the world can be done with voice or texting, many of these more advanced applications require more sophisticated mobile phones: the so-called 'smartphones', which offer full web access, cameras and graphics-enabled screens for viewing websites, photographs and videos. As smartphones become more common throughout the world, phone owners will be able to enjoy the full range of their features. Here are a number of features that are currently possible with smartphones.

Economic

Smartphones can be used as credit cards and loyalty cards, engage in barter and recycling; read QR/barcodes to find products, product prices, reviews and detailed information, find the best markets for prices for buyer or seller; pay parking meters; buy entertainment tickets; check in with airlines; pay for train, bus and subway journeys, and find location based information on local businesses and services.

An important example is the ability to conduct banking. As the United Nations agency International Telecommunication Union (ITU) states: 'There are now large numbers of people worldwide, especially in developing countries, who have a mobile phone subscription but no bank account – and increasingly, subscribers are using their phones for banking.'[45]

Cultural

Smartphones can disseminate and read, or listen to, music, audiobooks, podcasts, ebooks, lectures, speeches, sermons, discussions, articles, instructions and technical manuals; collaborate in novel writing; watch movies, videos and television programs; engage in online culture-related discussions; see graphics and videos of art, theatrical and dance performances; watch travelogues; play games, either individually or with other players located nearby or worldwide.

Political

Smartphones can facilitate political campaigns with texting and voice calls; conduct get-out-and-vote actions on election day; organise protests, support events and other demonstrations; rally hundreds of thousands of people to take political action by crowd gathering, texting, emailing, or making phone calls to targeted authorities.

Social

Smartphones enable participation in social media networks such as Facebook, MySpace and Twitter; manage virtual communities through online forums, email lists, blogs and wikis; create affinity/interest groups (instant, short- or long-term) for personal support, business or political/ social/environmental causes.

Health

Smartphones open access to health information (particularly HIV/AIDS), obtain emergency aid, and call for ambulances; receive online diagnostic help from both live sources of information and artificial intelligence medical databases. As the ITU has stated,

> Good examples include sending reminder messages to patients' phones when they have a medical appointment, or need a pre-natal check-up. Or using SMS messages to deliver instructions on when and how to take complex medication such as anti-retrovirals or vaccines. It's such a simple thing to do, and yet it saves millions of dollars – and can help improve and even save the lives of millions of people.[46]

Personal

Smartphones can assist health improvement through weight loss, stopping smoking and other programs, accessing nutritional information on grocery and restaurant food, and finding shopping information; obtain travel directions with turn-by-turn navigation; mark the location of a parked car for easy return; receive medication reminders; maintain a calendar, personal phone book, rolodex, 'to do' list, and personal organiser.

News/civic

Smartphones can receive emergency alerts, including severe weather and warnings for tsunamis, tornadoes and hurricanes; access instant global, national and local news; read newspapers and magazines; receive traffic reports; document police brutality, government oppression, and crimes; engage in on-the-spot, real-time public journalism, and photograph proof of automobile collision damage and other useful evidence.

Tools

Smartphones can be searched by voice, text or image. They can be used as a texting device, camera, video camera, audio recorder, video player, music player, compass, clock, alarm clock, calculator, decibel meter, dictionary, encyclopaedia, thesaurus, photo gallery, exercise trainer, flashlight, game player, instant interpreter, instant translator, language teacher, converter of text-to-speech and speech-to-text, location finder, map, navigator, notebook, pedometer, radio, QR/barcode reader, remote control – and, yes, even a telephone.

The future

Smartphones are moving into video chatting, video phone calls, pico projection (miniature projectors displaying cell phone content on a screen or wall), and air quality testing.

Conclusion

While most of these activities may not appear to be significant on a large scale, they all contribute to an equalisation of information distribution and to a slow but widespread change in society and how people obtain, process, share and use information. The use of one single device – a smart mobile phone – can instruct, educate, spread ideas, start and coordinate political and environmental movements, generate income, bring people together, change governments and public policy, save time, save money, and even save lives. Regardless of their social or economic level, all users of mobile phones have equal access to the information and features discussed in this chapter. While the poor may not be able to travel corporeally, they can travel virtually and, more importantly, information can travel to them.

British sociologist John Urry has stated that the automobile is the 'quintessential manufactured object produced by the leading industrial sectors and the iconic firms within 20th century capitalism', and the 'predominant global form of "quasi-private" mobility'.[47] I suggest that the roles of the automobile are rapidly being displaced – and indeed in many developing countries have already been displaced – by the far less expensive mobile phone. According to US analysis and research firm Plunkett Research, there were approximately one billion automobiles and light trucks on the road worldwide in 2010.[48] Compare that to the five billion mobile phones estimated to be in use worldwide by the end of the same year.

The result of the power and possibilities of mobile phones is undoubtedly social change. In which ways that will manifest, and how systemic that change will be, is dependent on conditions and events in each country and region. The peoples of the world are interconnecting into one vast electronic nervous system. The results may be astonishing.

Notes

1. L. Emberson, G. Lupyan, M. Goldstein and M. Spivey, 'Overheard Cell-phone Conversations: When less speech is more distracting', *Psychological Science*, 3 September 2010, *http://pss.sagepub.com/content/early/2010/09/03/0956797610382126*
2. *Ibid.*
3. *Ibid.*
4. 'Gartner Says More than 1 Billion PCs in use Worldwide and Headed to 2 Billion Units by 2014', *Gartner Newsroom*, *http://www.gartner.com/it/page.jsp?id=703807*

5. United Nations Conference on Trade and Development (UNCTAD), 'Information Economy Report 2010: ICTs, Enterprises and Poverty Alleviation', 2010, *http://www.unctad.org/en/docs/ier2010_embargo2010_en.pdf*
6. *Ibid.*, p. 69.
7. *Ibid.*, p. xi.
8. International Telecommunications Union, 'Ubiquitous Mobile', *ITU Statshot*, Issue 3, June 2010, *http://www.itu.int/net/pressoffice/stats/2010/06/index.aspx*
9. *Ibid.*
10. Google Goggles is a smartphone application that lets a user take a picture and search the web by image rather than by text, *http://www.google.com/mobile/goggles*
11. J. Chipchase, 'Shared Phone Use', *Future Perfect*, *http://janchipchase.com/2006/12/shared-phone-use*
12. Grameenphone, 'Every Freedom Counts – Village Phone', *http://www.grameenphone.com/index.php?id=79*
13. UNCTAD (2010) report, above note 5, p. 58.
14. S. Strauss, 'Twitter Co-founders Offer 5 Tips for Entrepreneurs,' *Tech Cocktail*, *http://techcocktail.com/twitter-co-founders-offer-5-tips-for-entrepreneurs-2010-10*
15. A. Sreberny-Mohammadi and A. Mohammadi, *Small Media, Big Revolution: Communication, Culture, and the Iranian Revolution* (University of Minnesota Press, 1994).
16. S. Burton, 'People Power Redux', *Time*, 157(4), 29 January 2001.
17. G. Griff, 'Text the Vote', *New York Times*, 13 August 2008.
18. *Ibid.*
19. W. Briggs, 'Sea Turtles, Cell Phones and the WTO,' *Communication World*, 1 February 2000.
20. *Ibid.*
21. San Francisco Department of Public Health, *http://www.SexInfoSF.org*
22. National Campaign to Prevent Teen and Unplanned Pregnancy, 'Case Study: Sexinfo: A sexual health text messaging service', *http://www.thenationalcampaign.org/resources/monster/MM_CaseStudySEXINFO.pdf*
23. L. Maynard, '#Haiti, by way of Twitter', Capture the Conversation, 13 January 2010, *http://www.capturetheconversation.com/social-community/haiti-by-way-of-twitter*
24. *Ibid.*
25. P. Dvorak, 'Texting Allows Multitude of Donors for Victims of Haiti Earthquake', *The Washington Post*, 15 January 2010.
26. *Ibid.*
27. D. Macsai, 'Haiti Earthquake Disaster: Google earth, online-map "absolutely crucial"', *Fast Company*, 14 January 2010, *http://www.fastcompany.com/blog/dan-macsai/popwise/haiti-earthquake-google-maps-web-tech*
28. Maynard, above note 23.
29. Macsai, above note 27.

30. Google, 'Staying Connected in Post-earthquake Haiti', *http://googleblog.blogspot.com/2010/01/staying-connected-in-post-earthquake.html*
31. Grameen Bank, 'Introduction', *http://www.grameen-info.org/index.php?option=com_content&task=view&id=16&Itemid=112*
32. Grameenphone, 'History', *http://www.grameenphone.com/index.php?id=63*
33. Grameenphone, 'About us', *http://www.grameenphone.com/about-us*
34. H. Rheingold, *Smart Mobs: The next social revolution* (New York: Basic Books, 2002).
35. Carrotmob, *http://www.carrotmob.com*
36. S. Corbett, 'Can the Cellphone Help End Global Poverty?' *New York Times*, 13 April 2008.
37. C. Partridge, 'Needy Ugandans Develop the Mobile-phone ATM', *The Sunday Times*, 24 October 2006.
38. 'New Uses for Mobile Phones Could Launch Another Wave of Development', *The Economist*, 24 September 2009.
39. Corbett, above note 36.
40. *Ibid.*
41. UNCTAD (2010) report, above note 5, p. 79
42. *Ibid.*
43. *The Economist*, above note 38.
44. M. Goldberg, 'Using Mobile Phones to Spot Counterfeit Drugs', *UN Dispatch*, 7 October 2010, *http://www.undispatch.com/using-mobile-phones-to-spot-counterfeit-drugs*
45. ITU Newsroom, above note 8.
46. *Ibid.*
47. J. Urry, 'The System of "Automobility"' *Theory, Culture and Society,* 21(4/5), 2004, pp. 25–39.
48. Plunkett Research, 'Automobile Industry Introduction', *http://www.plunkettresearch.com/Industries/AutomobilesTrucks/AutomobileTrends/tabid/89/Default.aspx*

Part 2
Structures for Sharing

5

Strangers in the swarm

Mike Kent

Abstract: What happens economically, culturally and socially in file sharing 'communities'? This chapter enters the Bit Torrent swarm and explores the complex, intricate and yet rule-bound relationships in this transitory community.

Key words: online file sharing, Bit Torrent, swarm, peers, seeds, leeches

> *No more mirror of being and appearances, of the real and its concept; no more imaginary coextensivity: rather, genetic miniaturization is the dimension of simulation. The real is produced from miniaturized units, from matrices, memory banks and command models – and with these it can be reproduced an indefinite number of times. It no longer has to be rational, since it is no longer measured against some ideal or negative instance. It is nothing more than operational. In fact, since it is no longer enveloped by an imaginary, it is no longer real at all. It is a hyperreal: the product of an irradiating synthesis of combinatory models in a hyperspace without atmosphere.*[1]
>
> Jean Baudrillard

The concept that 'miniaturized units, from matrices, memory banks and command models – and with these it can be reproduced an indefinite number of times' seems prescient of the transformations that emerge through identity as the cold war between people sharing files online, or when those pirating copyrighted material come into conflict with anti-piracy groups seeking to restore value to copyright ownership and control. In these transformations, people are reduced to numbers in a swarm of the torrent, rapidly exchanging information to complete a digital file and then going their separate ways. Therefore, in the context of this book, I am interested in the movement from the physical body, and how these new identities come together to form strong, yet transitory, communities of engagement. The chapter presents a brief history of online file sharing before turning to focus specifically on the largest peer-to-peer network, Bit Torrent, and its application. It then turns to identity and community in the Bit Torrent swarm, before briefly looking to the trends in the near future for these activities.

Many words attend 'community'. One is sharing. This chapter explores a particular type of sharing. I am interested in how digitally literate people use the internet to share information online. Much of the information exchanged is in violation of copyright. As these online pirates have become more closely persecuted by the controllers of copyright from the music industry and movie production houses, the process of sharing information online has evolved in ways that have created a new form of minimalist identity within a transitory community. While sites and services that facilitated file sharing were shut down (such as Napster), others with a more complex and mediated relationship with the transfer of information through the use of Bit Torrent file sharing (such as The Pirate Bay) rose up in their place. The individuals sharing the information became, on a technical level, a more tightly woven community. Through digital literacy, it was a form of elitism. At the same time, individual identities were subsumed in the swarm. This chapter explores this shell or simulacra of identity and community that remain in these transitory online spaces.

The history of file sharing

Sharing files on the internet has a long history with early platforms – particularly Bulletin Board Systems (BBS) – which allowed participants to both upload and download different files. While there were some concerns over the trading of copyrighted material in these fora, they were mitigated by the limitations of storage capacity and data transfer over what were, in the 1970s and 1980s, largely dial-up connections with slow modems.

The 1999 launch of Napster, however, brought more attention to the practice of file sharing, both for participants and those who were involved in the ownership and trade of copyrighted material. The service, designed by Shawn Fanning, made use of the MP3 format of music storage and playback to enable users to download music from each other's computers – to share music over the internet. This activity raised the concern of the commercial music industry, which shut down the service through the American legal system in July 2001. The company's brief lifespan mirrored the rise and fall of technology stocks in the dot-com bubble. Its philosophy of providing a free service to users mirrored that of the internet-related developments of that era.

While the music industry was able to claim victory in this attempt to protect its rights, other file sharing networks such as Gnutella, Grokster and Kazaa soon rose to prominence. These sites used a variety of methods to avoid the same fate as Napster, which included the decentralised open source model of Gnutella, and the use of off-shore servers and corporate structure in the case of Kazaa and Grokster.[2] These services became increasingly popular, as storage capacity and bandwidth increased. They were used not just in the distribution of music, but also video content such as film and television. Tellingly, the music and motion picture industries were able to take action successfully to stop this practice, in the case of those companies operating off-shore.[3] However, the decentralised Gnutella service continues to operate. It was relatively easy for industries dealing with copyright to shut down online services that facilitated file sharing that maintain an identifiable corporate body, even when companies went to great length to remove this structure from United States (US) jurisdiction.[4]

In 2003, the Recording Industry Association of America (RIAA) began a new strategy of suing individual people for sharing songs on peer-to-peer networks. This practice was later followed by similar organisations in other countries. In these cases, individual users were sued, often by being served with a letter of demand for a settlement of thousands of dollars, with the option of going to trial and facing potential judgments of hundreds of thousands of dollars.[5] These were remarkable campaigns aimed at the company's own consumers. In 2010 Manils et al.[6] noted that, in this climate of 'Cold War between users and anti-piracy groups', many file sharers took steps to hide their own identity.

In the BBS heyday, many networks were located within one geographic area[7] and members would often meet in person at events held to bring the BBS community together. As file sharing has been pushed more underground, not knowing who is involved in file sharing takes on a particular form. Rendering users anonymous, hiding their identity from each other is a safer way to engage with other file sharers on the net. However, paradoxically there is also a required level of trust. Users need to know if the content that they are receiving is what it claims to be and not a corrupt file, or worse malicious software designed to damage their computers or identify them to anti-piracy groups. There are also issues of reciprocity. There is the assumption that people will not only 'take' copies from a network, but will also provide other content for others on a network. Therefore, a certain level of identification is required to ensure that a balance is maintained. Similarly, the actual online networks that facilitate the exchange of files will need not to have a central technical or corporate structure that is subject to discovery and termination by anti-piracy groups.

Bit Torrent

In 2001 an online platform – Bit Torrent – was launched as a protocol that enabled this type of anonymous community. The program was written by Bram Cohen and designed to help the open source community by allowing large files associated with the Linux operating system to be transferred over the internet. The program allows an efficient method of distributing files between large numbers of people and can act as an inexpensive alternative to classic server based content distribution.[8] It allows users to distribute large files in a peer-to-peer network. It has been described as the 'King of File Sharing'[9] and is used so widely that it accounted for an average of 37.63 per cent of upstream traffic and 16.91 per cent of downstream traffic in the Asia Pacific region in 2010.[10] Other estimates place the volume of all internet traffic that can be attributed to Bit Torrent as ranging from 27 to 55 per cent globally.[11]

Bit Torrent works by breaking a particular file into a number of smaller pieces. These are then exchanged over a network so that many people can be both downloading parts of the file and uploading other parts of the file that they have already downloaded. This is in contrast to the more traditional model where a group of people would all be downloading the one file in its entirety from the same server. This process is enabled by the creation of a 'torrent'. This is a component of metadata that contains information about the files to be shared. Traditionally it also contained information about a particular torrent tracker that would monitor the torrent and identify 'peers' for file exchange. In this process the seed or person with the original file might only have to upload one copy of the complete file, and still be able to share it with many other users, each of whom would be part of the process of other people downloading the file.

This group of users all sharing the same torrent is known as a swarm. The larger the number of people in the swarm, the faster a file would be exchanged as there are more people with more pieces of the original file to exchange. Conversely, as people lose interest in the content being exchanged, particularly once they have a complete copy, the numbers decline in the swarm. So does the speed at which the file is transferred.[12] Seeds are users who have a full copy of the file; peers and leeches are those who do not yet have a full copy. The phrase 'leeches' is also used in a derogatory sense to describe someone who downloads a file, and then fails to maintain a connection to the swarm for others to download. By using the 'many to many' distribution method, the network is also able to overcome some of the limitations that other peer-to-peer networks encounter, allowing a faster connection for downloads than they allow for uploading files.[13]

Each swarm is unique to a particular file being exchanged. By operating as a protocol, rather than a formal and enduring network, Bit Torrent presents a very different type of challenge to any organisation that would want to close it down or regulate it. There is no central computer system or corporate body that can be closed down or prosecuted. Similarly, while the network establishes a link between all the computers in a swarm exchanging different pieces of the same file, the actual identity of each person is not immediately apparent to those involved. On the surface no one knows who they are sharing the file with, and they remain anonymous. This removes the next element where the network could be attacked, by hiding the identity of individual users.[14]

This process captures and continues the process of file sharing and improves upon it. Thompson describes Bit Torrent:

> You could think of Bit Torrent as a Napster redux – another rumble in the endless copyright wars. But Bit Torrent is something deeper and more subtle. It is a technology that is changing the landscape of broadcast media.[15]

Beyond the immediate utility of reducing the ability of the owners of copyrighted material to attempt to close down the file sharing network as they have in the past, Bit Torrent is changing the way in which information exchange is mediated. It creates a new model of many to many broadcasting and this has impacts beyond the immediate exchange of information over the internet.

Bit Torrent applications

There are many legitimate uses for this type of software, alongside exchanging Linux files. Many companies use it to distribute content; these include Blizzard Entertainment, which uses Bit Torrent to distribute data associated with its online games, including 'World of Warcraft'. Musicians such as Trent Reznor from Nine Inch Nails have distributed music using this service.[16] The United Kingdom government has also made use of Bit Torrent to distribute information.[17] For these and other organisations Bit Torrent can enable a relatively low cost and efficient way of distributing digital files, using its target audience to help distribute files, and being able to leverage more of the overall network resources available, not just its own.

While this type of technology can be used to distribute legitimate material in an efficient way, it needs to be acknowledged that the vast majority of Bit Torrent activity involves the illegal distribution of copyrighted material. A study by Layton and Watters in 2010 found that 89 per cent of all torrents in their sample involved the illegal distribution of copyrighted material and only 0.3 per cent was identified as clearly not breaching copyright.[18] It is this illegal context that frames the construction of identity in the swarm. Movies made up 43.3 per cent of the content available, compared to 29.1 per cent television programming and 16.5 per cent music. Tellingly, none of the material in these top three categories was found to be a legal distribution.[19]

Bit Torrent is having a significant effect on the traditional entertainment industry, impacting particularly on the way in which television is consumed. The ability of television content to be distributed and limited by geographic regions has been compromised by the greatly increased potential for people to share files over the internet using Bit Torrent.[20] This can have advantageous impacts for the industry. When the re-visioned series of *Battlestar Galactica* was aired in the United Kingdom in 2004 – before the US – the programme quickly became available online through Bit Torrent. When it did launch in the US the first episode was the most popular programme for the SciFi Channel in its history, largely as a result of word of mouth – or more precisely, speed of the swarm – generated by the online distribution. A similar effect was seen by a leak of the first episode of the new *Dr Who* series in 2005.[21] More recently, more mundane scheduling delays in popular television shows have been seen as a driver for the uptake of Bit Torrent as a preferred method of access,[22] and the negative impact of this has been seen in lower ratings in shows where distribution is delayed in one market.[23] As Thompson describes Bit Torrent, 'it pounds a final nail into the coffin of must see appointment television'.[24] It also starts to reconfigure how an audience for this type of entertainment needs to be imagined – no longer a community of geography, but a community of interest and a community in time.

While the impact on the distribution of television programming may be significant, Layton and Watters found that the most common file type in their sample of torrents was that of movies. The motion picture industry, clearly mindful that Bit Torrent may have a similar impact as Napster had on the music industry, has been particularly active in working against this type of file sharing. Rather than pursuing individual users, the motion picture industry has concentrated on shutting down websites that host the torrent addresses for people to join. It was also active in trying to shut down the torrent trackers. The largest and most famous of these trackers hosted by the Swedish based 'The Pirate Bay' was shut down in 2009.[25] However, unlike shutting down services such as Napster where the whole network could be destroyed, users of Bit Torrent quickly move to another website listing torrents.

Identities in the swarm

The sociologist Erving Goffman, in his seminal work *Presentation of Self in Everyday Life*, noted that people act differently in different settings.[26] Goffman suggests that we behave as if we are a theatre presenting different 'stages' to the world in different parts of our lives. We put on a different face or 'stage' for our bank teller than we do for our children. As our lives and identities start to converge online, this separation can break down – a collapse of context occurs. There is no distinction between avatar and corporeal identity. Such a change can be seen when a workmate reads our status updates of leisure pursuits on Facebook, when he or she knows we should be working on a report due on Monday morning.

At first glance, Bit Torrent takes this in a very different direction. Our identities are stripped back to the bare minimum necessary to find others and exchange data with them. We no longer have a clever online handle but are reduced to one of a number of 'peers', 'seeds', or 'leeches' in the swarm for any particular torrent. However, as Choffnes et al. note,[27] there is actually more to the identity and commonality of these transitory communities. Each of the strangers in the swarm shares an interest in the content, and is participating in the swarm at the same time. This commonality of interest and temporal presence are not as separated from traditional online communities as it might first appear. The factors that draw a group together to form a more traditional online community are very similar, even if the interaction between members is radically transformed.

Each swarm is more productive if more people are involved. Bit Torrent is designed so that each member of a swarm is actively participating in the process, giving data as well as receiving. It also relies on the altruism of seeders. It is seen as poor netiquette for users to leave a swarm as soon as they have a complete copy rather than stay connected to help others gain access to the material. However, it is also possible to use a variety of programs such as BitThief[28] to avoid uploading content and just download. Such 'freeloading' has been a considerable problem for other peer-to-peer networks. In 2005 some 85 per cent of the Gnutella community was considered to consist of freeriders.[29] Studies have shown, however, that Bit Torrent is distinguished by its high level of participation and a low level of this type of freeloading.[30]

This commitment to the swarm community also needs to be seen in the context in which users subject themselves to much harsher penalties for making material available, rather than just downloading, with penalties in many jurisdictions being much higher for distribution than for simply obtaining copyrighted material. One would expect each user to be in a 'prisoner's dilemma' decision as to whether or not to actively participate in the swarm,[31] yet there seems a commitment by many participants to contribute fairly to the process. Patrin and Hales[32] suggest that this may be in part because of a tendency for users to move to the most efficient swarms – the presence of freeloaders will make the swarm less efficient thus encouraging people to move to more efficient groups. This seems to be a somewhat circular argument.

While individuals are presenting a deliberately minimal identity in the swarm, the community exists beyond each individual swarm. As well as a transitory shared temporal interest in content, the users also congregate around websites that list torrent addresses. Many of these sites help to promote and encourage a cooperative virtual community as well as an ideology that encourages piracy. Most famous of these, The Pirate Bay, while having shut down its torrent trackers in 2009, claimed that this was only done because of the advances in Bit Torrent technology that rendered these services obsolete. When the site receives legal threats, it posts them on the site along with their often colourful responses.[33] At the bottom of the list, the site comments: 'We used to have a nice graph here, but it's simpler to just say: 0 torrents have been removed, and 0 torrents will ever be removed.'[34] Other sites, such as Demonoid.com, offer users advice on how better to hide their identities to protect their privacy from third party programs while using their service. These websites also allow users to post comments about particular torrents and communicate with each other. They also help to create and maintain a sense of community for those otherwise anonymous members of any swarm.

Other websites try to take this immediate anonymity away by requiring users to log-on and by monitoring the rations of members file sharing, much like the old BBS system, with the anticipation that this information about the participants in the swarm will be kept confidential within the website's community. Zhang et al., in 2010, estimated that there are more than 800 of these 'darknets' in use and that they are concentrated in North America and Europe.[35] This would seem on the surface to be consistent with the areas of focus for anti-piracy organisations.

The future

While these websites help to maintain a community, Bit Torrent is moving to a further decentralised network. Having bypassed the need for central torrent trackers, some swarms are now moving discussions to Twitter, with the hash tag for the discussion determined by each individual torrent's own infohash.[36] However, despite these moves to further decentralise the process, people using Bit Torrent are still largely vulnerable to being identified, mostly through their Internet Protocol (IP) address that identifies the computer device they are using on the network. Yet people continue to take risks to support the rest of the community. The sense of community and an individual's own identity within that community is still important.

The holders of copyrighted materials have, for the time being, changed tack and are now applying pressure to the next easily identifiable level of a file sharing network in the form of the internet service providers (ISPs) that deliver an internet connection to people in the swarm.[37] This new mode of control is taking a number of forms. In France, the UK and New Zealand there is legislation to cut off access to the internet for households that are accused of violating copyright three times.[38] In Australia, this focus is modified to try to have ISPs made liable for acts of copyright infringements by their subscribers.[39]

The idea that 27 to 55 per cent of all traffic on the internet consists of a protocol that is made up of at least 89 per cent of illegal transmissions of copyrighted material is truly staggering, and the threat it poses to the power of the owners of those copyrights is self-evident. The response to this and other file sharing services has been both arbitrary and severe. Those unlucky enough to be found and prosecuted face significant financial loss, while the fast majority of file sharers continue without sanction. This potential assault on people's wellbeing has changed the way in which they present their identities online.

Baudrillard presented four phases of the image. First, it is a reflection of reality, then it starts to mask and pervert a basic reality; next it starts to mask the absence of a basic reality and finally, at the fourth stage, it bears no relationship to any reality, it becomes its own simulacrum. While the identities in the swarm may be the simulacrum of our identities, they still generate a community of interest, located in the same time. A fragment of people's identities interested in the same content gather together online at the same time to 'ride the wave' of a particular torrent as it surges in popularity and peers. These transitory communities exist for a brief period in time; yet people show a commitment to their wellbeing and a sense of obligation to participate in a meaningful way. Apple has, to date, rejected a Bit Torrent App for the iPhone, but it has been embraced by the android operating system. The next stage of this process will be people moving through their community of the 'real' while their mobile phones act as their online agents in a simulacrum of the real through Bit Torrent. They walk through their community – strangers in the swarm.

Notes

1. J. Baudrillard, *Jean Baudrillard, Selected Writings*, Mark Poster (ed.) (Stanford: Stanford University Press, 1988), pp. 166–84.
2. S.A. Hetcher, 'The Music Industries' Failed Attempts to Influence File Sharing Norms', 7 *Vanderbilt Journal of Entertainment Law and Practice* 10(11), 2004, pp. 10–40.
3. Sharman Networks, owners of Kazaa, were incorporated in Vanuatu and resided in Australia.
4. While both Kazaa and Napster have been relaunched, they are now organisations where people can pay for legitimate content, rather than places where people can freely exchange files.
5. D. Kravets, '$675,000 RIAA File Sharing Verdict is "Unreasonable"', *Wired Magazine*, 5 January 2010, *http://www.wired.com/threatlevel/2010/01/riaa-verdict-is-unreasonable*
6. P. Manils, A. Chaabane, S. Le Blond, M. Ali Kaafar, C. Castelluccia, A. Legout and W. Dabbous, 'Compromising Tor Anonymity Exploiting P2P Information Leakage', INRIA France, 12 April 2010, *http://hal.inria.fr/docs/00/47/15/56/PDF/TorBT.pdf*
7. The need to dial-up directly to many of these services limited the popular area of service to that within the cost of a local phone call.
8. M. Izal, G. Urvoy-Keller, P.A. Biersack, A. Felber, A. Al Hamra and L. Garces-Erice, 'Dissecting BitTorrent: Five months in a torrent's lifetime',

Proceedings of Passive and Active Measurements (PAM), Antibes Juan-les-Pins, France, April 2004, *http://www.pam2004.org/papers/148.pdf*

9 S. Patarin and D. Hales, 'How to Cheat BitTorrent and Why Nobody Does', University of Bologna, Dept. of Computer Science, May 2005, Technical Report UBLCS-2005-12, *http://cfpm.org/~david/papers/19-eccs06.pdf*

10 For a more detailed breakdown of Bit Torrent and other internet traffic in different regions of the world see Ernesto, 'BitTorrent Still Dominates Global Internet Traffic', *TorrentFreak*, 26 October 2010, *http://torrentfreak.com/bittorrent-still-dominates-global-internet-traffic-101026/?utm_source=feedburner&utm_medium=feed&utm_campaign=Feed%3A+Torrentfreak+%28Torrentfreak%29*

11 Ernesto, 'BitTorrent Still King of P2P Traffic', *TorrentFreak*, 18 February 2009, *http://torrentfreak.com/bittorrent-still-king-of-p2p-traffic-090218/*

12 Patarin and Hales, above note 9.

13 C. Thompson, 'The BitTorrent Effect', *Wired Magazine*, issue 13.01, January 2005, *http://www.wired.com/wired/archive/13.01/bittorrent.html*

14 As I will explore later, this is not to say that individual identities are completely or safely hidden just by the use of the protocol.

15 Thompson, above note 13.

16 G. Sandoval, 'Nine Inch Nails Releases Internet Album', *CNet.com*, 3 March 2008, *http://news.cnet.com/8301-10784_3-9884180-7.html, accessed 19 October 2010.*

17 Ernesto, 'UK Government uses BitTorrent to Share Public Spending Data', *TorrentFreak*, 4 June 2010, *http://torrentfreak.com/uk-government-uses-bittorrent-to-share-public-spending-data-100604/*

18 The majority of the rest, some 9.1%, was pornography where the copyright was hard to determine: R. Layton and P. Watters, 'Investigation into the Extent of Infringing Content on BitTorrent Networks', Internet Commerce Security Laboratory, University of Ballarat, April 2010, *http://www.afact.org.au/research/bt_report_final.pdf*

19 Although given the reluctance of the manufacturers and distributors of this kind of content to make use of this technology, this is hardly a surprise.

20 T. Leaver, 'FlashForward or FlashBack: Television distribution in 2010?', *Flow*, 11(5), 2010, *http://flowtv.org/2010/01/flashforward-or-flashback-television-distribution-in-2010-tama-leaver-curtin-university-of-technology/*

21 M. Pesce, 'Piracy is Good? How Battlestar Galactica Killed Broadcast TV', *Mindjack*, 13 May 2005, *http://www.mindjack.com/feature/piracy051305.html*

22 Leaver, above note 20.

23 T. Leaver, 'Watching *Battlestar Galactica* in Australia and the Tyranny of Digital Distance', *Media International Australia*, vol. 126, February 2008, pp. 145–54, *http://www.tamaleaver.net/cv/tyranny_postprint.pdf*

24 Thompson, above note 13.

25 D. Kravets, 'Pirate Bay Retires World's Largest BitTorrent Tracker', *Wired Magazine*, 17 November 2009, *http://www.wired.com/threatlevel/2009/11/pirate-bay-shutters-tracker*

26 E. Goffman, *Presentation of the Self in Everyday Life* (New York: Anchor Books, 1959).

27 D. Choffnes, J. Duch, D. Malmgren, R. Guimera, F. Bustamante and L.A. Nunes Amaral, 'Strange Bedfellows: Community identification in BitTorrent', Proceedings of the 9th International Conference on Peer-to-Peer Systems, San Jose, CA, 27 April 2010, *http://www.usenix.org/event/iptps10/tech/full_papers/Choffnes.pdf*
28 T. Locher, P. Moor, S. Schmid and R. Wattenhofer, 'Free Riding in BitTorrent is Cheap', Proceedings of HotNets-V, Irvine, CA, November 2006.
29 M. Ripeanu, M. Mowbray, N. Andrade and A. Lima, 'Gifting Technologies: A BitTorrent case study', *First Monday*, 11(11), November 2006, *http://firstmonday.org/htbin/cgiwrap/bin/ojs/index.php/fm/article/view/1412/1330*
30 *Ibid.*, and N. Andrade, M. Mowbray, A. Lima, G. Wagner and M. Ripeanu, 'Influences on Cooperation in BitTorrent Communities', Proceedings of the 2005 ACM SIGCOMM Workshop on Economics of Peer-to-Peer Systems, 22 August 2005, Philadelphia, PA, *http://people.cs.uchicago.edu/~matei/PAPERS/p2pecon.05.pdf*
31 S. Jun and M. Ahamad, 'Incentives in BitTorrent Induce Free Riding', Proceedings of the 2005 ACM SIGCOMM Workshop on Economics of Peer-to-Peer Systems, 22 August 2005, Philadelphia, PA, *http://www.cs.sfu.ca/~fedorova/Teaching/CMPT401/Spring2008/bittorrent-free-riding.pdf*; Patarin and Hales, above note 9.
32 *Ibid.*
33 Some of these responses are quite amusing but use strong language: see The Pirate Bay, *http://thepiratebay.org/legal*
34 *Ibid.*
35 C. Zhang, P. Dhungel, D. Wu, Z. Liu and K.W. Ross, 'BitTorrent Darknets', Proceedings of IEEE Conference on Computer Communications (INFOCOM'10) San Diego, CA, March 2010.
36 E. Van Buskirk, '"Torrent Tweets" Marries BitTorrent to Twitter', *Wired Magazine*, 6 August 2010, *http://www.wired.com/epicenter/2010/08/bit-torrent-and-twitter*
37 D. Kravets, 'Copyright Lawsuits Plummet in Aftermath of RIAA Campaign', *Wired Magazine*, 18 May 2010, *http://www.wired.com/threatlevel/2010/05/riaa-bump*
38 This is itself a transformative expansion of the concept of identity for file sharers – expanding to include a whole household of people.
39 The latest attempt to have this applied in the courts failed in February 2011: see B. Head, 'iiNet Wins Landmark Copyright Stoush', *Itwire*, 24 February 2011, *http://www.itwire.com/it-industry-news/listed-techs/45408-iinet-wins-landmark-copyright-stoush*

6

Status (update) anxiety: social networking, Facebook and community

Amanda Evans

Abstract: Facebook remains at the top of social networking sites, continually being challenged by other options such as Google+. Yet when social networking spills into oversharing, the simple act of constructing a status update can have an impact on family, friends, reputations and employment. This chapter probes the anxiety that can – and often should – emerge through the act of updating Facebook status.

Key words: Facebook, social networking, belonging, identity, community, anonymity

> *As of this morning, 500 million people all around the world are actively using Facebook to stay connected with their friends and the people around them. This is an important milestone for all of you who have helped spread Facebook around the world. Now a lot more people have the opportunity to stay connected with the people they care about.*[1]
>
> Mark Zuckerberg

Since its inception in February 2004,[2] Facebook has had a meteoric rise to the top of the social networking ladder. Competing for subscribers with other social networking sites like MySpace, Bebo and Twitter, Facebook has emerged as the one SNS (social networking site) where students, teachers, mothers, fathers, grandparents, companies, bands, magazines and retail outlets cluster. Seemingly innocent, Facebook statuses are updated, commented upon, liked and deleted in an instant. What happened last night or what may happen tomorrow can intrigue, infuriate or bore, as friends randomly scroll through status updates. But, for all of the apparent frivolity and posturing, what is the cost to the individual of the personal (over)sharing of information? What lurks behind those innocent photos of Stevo's 21st? In essence, what is the social cost of social networks?

It's all about me

The perceptible anonymity of MUDs,[3] chat rooms and message boards has been replaced by the overt nonymity of the Facebook network. The choice of profile pictures and 'about me' descriptions offer a projection of a virtually desirable self and are littered throughout the internet. Social networks like Facebook provide a sense of belonging and identity performed within a community imagining. This community is neither static nor stable, as is witnessed by the relative ease of one 'friend' exiting while another crosses the social threshold with an intense desire to belong. The apparent innocuousness of communication requires further understanding to ensure that members of these communities are not vulnerable to institutions and agencies that can data mine this information for their own purposes. It was recently revealed, via Freedom of Information, that in 2008 US Homeland Security encouraged overt cyber snooping of potential US citizens, declaring that officers from the Office of Fraud Detection and National Security (FDNS) might 'friend' suspected fraudsters on sites like Facebook, by taking advantage of 'narcissistic tendencies' to learn about their daily activities. Weinberger reports that 'this provides an excellent vantage point for FDNS to observe the daily life of beneficiaries and petitioners who are suspected of fraudulent activities'.[4] The trust displayed by those creating Facebook profiles may be described as overly romantic, but perhaps this indifference has more to do with belonging and the need for social connectedness in a rapidly changing virtual world.

Community beliefs are strengthened by those who reside within the consensual normalities. The social networks that people find themselves drawn to can also effectively stabilise the community in which they imagine themselves. The most obvious community frameworks are often the most dominant and ideologically incontrovertible: religious beliefs, sovereign rights, national pride and youth culture. The unquestionable nature of community beliefs is both clear and disturbing. As Benedict Anderson reveals about nationalism, 'it is imagined, because, regardless of the actual inequality and exploitation that may prevail in each, the nation is always conceived as a deep, horizontal comradeship'.[5] Anderson's analysis is pertinent when exploring the explosive construct of social networking, particularly through his emphasis on the ideological construction of comradeship. Imagined communities are not facile groupings that appear and disappear. It is important that the relationship between social networking and community be stressed as they are difficult to separate.

Communities are dependent upon the instability and dynamic nature of identity. Identities are changed and moulded in relation to the emptiness that is preoccupied with the performance of a self(s). The performance of visibility is an act of community belonging, the consensual agreement to live under the sign of that community. As Poole states, '[t]he nation is not only a form of consciousness; it is a form of *self-consciousness*. A community is a nation only if its members *identify* themselves and each other through their membership of it'.[6]

The signs of a community are constructed as visible identities and attach themselves to cultural texts. The manner in which this attachment is performed relies upon higher and lower degrees of visibility. Signs are ordered and presented to accommodate the purpose of the present self. For example, feminists are able to recognise other feminists through the mobilisation of particular cultural resources, but the overt fact remains that there is not one, singular feminist community. Identity and community focus upon the importance of belonging. As Elspeth Probyn argues,

> It is of the utmost importance that we take into account this desire to belong, a desire that cannot be categorized as good or bad, left or right – in short, a desire without a fixed political ground but with immense political possibilities.[7]

This desire to belong, to immerse the self in significance, is relevant to the dynamic and free-floating nature of community. This creates a space where the signs presented to the self from the community create a continuation of belonging, a site of homologous imaginings. There must be an agreement to the signs that surround and are dispersed by a network in which they imagine their signification in relation to others. It is at this point that the self, community and social network are at their most visible.

Imagined communities should be celebrated and applauded, but in a virtual world where identity is multi-faceted and ever-changing, should we be concerned about the iceberg that lies beneath? For every 'friend researcher' in the Facebook community there is a bored viral antagonist trolling the fringes looking for profiles, pages and groups to exploit. How much should people keep explicit? In a world tinged by identity theft and cyber crime, how safe are our virtual identities and how trustworthy are people's profiles? Would you trust Ronald K. Noble, Head of Interpol?

> Just recently Interpol's Information Security Incident Response Team discovered two Facebook profiles attempting to assume my identity as Interpol's secretary general. One of the impersonators was using this profile to obtain information on fugitives targeted during our recent Operation Infra Red.[8]

This example highlights the currency of the new millennium: information. Whoever controls the social network controls the flow of information. What makes this new currency so powerful is the control that it bestows on those who possess it. While cyber criminals can cover their tracks, the majority of SNS users are leaving dirty, great, big, muddy footprints all over the virtual landscape. In essence, those who playfully flit through cyberspace are disproportionate to those who can understand and manipulate the technology and then effectively hide the evidence. Even privacy settings cannot withstand the power of a skilled techno-criminal who wants to access a profile. Facebook, the organisation, has firmly placed the responsibility for identity protection firmly in the hands of its users. Therefore, Facebook is an identity gamble and one where the community itself must scrutinise one another and propose a directive of good taste and acceptable behaviour.

Watching the self (being watched)

What better way to ensure self-regulation and self-surveillance than to introduce a visible nonymous virtual reality? This virtual panopticon ensures that participants are overtly aware of their identity claims and the self-performance that ensues. The community bolsters this compliance by 'outing' non-conformists and less literate members by holding them up to public ridicule. A recent case in the UK involved a woman being sacked after forgetting she had added her boss as a friend on Facebook. Her status update at 6:03 pm read:

> OMG I HATE MY JOB!! My boss is a total pervy w***** always making me do s*** stuff just to p*** me off!! W*****!

The response from her boss was swift and decisive; at 10:53 pm he left the ultimate comment to her status update:

> Hi, I guess you forgot about adding me here? Firstly, don't flatter yourself. Secondly, you've worked here 5 months and didn't work out

> that I am gay? I know I don't prance around the office like a queen, but it's not exactly a secret. Thirdly, that 's*** stuff' is called your 'job', you know what I pay you to do. But the fact that you seem able to f***-up the simplest of tasks might contribute to how you feel about it. And lastly, you also seem to have forgotten that you have 2 weeks left on your 6 month trial period. Don't bother coming in tomorrow. I'll pop your P45 in the post, and you can come in whenever you like to pick up any stuff you've left here. And yes, I'm serious.[9]

This sacking highlights a concern for the Facebook community: has the need for social connectedness replaced the skills and tools of self-preservation? SNSs encourage interaction from a geographically disparate space, often exploiting people's desire to socially connect in cyberspace. This distance reinforces the apathy illustrated by this female worker's forgetfulness of 'friending' her boss and then naively updating her status attacking him. The desire to be popular and visible in the social network places a heavy burden on the idealistic construct of the virtual community that is Facebook. If there is no physical interaction or dealings with Facebook friends, then how do participants keep track of these associations? What effort is required to maintain these relationships? As Gray posits, 'the fantasy of virtual communities is that we can enjoy the benefits of community without its burdens, without the daily effort to keep delicate human connections intact'.[10]

Facebook provides a sense of belonging, an identity performed within a community imagining. The invocation of imagined communities is not intended to be a model of cultural change. It is a way to disclose the ideologies and hegemonic apparatuses that are present throughout cyberspace. Facebook offers much to this imagining:

> It is *imagined* because the members of even the smallest nation will never know most of their fellow-members, meet them, or even hear them, yet in the minds of each lives the image of their communion.[11]

Given the arguments presented, Facebook is an unavoidable, unpredictable and undervalued social and political force. While Facebook seems innocuous and frivolous, the fact that 500 million people openly filter their (virtual) identity through the network confirms that it is not only a powerful social and cultural force, but a site prime for exploitation and manipulation.

This sense of community, of veiled (be)longing, does come at a cost: is the self permanently transformed or will self-preservation re-enter the domain and reinscribe our virtual selves? Social identity is a crucial aspect in the understanding of Facebook and its impact within the social media and culture. It is easy to roam this virtual landscape, locating site-specific sameness/difference with this movement and, it can be argued, creating a space for permanent self-transformation. However, when we log out, close the laptop, shut down the PC/Mac, how is this virtual self altered? There is no denying the fact that our virtual and actual identities are intertwined. But the tangible reality is this: the woman I am now and the girl that I was (who my Facebook and geographically tangible friends engage with) remains when I log out of Facebook. She is at once a woman, mother, wife, academic, daughter, friend, teacher, sister, school friend, colleague, cousin, niece and aunt. This list continues to expand.

Notes

1. M. Zuckerberg, '500 Million Stories', *Facebook*, 21 July 2010, *http://blog.facebook.com/blog.php?post=409753352130*
2. In February 2004, 'the facebook' was launched for Harvard University students and then spread quickly to include Stanford University and Yale University students. By August 2006 the 'Facebook' we now know was fully functional.
3. Multi-User Domains.
4. S. Weinberger, 'US Government Monitoring Social Networking Sites', *AOL News Online*, 15 October 2010, *http://www.aolnews.com/nation/article/homeland-security-monitoring-social-networking-sites/19675854*
5. B. Anderson, *Imagined Communities* (London: Verso, 1991), p. 7.
6. R. Poole, 'Nationalism: The last rights?', *Arena Journal*, No. 4, 1994–95, p. 54.
7. E. Probyn, *Outside Belongings* (New York: Routledge, 1996), p. 9.
8. 'Cyber Criminals Assume Interpol Chief's Identity', *ABC News Australia Online*, 17 September 2010, *http://www.abc.net.au/news/stories/2010/09/17/3015321.htm*
9. J. Moult, 'Woman Sacked on Facebook for Complaining about her Boss after Forgetting She Added him as a Friend', *Daily News Online*, 14 August 2009, *http://www.dailymail.co.uk/news/article-1206491/Woman-sacked-Facebook-boss-insult-forgetting-added-friend.html*
10. J. Gray, 'The Sad Side of Cyberspace', *The Guardian*, 10 April 1995.
11. Anderson, above note 5, p. 6.

7

Becoming Mireila: a virtual ethnography through the eyes of an avatar

Faracy Grouse

Abstract: This chapter constructs a virtual ethnography of Second Life. Particularly, the focus is on virtual sex and the configuration of 'consent' in such environments. When genitals do not touch, how do the rules of intimacy transform legally and culturally?

Key words: Second Life, virtual ethnography, avatars, virtual sex, feeders, rape, consent

I recently read an article about a virtual (or 'virtual') rape on the popular MMORPG Second Life.[1] Initially, I was sceptical that such an act was even possible, let alone merited attention. However, days after I read the article, the idea still haunted me. The incident which led to this phenomenon involved a teenage girl in Belgium who had infiltrated the adult section of Second Life, where her avatar was sexually accosted by another avatar. The newsworthy portion of the story was that she subsequently reported it to Brussels police as a rape. As a survivor of non-virtual sexual violence, I am eternally curious – if not slightly paranoid – about what triggers people to commit these acts. Regina Lynn dedicated an entire column to this story and writes:

> There is no question that forced online sexual activity – whether through text, animation, malicious scripts or other means – is real; and is a traumatic experience that can have a profound and unpleasant aftermath, shaking your faith in yourself, in the community, in the platform, even in sex itself.[2]

While agreeing with the mental trauma that forced online sexual activity can create, Lynn's views, much like my own, were still in the grey area regarding whether or not such activities could actually be classed as rape.

Entry

Second Life (SL) is an interactive platform. It seems logical, therefore, to study it by interacting with it. While my immediate response to the concept of virtual sex – let alone virtual rape – between avatars was sceptical at best, I believe the intrinsic value of SL as a cultural entity deserves to be experienced before being judged. I decided that the best way to make an informed judgment would be to venture into Second Life myself, as a 30 year-old anthropologist. In the spirit of Alfred Kinsey, I decided to take research into my own hands. And body. I created the Second Life avatar, Mireila Galvanaldo, as a means to better understand the culture of virtual human interaction by becoming part of it. I wanted to see first hand what aspects of Second Life could lead to sexually deviant behaviour and, more importantly, to try to uncover how the ability to act out one's fantasies in avatar form could influence real life behaviour.

Before embarking on this exploration, I felt that I needed to explain what I was doing to my husband. Even though it would be as an avatar, I would technically be engaging in sexual activity with beings other than him to find out about their culture. I titled my project 'a virtual ethnography[3] of the sex lives of Second Life avatars'. I deployed observation, often attended by unobtrusive research methods,[4] to gauge the interactions between other avatars. But, as it is impossible to know what players are saying to each other via private instant messaging (IM), it would be necessary for me to participate on some level.

As a great admirer of Henry Jenkins, an MIT professor who famously defended violent video games,[5] I was curious about his views of Second Life, and the socially unacceptable behaviour within it. He writes via his weblog:

> Whatever the value of your criticism of Second Life may be, acting like a jerk in a virtual world is no different than acting like a jerk in the real world. This suggests the actions of someone who imagines virtual worlds as simply a playground where individuals

> can do anything they want and not expect any social consequences. It suggests the actions of someone who has contempt for anyone who takes what's going on in such a space seriously and wants to show his contempt by bearing his rump to the world. Here's hoping that we can debate the issues surrounding virtual worlds with a bit more civility and maturity in the future.[6]

I wondered if Jenkins' attitude regarding inappropriate behaviour also encompassed sexual activity between avatars. More importantly, did sexual behaviour in an online environment impact on offline life? With my husband's (grudging) blessing, I commenced my research to find some answers.

To me, the creation of an avatar runs much deeper than a mere representation of a computer user in a game. It gives its creator the opportunity to be the person or being that they want to be, independent of what genetics, society or life circumstances have allocated for them. Tom Boellstorff, author of *Coming of Age in Second Life*, defines avatar historically.

> The word *avatar* itself goes back to ancient Sanskrit which referred to the incarnation of the Hindu god (particularly Vishnu). With reference to cybersociality, the term was probably first used in the virtual worlds Habitat and Ultima IV in the mid-1980s, as well as in Neal Stephenson's 1993 science fiction novel *Snow Crush* (Morningstar and Farmer 1991; Stephenson 1993: 470). While 'avatar' ('avie' or 'av' for short) historically referred to incarnation – a movement from virtual to actual – with respect to online worlds it connotes the opposite movement from actual to virtual, a decarnation or invirtualization.[7]

The slippage between states, spaces and identities is clear from Boellstorff's statements. But the aim of my research was to find out if the opposite is now happening. Through my observations, interviews with other players and gauging my own personal changes, I wanted to find out if we are actually becoming our avatars.

Upon registering with Second Life, I was given the choice of four female starter avatars. I chose one called 'Girl Next Door' because out of the four she looked the most like me: a brunette with a fair complexion. That was where our similarities ended. I was asked to choose a name and a home region. Not knowing how much of my *real life* (RL) self I wanted to expose, I named her Mireila Galvanaldo and made her from London. Players are allowed to choose first names. I chose Mireila because it is an unusual name that I like and, as my own last name begins with G, I chose Galvanaldo as it was the most interesting of the G list of approved SL surnames. I am sure that I also wanted to make my avatar closer to what I – a Jewish-Irish-Norwegian woman from Minnesota – would call exotic. The act of choosing this vaguely Latin sounding name was my first taste of being able to live out desires vicariously through my avatar.

For my first session, I wandered haplessly through virtual Hyde Park, London. There were so few avatars present that I was actually logged off by the system for lack of player interaction. During my second session, I was determined to meet someone. Again, I wandered around Hyde Park, but this time I ventured into the shopping districts and into a pub. There I sat, looking forlorn with a glass of virtual white wine, hoping someone, anyone else, would approach me. I watched Furries[8] and Nekos[9] dancing happily to techno music while the human female avatars posed in various skimpy club-ware outfits. The human male avatars, invariably tall, muscular and young, stood along the walls watching.

After my first two sessions, I was less than impressed. My notes read:

> This is boring; everyone is ridiculously tall and physically fit. I can't understand how millions of people could be hooked on this game. I seriously question the 'Love your Life' slogan that SL uses in its advertising. What kind of real lives do these people live to want to escape to this?

It was later that I made the connection that this was the place where these people could *be* willowy and beautiful. Before this minor epiphany, I was under the false impression that everyone was as honest with their avatar as I intended to be. I decided it was time to start changing Mireila to see if a different appearance would alter how other players interacted with her and, more importantly, how I felt as her. After several humiliating attempts to change her clothes, one of which resulted in a walk around Knightsbridge in her underwear, I figured out how to give her a new dress. Clad in a pink, form-fitting halter dress, she looked slightly more normal in the SL world. She still, however, lacked a deep sun tan, sparkling eyes and movable hair.

I observed among the humans that everyone who was not a vampire or black was quite tanned. There were notably very few black avatars but a fair number of vampires. Apparently above average height and a deep suntan were attributes that people wanted in their second life. Mireila, still with her original body dimensions, was substantially shorter than the other female avatars. She also had a comparatively small chest. She stuck out in a crowd because she looked more like a real human being. I wondered what constituted the *erotic capital* of Second Life.[10] Did the creators of these avatars think they were beautiful, or did they believe other players thought they were beautiful?

Hakim defines erotic capital as 'a combination of aesthetic, visual, physical, social and sexual attractiveness to other members of your society, and especially to members of the opposite sex, in all social contexts'.[11] Again in Hyde Park, I took note of the female avatars that seemed to attract the most attention from male avatars. They were not the tall, willowy creatures in barely-there shorts and bra tops, but more realistic looking creations. I conjectured that the tall, slim, android Barbies were too common to be noticed. Women of colour tended to be interacting with numerous avatars, as were the curvier female avatars. This was apparent from the typing gesture they displayed. This meant they were engaged in IM conversations. Many of the slim female avatars danced or engaged in some other solitary physical activity in a corner for long periods of time. When I attempted to approach them, they became more engrossed in their activity. I felt like my presence was disturbing them.

The male avatars stood stationary, seemingly sizing up their environment or what I would term *on the prowl* for mates, walking or flying from one area to another without obviously taking part in any activity other than chatting up other players. My personal encounters with this environment entailed brief IMs, starting with a standard greeting such as 'hello Mireila' followed by a chat-up line such as 'are you single?' Already I was beginning to note the different modes of social etiquette and space based on the gender of avatars. Henry Jenkins touches on this topic:

> Perhaps, our sons – and daughters – need an unpoliced space for social experimentation, a space where they can vent their frustrations and imagine alternative adult roles without inhibiting parental pressure. The problem, of course, is that unlike the 19th century 'boy culture,' the video game culture is not a world children construct for themselves but rather a world made by adult companies and sold to children. There is no way that we can escape adult intervention in shaping children's play environments as long as those environments are built and sold rather than discovered and appropriated.[12]

This raises the question: is SL an unpoliced space and, if so, do the same social constructs apply to the male and female players as they do in the real world? Because SL is a world based on avatars, does the chosen gender of one's avatar influence behaviour within a virtual environment? I will touch on the subject of gendered behaviour and avatar gender switching later in this chapter.

Stripping Mireila

Tired of Hyde Park, I decided to move to another location. Anxious to get to the core of my research, I typed in the words 'sex' and 'adult' to see what locations would emerge. The top listed location was called 'Extreme Sex Empire'. I teleported there, only to find out that I needed to go through age verification to enter, thus proving that SL was at least attempting to keep minors out of the adult areas.[13] So, after entering my credit card and other personal information into a SL database, I was allowed inside. Once there, I was surrounded by hundreds of naked, predominantly white, male avatars walking around with erect penises. The surroundings were pleasant enough, with swaying palm trees, sandy beaches with turquoise water and a plethora of shimmering waterfalls. The female avatars who were not completely naked were wearing revealing lingerie. What struck me, however, were how few women were there. I looked at the room's chat on the side of the screen, and there was mention of players entering as male avatars and altering their appearance to become female. As time went on I witnessed this happen as a male avatar entered and proceeded to transform into a leggy, blonde female avatar. I wondered how many women were operating the female avatars and how many players only used female avatars in the regions devoted to sex.

Mireila walked around, and was finally taunted by the other players for her outfit. Out of curiosity more than a desire to assimilate, I took Mireila's clothes off. But since she was still using her original skin, her underwear was part of her. Nonetheless, she was approached by several male avatars, one of whom invited her to sit next to him on a beach recliner. On this recliner were two animation balls – one blue for male, one pink for female. He spooned and petted Mireila. I started to ask him questions about how long he had been playing SL and if he looked like his avatar in reality. He told me he did. He then offered to get me a new skin which had a birthday suit option. Not knowing how to get one myself, I accepted and changed into it. Fairly soon after this, he asked if I had had sex on SL yet. I told him no. He offered to introduce me to it, but I declined his offer. He politely moved on to another area. Mireila, however, was getting significantly more attention in the skin he had given her. Moreover, I had observed a case of asking for consent before sex.

Through the construction of an avatar, there is a way of being who you would like to be. Therefore, I decided to take this opportunity to look how I would like to look. Contrary to the SL trend, I remained short, as I am in reality. However, I chose to thicken Mireila's frame, and also the girth of her hips, and round out her buttocks to give her a fuller, hourglass figure. I gave her a light olive complexion and huge, sparkling, green eyes. Finally, I found the longest brunette hair in my collection of free accessories and put it on. I thought she was beautiful. She was the 'me' who I would like to have looked like in reality. She was exotic in that she did not look like any of the other female avatars I had seen. Through her, I could know what it was like not to have cellulite, a tummy bulge or post-pregnancy stretch marks. I was beginning to understand the joy of this game. Also, the more time and effort I spent creating Mireila's presence and appearance, the more I grew attached to her. I started to call her Miri. When I went out as the new and improved Mireila, she immediately attracted a lot of attention from both male and female avatars. One of the notable comments she received was 'you don't look like all the other girls'. This I liked. She was twice the width of most of the other female avatars and much shorter. She was, indeed, different. It made me, as her human creator, feel special as well.

I was experiencing the Proteus effect. The Proteus effect refers to how identity selection determines behaviour.[14] As SL is ultimately a role-playing game, all the players are occupying a role and their avatar is the ultimate tool. The effect of how other players interact with the created avatar translates into our lived – offline – experience.[15] It was as if my choices were being validated. This feeling of acceptance translated into my everyday real life as well. I began to feel more attractive and interesting. Oddly, I started to feel like my real life was a game. Whenever I was in a crowd of people I felt the urge to right click and fly above it. When I was bored in my surroundings, the first thought that popped into my mind was to teleport somewhere else. The sound of real wind reminded me more of the ambient atmospheric sounds of SL than a real meteorological condition. Moreover, I craved the ease and ability to start a conversation or completely disappear from a social setting at the click of a button. Alarmingly, I begin to crave being in SL and, more shocking still, I had begun looking to find out the existence of the real life versions of some of the places I had visited.

Most of the players I observed chose to make their virtual incarnations tall and thin. Secondly, aside from the furry culture which I did not delve into, they chose to make them white. Third, the men were almost unanimously athletic with a full head of hair. The women were slim with exceptionally long legs, necks and, with a few exceptions, long hair. Therefore, I used Mireila as a canary in the mine to gauge the limit of SL believability. We should study online popular culture by asking questions not only of others, but ourselves. Why do we choose what we choose? What are our motivations? They remain to be free of danger, warm and fed. After these functions are activated, they may be to attract and maintain a mate for companionship and possible reproduction. Since there is no actual physical danger or risk of being hungry or homeless in SL, players can focus on aspects of their lives that are higher in the hierarchy of needs.[16]

Unfortunately, from my period of observation, it did not seem as if there was much progression beyond the seeking of a mate, or someone with which to mate. I think there was an element of respect and surprise towards a player who is brave enough to be unique, but they are afraid to be that way themselves. If anything, Second Life is a prime example of behavioural confirmation:

> There is good reason to believe that our avatars change how we interact with others. Behavioral confirmation offers one potential pathway for this change. Behavioral confirmation is the process whereby the expectations of one person (typically referred to as the perceiver) cause the other person (typically referred to as the target) to behave in ways that confirm the perceiver's expectations.[17]

In an environment so seemingly afraid of veering from normative parameters, it is quite surprising to think that deviant behaviour, sexual or otherwise, could take place in SL. Unless the signals between perceiver and target were crossed, it could be assumed that the 'deviant' behaviour was actually quite normal. In other words, SL did not seem like a place with sufficient individuality to promulgate deviant activity.

I decided it was time for Mireila to ask some deeper questions. I took her to the darkest reaches of SL to talk and perhaps even interact with the players there. She went to bondage clubs, forced sex rooms and even wandered through the bestiality regions. She engaged another female avatar in the forced sex room, asking her companion if she had ever wanted to do what she was doing in SL in real life. Her response was that SL was a way to behave in a way not possible in real life. Again, it was hard to know if this was an honest answer, because the very fact that her actions were being questioned could have made her reflect what she thought I wanted to hear. When I asked her if she always played using a female avatar she quickly disappeared.

I had visited numerous sex regions, but all – even the ones devoted to bestiality – had avatars running around engaging in very similar sex acts, whether with humans or animals. The sex using animations were all labelled. There were shops where players could buy further animations, but from what I observed permission had to be obtained before the animation of another player could be activated. In short, a player had to make a conscious choice to be in a place where such animations existed to take part in any sort of avatar sex, all of which were strictly for adult players. Furthermore, to actually engage in any sexual activities, a player needed to sit on or by an animation ball or to give permission. The grey areas in consciousness, choice and decision-making I found with regard to consensual sex were whether sitting or lying in a place of animation constituted permission for another player to engage an avatar in sex. I had three different experiences with this.

The first kind involved another player starting a conversation with me, and then agreeing to go to a sex animation place together and choosing which animations to use before the sex commenced. Further conversation tended to continue during these kinds of encounter, with frequently the invitation to teleport back to the 'home' of the other player where we would engage in further animation-generated sex. The animations in the homes of these players were not all clearly labelled, but required the players to control them with the keyboard. If a virtual rape were to take place, it would seem most likely that it would happen within the realms of a private home. While I had met all of the players with whom I had engaged in sex in adult areas, it did not mean that everyone they brought back to their home was a consenting adult. I had been offered to teleport back to homes in places outside of sex areas which were open to players of all ages. To be teleported, I needed to accept the invitation by pressing 'accept' before the action could occur.

The second kind of sexual experience started with Mireila sitting on a chair or lying in an area with a sex animation. In essence, she was waiting to see if someone would come and engage her. Sometimes a player would ask if he or she could join her, which meant that by sitting or lying near her, their avatars would automatically animate. The other way was when there was no conversation and another player simply got close enough to her so that the player's avatar would engage in sex with her avatar. The latter instance could be considered to be inappropriate etiquette, but could it be called rape? According to Rapecrisis.org, the definition of rape in UK law is:

> The offence of rape (sec 1(1) SOA 2003) can only be committed by a man; however, a woman can be charged with, or convicted of rape as a secondary party. For example, a woman may be convicted of rape where she facilitated (helped) a man who has raped another person.
>
> The main provisions of the Act include the following:
>
> - Rape is widened to include oral penetration
> - Significant changes to the issue of consent and the abolition of the Morgan defence
> - Specific offences relating to children under 13, 16 and 18
> - Offences to protect vulnerable persons with a mental disorder
> - Other miscellaneous offences
> - Strengthening the notification requirements and providing new civil preventative orders.[18]

What I found strangest about this definition was that only men could actually rape, while women could be convicted if, and only if, they assist a man. Furthermore, there was no mention of avatars, male, female or otherwise. For me, the definition of rape is sexual activity which goes against the will or consent of one or more of the parties involved. As young children and those classified as vulnerable individuals are not by definition qualified to give consent for sex, for any qualified adult or other person to engage such a person would be rape.

Consent is not as clearly offered as saying 'yes'. As many sexually active adults can attest, not every consensual sexual encounter involves a question and answer session. Citing UK law, Rape Crisis defines consent as '[i]f she agrees by choice, and has the freedom and capacity to make that choice'. Rape Crisis clarifies this statement:

> In the offences of rape, assault by penetration, sexual assault and causing a person to engage in sexual activity without consent,

> The person (A) is guilty of an offence if (s)he:
>
> - acts intentionally;
> - (B) does not consent to the act; and
> - does not reasonably believe that B consents.
>
> Deciding whether a belief is reasonable is to be determined having regard to all the circumstances, including any steps A has taken to ascertain whether B consents (subsection (2) of sections 1–4). It is likely that this will include a defendant's attributes, such as disability or extreme youth.

As lack of consent is a key element in rape, this definition holds much of the answer to my question of whether or not rape is possible in SL. As nearly all sexual activity in SL involves choice – entering a sex area, sitting by an animation ball, or going back to a player's home – it seems clear to me that, on some level, sexual activity in SL requires all participants to choose to be involved. Beyond that, avatars and other virtual entities are not included in the definition of who can legally commit rape. Therefore virtual 'rape' does not exist.

Arching back to Jenkins' statement, perhaps his comment is even more relevant: '[A]cting like a jerk in a virtual world is no different than acting like a jerk in the real world.'[19] Does that mean that people who go around committing sexual 'crimes' in SL do so in real life? If they do, does the fact that they can experiment with and visualise these acts make them more enticing, or serve as a release of sexual aggression in a reasonably safe way? I hope it is the latter. The players who were willing to answer my questions told me that it was a harmless release, akin to masturbation. But then again, they were the players who asked my consent for sex. The others are still a mystery, as is the effect of what being able to choose and act out their fantasies is on their real life.

I found the experience of virtual sex interesting from a research point of view but, despite its blatant sexuality, very cold. As a happily married researcher, I was able to sit back and watch the virtual sex acts from a detached point of view. Even when I was single, the prospect of a relationship without an analogue, physical aspect lost its steam almost immediately. I can appreciate, however, that other people feel otherwise. I can also see where the ability to engage sexually through an avatar could serve people in long-distance relationships very well. I encountered numerous players who admitted to being in committed relationships and that they used SL as a place to find, or meet up with lovers with whom they were having affairs. In this last instance, I do believe SL can have a direct influence on real life.

Feeders

Realising that I had not viewed fat avatars, I typed the word 'fat' into the search bar and discovered Buffet Island. It was here that I discovered something called 'feeding'. Feeding involves one player attaching a tube to another player and effectively force feeding that player to become fatter and fatter like a veal calf. It was a fetish which I had never heard of before, so I was intrigued to find out more. Once on the island I looked around and found tables full of virtual food, a pig being roasted over a spit, and a number of players being 'fed' with tubes and increasing in size. I was approached by a male avatar who offered to feed me. What I discovered was that I had to then control my avatar to increase my own size. I had not purchased a special 'fluffy' skin as the overweight ones were called. I could not satisfy his desire to make me suitably fat. He moved on to a larger player and fed her with greater success. What I found odd was that the male avatars in this region appeared to be of average human size. While not showing the obvious musculature of the other regions, they were not obese either. The women ranged from curvy to enormous, some displaying avatars which would be classified as morbidly obese, whom I assumed had been 'fed'. I failed to engage any of the players in this region in any meaningful conversation as Mireila, with her still relatively small figure, was clearly an outsider. I left Buffet Island, confused and insulted. In real life I am a healthy, curvy, size 14 woman. It was only in Buffet Island that I saw avatars anywhere near my own size, and it was then looked upon as a fetish.

I wondered if I were to make Mireila my own size she would be looked upon as a freak. By this point, I was used to logging onto SL and spending an hour or more there every night. Mireila was a familiar sight, but I wanted to make her an even more familiar sight. That is, I wanted to make her actually look like me. I bought what looked like an application for curly hair, but it turned out to be a complete avatar called 'Heavenly'. I put it on, and suddenly Mireila disappeared and a tall, slim and very different avatar appeared. My first reaction was to stop playing altogether. This 'Heavenly' creature looked just like every other avatar. I realised at this point how much of myself I had begun to associate with

Mireila. I could not relate to this avatar so I had no emotional investment in her welfare. Mireila in 'Heavenly' form wandered around having casual sex with both male and female avatars for the experience of it. I used her to test the boundaries of what was possible on SL. The fact that I did this makes me seriously wonder what someone with a predatory nature could do if they created an avatar through which they could act out their wildest fantasies in a detached way. Contrary to what might seem obvious, I derived no sexual pleasure from watching this avatar behave in ways I would never do myself. It was morbid fascination at best, and icy detachment the rest of the time. I lost interest in SL within two sessions of this experimentation. When I finally managed to figure out how to change back into the old Mireila, the sex stopped completely. I would not let *my* Mireila engage in anything I would not do myself. Conversely, what Mireila did were behaviours that, under the right circumstances, I would do in person.

Self

My last experiment was to see how having an avatar that closely resembled me in real life would affect my behaviour. I was also intrigued by how an avatar that looked like me would be viewed by other players. First, I lightened my skin to match my pale complexion. Next, I increased Mireila's hips, stomach, buttocks and thighs and added body fat which looked like cellulite. I added pubic hair to her genitals and gave her a rounder face with softer features. Unfortunately, I was unable to change her lips to look like mine. Finally, I found a hair application which looked similar to my own: either long and curly, or in two ponytails. I found a private room to take a picture of her nude, once again to see her full body.

This photograph brought out all of my own insecurities and magnified them. When she got dressed, however, and I took her out to interact with other avatars, she proved to be mysteriously attractive to the other players. Unlike Mireila when she was in her 'Heavenly' form, I did not want anyone to touch her. While I enjoyed the attention I received, I was quite reserved in my interactions. She was becoming more and more like the real me. I took her to one of the beaches on SL to see if anyone would dare make a comment on her body. The few that she did receive were only after another player had spent at least five minutes talking with her in private IM. These conversations were non-sexual in nature, even though the location allowed for sex. The comments about her physical form were complimentary, again appreciating that she was different. Much like my interactions in real life, Mireila's interactions when looking like this were fewer, but more profound. Because she looked like me, I acted like myself even while in SL. Each interaction resulted in being added to that player's contact list.

Avatars have the potential to give us great insight into human motivation. But given my own experience, I also think they have the ability to subtly alter our behaviours just as we alter theirs if we choose to let them. We are living in an age when intimacy no longer requires face to face, or flesh to flesh contact. Is this necessarily a good thing? We are already at a point in time when people are filing for divorce on the grounds of online infidelity. The more time we spend in our virtual incarnations, the more our lives will revolve around the actions we make them do. As sex turns digital, a change in the definition of rape could be next.

Notes

1. R. Lynn, 'Virtual Rape is Traumatic, but is it a Crime?', *Wired*, 5 April 2007, *http://www.wired.com/culture/lifestyle/commentary/sexdrive/2007/05/sexdrive_0504*
2. *Ibid.*
3. V. Paech, 'A Method for the Times: A meditation on virtual ethnography faults and fortitudes', *Nebula*, No. 6.4, December 2009.
4. A. Kellehear, *The Unobtrusive Researcher* (Sydney: Allen and Unwin, 1993).
5. H. Jenkins, 'Complete Freedom of Movement: Video games as gendered play spaces', in J. Cassell and H. Jenkins (eds), *From Barbie to Mortal Kombat: Gender and Computer* Games (Boston: MIT Press, 1998), pp. 262–97.
6. H. Jenkins, 'A Second Look at Second Life', Confessions of an Aca-Fan: The Official Weblog of Henry Jenkins, 30 January 2007, *http://henryjenkins.org/2007/01/a_second_look_at_second_life.html*
7. T. Boellstorff, *Coming of Age in Second Life: An anthropologist explores the virtually human* (Princeton: Princeton University Press, 2009), p. 128.
8. Avatars that take on animorphic forms.
9. Avatars that have both human and feline attributes.
10. C. Hakim, 'Erotic Capital', *European Sociological Review*, 26(5), 2010, pp. 499–518.
11. C. Hakim, 'Attractive Forces at Work', *Times Education Supplement*, 3 June 2010.
12. Jenkins, above note 5.

13. T. Pratt, K. Holtfreter and M.D. Reisig, 'Routine Online Activity and Internet Fraud Targeting: Extending the generality of routine activity theory', *Journal of Research in Crime and Delinquency*, 47(3), 2010, pp. 267–96.
14. N. Yee and J.N. Bailenson, 'The Proteus Effect: The effect of transformed self-representation on behavior', *Human Communication Research*, No. 33, 2007, pp. 271–90.
15. *Ibid.*
16. A. Maslow, 'A Theory of Human Motivation', *Psychological Review*, No. 50, 1943, pp. 370–96.
17. Yee and Bailenson, above note 14.
18. Rape Crisis England and Wales, 'Definition of Rape', *http://rapecrisis.org.uk/Definitionofrape2.php*
19. Jenkins, above note 6.

8

Taste is the enemy of creativity: disability, YouTube and a new language[1]

Katie Ellis

Abstract: Disability is everywhere and therefore nowhere. Although present in popular culture, its function is rarely of benefit to those with impairments. However, social media do provide options for diverse communities and citizens to communicate, resist, challenge and create a consciousness through popular culture. This chapter explores the new uses of new media, with attention to YouTube and its comment function.

Key words: disability, impairment, discrimination, YouTube, social media, social model of disability, universal design

When I was 18, I had a massive stroke. Obviously, this was totally, totally unexpected. My long hair was shaved for life-saving neurosurgery and the lime green Betty Boo T-Shirt I had just bought off my younger sister was cut from my body, never to be seen again. I spent the next three months in hospital learning to walk and live independently again. Four months after that were spent in outpatient rehabilitation. I even learnt how to type one handed. While my friends were clubbing and discovering that ritual of transition into adulthood that comes with being 18, I was wearing Thrombo Embolic Deterrent stockings, Velcro sneakers and a bike helmet to protect my head. My carefree days were gone. I was medicalised. I started to listen attentively to people who seemed to have more authority over my life's direction than I did. Instead of returning to University studies when I felt I was ready, I waited until the following year. I avoided telling anyone about my stroke until my last semester of study when I pitched a documentary to my Advanced Screen Production tutorial about learning to walk again. My first steps had been captured on video. The film was made and screened for the first time at the Film and Television Institute in Fremantle, Western Australia. I won best documentary at that festival and received a High Distinction grade in the unit for which it was made. The fact that I had screened a film about illness and disability in a cinema totally inaccessible to wheelchair users is an irony that only dawned on me several years later.

Disability streams through every facet of popular culture, yet mainstream media often frames the disability experience around the 'expert opinions' of doctors, parents, and educators rather than anyone actually experiencing this socially constructed phenomena. Likewise, popular Hollywood films individualise disability by constructing it as a personal problem that can be overcome through hard work, determination and an exemplary personal attitude. Described by Barnes as the 'super cripple', this stereotype attributes magical or superhuman qualities to people with disability.[2] Films such as *My Left Foot*, *Rain Man*, *Forrest Gump* and *Born on the Fourth July* allow audiences to reassure themselves that if the disabled person tries hard enough he or she can appear normal.[3] In these films, disability is primarily presented as a personal tragedy where the individual is struck down by impairment and must rise above it, often with the help of a nondisabled person, in order to move on with their life.

As a disability cultural movement emerged in the 1990s, activists, academics and media producers argued that citizens with disabilities should be in charge of their images. Further, the resultant images must make the able bodied audience feel uncomfortable in order for social change to occur.[4] New participatory media such as YouTube has seen a realisation of this vision. The platform has afforded people with disability a new voice, a way to tell their stories and force the nondisabled world to take responsibility for systemic ableism. This chapter considers the techniques adopted in the YouTube film *In My Language*, made by a woman with autism, and a series posted by the Disability Rights Commission as it demonstrates how disability is a social construction dependent on environment and prejudicial attitudes.

Disability is a social construction

In order to situate disability in a cultural and political position, Michael Oliver redefined it as a social construction. He separated disability and impairment:

> We define impairment as lacking part or all of a limb, or having a defective limb, organ or mechanism of the body; and disability as the disadvantage or restriction of activity caused by a contemporary social organization which takes little or no account of people who have physical impairments and thus excludes them from participation in the main stream of social activities.[5]

Social models of disability described by Oliver highlight the disabling impact of the built environment on people who have impairments. The barriers to full participation in social life can be grouped together under three main categories: environment, attitudes, and organisations. This chapter expands the theorisation of an inaccessible built environment to include narratives, characters and images.[6] While disabling images can be easily identified, locating the 'problem' of disability in an individual's 'damaged body', so too must we consider the potential of images and media to problematise disability and highlight the disabling impacts of certain environments, attitudes and organisations.

The 'Talk!' series of short films produced for YouTube by the Disability Rights Commission[7] provide rich interpretative grounds for considering how disability is socially constructed through an unadaptive environment and prejudicial attitudes. These films follow the experiences of Robert, an able-bodied employee of a large corporation bestowed with the task of looking into what his company should do about the new Disability Discrimination Act. He is instructed to do sufficient to stay ahead of their competitors in the corporate world. Given that his cousin is disabled, Robert thinks he knows what it is like 'for them' but agrees that the company should not spend too much money, especially due to the fact that no one with a disability currently works for them. Uninspired by the task, Robert falls asleep at the computer only to wake up in a world where having no impairment is a disabling barrier. He is unable to communicate in sign language on the street, he is stuck in the rain as wheelchair taxi after wheelchair taxi drive past him, and later cannot get home by the 'wheelchair only' lane. Condescension surrounds him.

Although he is an attractive man, Robert finds it difficult to gain female attention in this parallel universe. He is treated like some kind of sexual novelty. The purpose of the film – and, indeed, the imperative of academic/activist Christopher Newell – is to demonstrate how the exclusion of disability is internalised. Newell discussed an overwhelming 'lifelong and daily socialization' regarding his romantic potential.[8] The 'Talk!' films explore this internalisation by creating a world where the nondisabled are disabled by the actions and attitudes of people with impairments. When Robert is unable to read a form written in Braille or when people in a night club rub his head and tell him how brave he is for coming out, and how great his mates are for taking him to places, it is clear that Robert is not the problem. The problems emerge from the environment, not his body. Discrimination and injustice emerge through the structures, strategies, opinions and oppressions that confirm on a daily basis an unwillingness to accommodate the needs of people with impairments. This unwillingness is evident through both the physical environment and the prejudicial attitudes of people around him. Robert's inability to communicate via Braille or sign language is clearly more about dominant communication practices than any deficit on his part.

By creating a world where the nondisabled are disabled by the actions and attitudes of people with disability, these films reveal the ways in which disability is socially constructed. As Christopher Newell argues, 'many of us have impairments, yet whether or not they become a disability depends upon physical structures and norms'.[9] In the early 1980s, Vic Finklestein illustrated this contention with the simple story of a fictional place where everyone uses a wheelchair. The physical world is structured accordingly, as are social relationships and it is the 'able-bodied' visitors to the world who are disabled:

> It is easy to imagine that in a community where everyone uses wheelchairs and determines their own social environment that the architecture would soon reflect the character of the residents. Door and ceiling heights, for example, could be lowered substantially. If now, able-bodied people were to live in this community they would soon find that they were prevented from 'normal' social intercourse – they would be constantly knocking their heads against the door lintels! Apart from bruises the able-bodied would inevitably find themselves prevented from using the wheelchair-user designed environment and aids. They would lack jobs and become impoverished – they would become disabled![10]

'Talk!' explores this concept with a world that is unwelcoming toward Robert simply because he is able bodied. Fellow diners are outraged by his mere presence in a restaurant and there is no possible way for him to be successful at a job interview, because it has not even occurred to the company that someone with Robert's type of body would apply. They had not accommodated for him and so could not cope with his needs.

A questioning of deeply entrenched accounts of normalcy, as they exclude people with disability, is vital to a discourse on human rights.[11] A disabling social environment has been established around a variety of norms that dictate who is included and who is excluded. The disabling social world established against the able bodied in 'Talk!' provides opportunity to reflect on disability in socio-political ways: as a social issue that demands a human rights response. The ways in which Robert's body is marginalised and patronised provide a provocative comparison with the ways in which citizens with disabilities are socially disabled in the real world. People with certain bodies are oppressed. Others are accorded the right to speak on their behalf:

> When we think about disability we are thinking about some of the most entrenched accounts of normalcy – that which is nice, normal and natural. In particular, we see that medical accounts of disability are so dominant that so often I find people failing to understand the distinction between the impairments that I have and the way in which society regards me.[12]

Traditional media individualises disability by emphasising the importance of personal attitude, rather than inaccessible attitudes, environments or organisations in a way that naturalises the exclusion of people with disability. Often shaped as 'inspirational heroes', the narrative and iconography perpetuate the individualisation of disability and do not acknowledge the way in which people with disability are disabled by society.[13] Just as 'Talk!' reveals ability and disability as a series of social choices, the YouTube film 'In My Language' confronts audiences with social disablement.

Lessons from Picasso

Impairment in general is difficult to watch on screen as it reminds audiences of mortality. Films which highlight the intersection between disability and impairment are particularly confronting as they force audiences to consider their own role in the social disablement of people with impairments. Similarly, audiences must admit the possibility that they too may one day acquire impairments. By recognising that social structures are organised in a way that empowers people without disabilities, the 'Talk!' films problematise the Hollywood-infused ideology that people with disability can achieve equality if they work hard enough and remain positive about their limitations.

In stark contrast, by facilitating an insider's look at the experience of autism and the intersecting experience of impairment and social disablement, the YouTube film, 'In My Language', introduces a more confronting representation.[14] These films do not attempt to aestheticise impairment in order to make it entertaining or more acceptable to a nondisabled audience. David Hevey claims that this is the first step in offering adequate representations of disability that could impact on social change:

> Picasso said that taste was the enemy of creativity and, eventually, those disabled artists who pursue that path of affecting taste will find their work stagnate, since they are facilitating an outsider's vision of themselves.[15]

Following his experiences in disability arts community projects, Hevey believes that people with disability often fall into a representational trap of making films which naturalise disability as a personal tragedy, rather than expose disability as dependent on a disabling context. Although Hevey refers specifically to the potential of community film-making in a time before YouTube, he maintains that an active audience is integral to revealing how modes of exclusion are naturalised through modes of representation. Because of the competing interests that invariably occur in community projects, Hevey's vision for disability representation rarely emerged. YouTube offers new possibilities because it granted users the ability to produce and distribute their own content. As Ellis and Kent argue, YouTube may prove more successful than community based advocacy, because it allows web-literate people to post their own content.[16] Active audiences engage with that content in the comments following each piece. YouTube is not bound by the same funding and philosophical constraints as community video projects and disability film festivals.

YouTube has a growing community of people with disability. A number of grassroots videos have emerged that question social interpretations of the experience of disability and the tendency of the media to value the 'expert opinion' of people who have no direct personal experience of living with disability. YouTube is structured to allow the users to comment following each video. This has resulted in lively discussions that see commentators questioning perceptions and experiences. This feature of YouTube invites a consideration of production, text and reception in line with the recommendations of several theorists within disability media studies.[17] In this post-structural model, the film-maker and spectator have equal weighting. Ideology and context are acknowledged. While wanting to effect social change is an important starting point for a film-maker, audience reception is crucial to the acceptance of this change. An active audience engaged in politics accepts social responsibility.[18] YouTube has an active audience, with the potential to enact lasting change. YouTube is not minority media. Videos can be (and are) viewed by millions of people and can even be translated into other languages.[19]

Amanda Baggs' 'In My Language' depicts people with autism, including herself, as a linguistic minority and questions who has 'the right to communicate and define one's own identity within the culture'.[20] Baggs offers a radically different way of representing disability, beyond the deficit and super cripple stereotypes. The film-maker's way of interacting with the world is valued:

> The first part is in my 'native language,' and then the second part provides a translation, or at least an explanation. This is not a look-at-the-autie gawking freak show as much as it is a statement about what gets considered thought, intelligence, personhood, language, and communication, and what does not.[21]

The film does not aestheticise impairment in order to make it entertaining or easier to watch, and therefore highlights the intersecting experience of impairment and social disablement. Baggs is seen in the film rocking back and forward, making a constant 'e' sound and performing repetitive behaviours such as running a tap and moving her fingers across a keyboard. The film has encouraged an active and energetic cultural conversation through YouTube's format which allows the film-maker to provide context and the audience to comment. Some agree with Baggs' critique of socially constructed notions of personhood.

> Unfortunately, when people (scientists or general public) find somebody not understandable, they just label them as 'strange', 'deficient' or 'inferior'. It happens to people with autism or other mental conditions, but also happens to another race (black, Asian) ... We use our self-centered, over-simplified standard to judge other beings. After watching your video, i realize that how foolish and arrogant we are ... Thank you![22]

Often, people with disability are not treated as the experts in the narrative of their own lives.[23] Instead, narratives are offered which reassure the able of their own normality. Baggs confronts this ubiquitous representation by suggesting that the problem lies with people who do not understand the experience of autism rather than those who have autism themselves. She adopts Hevey's recommendation to confront audiences with their own prejudices.

However, others do not believe that Baggs is offering a critique of restrictive interpretations of communication:

> How can you even begin to claim that you're having a conversation, when you're not even establishing any sort of sense? You're like a homeless man screaming at parked cars and calling it a 'debate'.[24]

Yet Baggs is communicating, both through the film and her activity in the YouTube forum. Baggs comments that her film is a statement on who is valued rather than a 'gawk at the autie film'. Many representations of autism in the media and cinema present the person with autism as an inspirational hero or as somebody whose life is not worth living. Depictions that suggest that a disabling social world is responsible for exclusion are never seen in the mainstream. The potential contradictions of this were debated by the YouTube community:

> Wonderful video, but I have to ask: should thinking – any kind of thinking – equal personhood? Is that all there is to a person? Is that all that we should value and protect? It seems that your argument would lead to a marginalization of those things and people that cannot think.[25]

Narrative is vital to a confrontation of otherness.[26] For Kestrell Verlanger 'In My Language' is an eloquent example of the new language available through new media such as YouTube:

> [W]hile other cultural groups are constructing categories of taste about the value of new media over old, people with disabilities are always experimenting with new tools and technologies that will allow them to participate in the culture at large. Often it is the mere act of participating, of breaking into cultural conversations, which becomes a political act.[27]

Verlanger claims that, for this reason, people with disability are often the earliest adopters of new technologies. Video streaming sites such as YouTube provide a new opportunity for media representation by putting control into the hands of people with disability. However, in order for YouTube to be effective to the disparate disability communities, it must allow access for all. Universal design and accessibility measures should be put in place so that people with many different types of impairment can access this powerful platform.

Digital disability

While YouTube empowers certain groups within the disability community, it disables others. In a 2008 survey of the accessibility of social networking sites, YouTube was given only one star.[28] This was flagged as an issue in the comments following the DRC films. The DRC listened to the active audience and has progressively made the films more accessible as YouTube itself has become more accessible. This process was enacted first by including a sign language translator, and then later by the introduction of subtitles.

As a way to participate in social networks and advocate for a more equitable and accessible world, the web is a crucial platform for people with disability. Communication can take place in many different ways: through text, still images, moving images, and sound. The opportunity to be a user creating user-generated content has proved invaluable to people with disability. For example, without captions, people with hearing impairments cannot authentically experience YouTube videos. For this reason, measures to improve access for people with disability have become increasingly important to this group.

The recent trend toward mobile applications and internet usage suggests the majority of internet users would benefit from accessibility options, thus making it broadly relevant beyond the niche groups of people with disability, the elderly and people in the developing world.[29] Digital information is most useful when it can be accessed by users with different needs in different ways. For example, people with vision impairment have adopted podcasts while people with hearing impairments opt for video blogging.[30] As these YouTube videos demonstrate, the social and personal commentary enabled via broadband telecommunications advances a social understanding of disability that moves beyond and between the individual and social divide.[31]

In 2009, Ken Harrenstien, a software engineer for Google/YouTube, announced on his blog that YouTube could now automatically caption all of its videos:

> [M]ore and more people are becoming aware of how useful captions can be. [...] captions not only help the deaf and hearing impaired, but with machine translation, they also enable people around the world to access video content in any of 51 languages. Captions can also improve search and even enable users to jump to the exact parts of the videos they're looking for.[32]

This change and recognition demonstrates that 'technologies and innovations designed to improve access by the disabled actually enhance access for all users'.[33] YouTube's enhanced accessibility features are of great benefit to all people. This is particularly so in light of the recent mainstreaming of video search technology.[34] This demonstrates the broader benefits of not treating users with disability as an afterthought. Harrenstien's argument that captions improve search highlights the need to think about constructions of ableness rather than disability as deficit.[35] While a focus on users with disability is highly unusual, in this case it has done much to move Google towards its aim of making information accessible to all.[36]

By building accessibility into the initial template, end-users will recognise the value of increasing accessibility.[37] Now that internet giants such as Google and YouTube have started a conversation about accessibility, end-users are becoming more aware of the far reaching benefits of accommodating for people with disability. This productive space of debate raises more questions and concerns about what are – actually – unacceptable platforms for a community of users.

> Once upon a time we had accounts of women as inherently inferior, based on so-called scientific accounts. Once upon a time we cherished myths of different creeds and races as other, even constructing a science of phrenology [...] Yet the medical account that has been so central to the oppression of so many social groupings and narration as other is even more pernicious when we think of [...] disability.[38]

Newell calls for a respectful narration of the lives of people with disability, beyond that of 'special needs' in order to reveal the oppression that people with disability experience as something from which all people need to be liberated.[39] While a more rigorous investigation of Disability Studies within the burgeoning field of Internet Studies is required, in light of the exciting debates on YouTube and its improving accessibility measures, the discipline of Disability Studies needs likewise to embark on an examination of internet technologies.[40]

This is especially important given recent calls to interrogate ableism rather than disability in these types of discussion.[41] The broad uptake of mobile devices to access the web confronts many of the same access issues that people with disability routinely experience. If web designers continue to ignore accessibility, mobile internet users, like many people with disability, will find themselves disabled by the network. In the context of the digital divide, the obstacles faced by people with disability shed light on the potential problems each user can encounter if excluded from the web.[42] It takes the 'world wide' from the web.

In articulating his vision for a platform to share information, Tim Berners-Lee believed that access for everyone regardless of disability was a crucial factor.[43] Although integral, disability is rarely foregrounded as a case study or recognised for its potential to move grand visions forward. Digital technologies, including the internet, broadband and advanced telecommunications have the potential to revolutionise our lives and have been held up as a way to eradicate disability, yet disappointingly continue to 'build in' disability at the point of production.[44] YouTube demonstrates the way in which people with disability can be both empowered and disabled by the network. While accessibility issues demonstrate a continuing existence of social prejudice regarding the exclusion of people with disability, this prejudice is being exposed. YouTube, with its vibrant disability activism community is leading the way in creating a socio-political space, offering a new language beyond the comfortable discourses of mainstream media, in which to confront disability.

Notes

1. An earlier version of this chapter was shortlisted for the inaugural Telstra-TJA Christopher Newell Prize for Telecommunications and Disability.
2. C. Barnes, *Disabling Imagery and the Media: An exploration of the principles for media representations of disabled people* (Krumlin: Ryburn Publishing, 1992), *http://www.leeds.ac.uk/disability-studies/archiveuk/Barnes/disabling%20imagery.pdf*
3. *Ibid.*

4. D. Hevey, 'Controlling Interests', in A. Pointon and C. Davies (eds), *Framed: Interrogating disability in the media* (London: British Film Institute, 1997), pp. 209–13.
5. M. Oliver, *Understanding Disability: From theory to practice* (New York: St Martin's Press, 1996), p. 22.
6. D. Mitchell and S. Snyder, *Narrative Prosthesis: Disability and the dependencies of discourse* (Ann Arbor: University of Michigan Press, 2000).
7. Disability Rights Commission, 'Talk', Disability Rights Commission Channel, *YouTube*, 26 July 2007, *http://www.youtube.com/user/DisabilityRightsComm*
8. G. Goggin and C. Newell, *Disability in Australia: Exposing a social apartheid* (Sydney: UNSW Press, 2005), p. 200.
9. C. Newell, 'From Others to Us and Human Rights Education', in C. Newell and B. Offord (eds), *Activating Human Rights in Education: Exploration, innovation and transformation* (Deakin West: Australian College of Educators, 2008), pp. 77–86.
10. V. Finkelstein, 'Attitudes and Disabled People: Issues for discussion', World Rehabilitation Fund, 1980, *http://www.leeds.ac.uk/disability-studies/archiveuk/finkelstein/attitudes.pdf*
11. Newell, above note 9.
12. *Ibid*., pp. 78–9.
13. G. Goggin and C. Newell, 'Fame and Disability: Christopher Reeve, super crips, and infamous celebrity', *M/C Journal*, 7(5), 2004, *http://journal.media-culture.org.au/0411/02-goggin.php*
14. A. Baggs, 'In My Language', *YouTube*, 14 January 2007, *http://www.youtube.com/watch?v=JnylM1hI2jc*
15. Hevey, above note 4, p. 213.
16. K. Ellis and M. Kent, *Disability and New Media* (New York: Routledge, 2010).
17. See K. Ellis, *Disabling Diversity: The social construction of disability in 1990s Australian national cinema* (Saarbrücken: VDM Verlag, 2008); T. Shakespeare, 'Art and Lies? Representations of Disability on Film', in M. Corker and S. French (eds), *Disability Discourse* (Buckingham: Open University Press, 1999), pp. 64–172; L. Ferrier, 'Vulnerable Bodies: Creative disabilities in contemporary Australian film', in I. Craven (ed.), *Australian Cinema in the 1990s* (London: Frank Cass & Co, 2011).
18. Hevey, above note 4, p. 213.
19. M. Jackson. 'Fluidity, Promiscuity, and Mash-Ups: New concepts for the study of mobility and communication', *Communication Monographs*, 74(3), 2007, p. 409.
20. K. Verlanger, 'Disability and Participatory Culture', *Beyond Broadcast: Mapping Public Media*, 9 February 2008, *http://www.beyondbroadcast.net/blog/?p=124*
21. Baggs, above note 14.
22. *Ibid*., comment.
23. G. Goggin, 'Disability and the Ethics of Listening', *Continuum*, 23(4), 2009, p. 493.

24. Baggs, above note 14, Comment.
25. *Ibid.*, comment.
26. Goggin, above note 23, p. 494.
27. Verlanger, above note 20.
28. AbilityNet Web Accessibility Team, 'State of the eNation web Accessibility Reports: Social networking sites', January 2008, *http://www.abilitynet.org.uk/docs/enation/2008SocialNetworkingSites.pdf*
29. M. Zajicek, 'Web 2.0: Hype or Happiness?' A Keynote presented at the 16th International World Wide Web Conference: Banff, Canada, 7–8 May 2007, *http://www.w4a.info/2007/prog/k2-zajicek.pdf*
30. G. Goggin and T. Noonan, 'Blogging Disability: The interface between new cultural movements and internet technology', in A. Burns and J. Jacobs (eds), *Use of Blogs* (New York: Peter Lang, 2006), p. 166.
31. See *ibid.* K. Ellis. 'A Quest through Chaos: My narrative of illness and recovery', *Gender Forum*, 26(2), 2009, *http://www.genderforum.org/issues/literature-and-medicine-ii/a-quest-through-chaos*
32. K. Harrenstien, 'Automatic Captions in YouTube', *The Official Google Blog*, 19 November 2009, *http://googleblog.blogspot.com/2009/11/automatic-captions-in-youtube.html?utm_source=feedburner&utm_medium=feed&utm_campaign=Feed:+blogspot/MKuf+%28Official+Google+Blog%29*
33. K. Ellis and M. Kent, 'iTunes is Pretty (Useless) When You're Blind: Digital design is triggering disability when it could be a solution', *M/C Journal*, 11(3), 2008, *http://journal.media-culture.org.au/index.php/mcjournal/article/viewArticle/55*
34. D. Whitney, 'Search Engines Lead Way to Video', *Television Week*, 27(2), 2008, p. 14.
35. See F.K. Campbell, *Contours of Ableism: The production of disability and abledness* (New York: Palgrave Macmillan, 2009); G. Goggin, 'Innovation and Disability: Critique of ability', *M/C Journal*, 11(3), July 2008, *http://journal.media-culture.org.au/index.php/mcjournal/article/viewArticle/56*
36. Information Gatekeepers Inc, 'Telecommunications Mergers & Acquisitions', 2006, *http://books.google.com/books?id=d8osxelUx-MC&pg=PP2&dq=youtube+telecommunications&ei=hHhBS-DNNZCclQSSsOnDAQ&cd=2#v=onepage&q=youtube%20telecommunications&f=false*
37. B. Gibson, 'Enabling an Accessible Web 2.0', Keynote presented at the 16th International World Wide Web Conference, Banff, Canada, 7–8 May 2007, *http://www.w4a.info/2007/prog/k1-gibson.pdf*
38. Newell, above note 9, p. 79.
39. *Ibid.*, p. 83.
40. Ellis and Kent, above note 16.
41. Campbell, above note 35.
42. I. Liccardi et al., 'The Role of Social Networks in Students' Learning Experiences', Working Group Reports on ITiCSE (Innovation and Technology in Computer Science Education), 2007, *http://eprints.ecs.soton.ac.uk/14907/2/ITiCSE2007_WG4.pdf*

43. T. Berners-Lee, 'World Wide Web Consortium Launches International Program Office for Web Accessibility Initiative', 22 October 1997, *http://www.w3.org/Press/IPO-announce*
44. G. Goggin and C. Newell, *Digital Disability: The social construction of disability in new media* (Oxford: Rowman and Littlefield, 2003), pp. xiii–xv.

Part 3
Professions, Production, Consumptions

9

The sound of a librarian: the politics and potential of podcasting in difficult times

Tara Brabazon

Abstract: Quite unexpectedly, the Information Age has not provided a golden era for librarians. The de-skilling of information literacy and a decline in public funding has resulted in librarians fighting for their professionalism, knowledge and ability, as much as for their jobs. This chapter explores how libraries and librarians are using podcasts not only to fulfil an outreach function to build a community of users, but to demonstrate the value of an information professional in an age of excessive information.

Key words: librarianship, information management, information literacy, iPod, podcasting

Michael Moore's *Stupid White Men* was a publishing success story of the early 2000s. It featured a great title and defiant argument, but it had a troubled passage to fame. The first 50,000 copies of the book came off the press on the night of 10 September 2001. Not surprisingly, a critique of George W. Bush was not seen as appropriate in the aftermath of 9/11. But as the weeks passed after this inopportune printing, the publishers – ReganBooks/HarperCollins – demanded a 50 per cent rewrite of the book. They also wanted a $100,000 cheque from Moore to pay for the reprint. With the publisher and writer at a standoff, the book was to be pulped.

The reason it survived and thrived was thanks to librarians. On 1 December 2001, Michael Moore was booked to speak to one hundred people in New Jersey. He did not deliver the planned speech but relayed the story of his soon-to-be-doomed book. In that crowd, Ann Sparanese, a librarian from New Jersey, was disgusted at the censorship. After the talk, she went home, logged on and started typing. She left messages on sites for politically progressive librarians, detailing HarperCollins' behaviour. Sparanese asked forum participants to write to the publisher and demand the release of *Stupid White Men*.

Thousands of librarians peppered the publisher's offices with letters. In disgust, HarperCollins contacted Moore and asked him what he had done, because 'now we're getting hate mail from librarians'.[1] To silence them, the publishers released the book with little advertising, book tours or publicity. The internet, in those early days of the read write web, was used to convey information about the release. Within hours, the first 50,000 copies were sold. By the next day, *Stupid White Men* was the Amazon.com number one best seller. By the fifth day, the book was in its ninth printing and at the top of the *New York Times* best seller list. It stayed there for five months.

It is no surprise that librarians were the first voices to affirm the value of democracy, justice and dissent. As a profession, librarians have faced excessive spin doctoring about the Information Age and managed the budget cuts as a consequence of it.[2] As librarians were reclassified as information managers and libraries transformed into media centres and information commons, new priorities emerged. Against this digital tide, members of the profession transformed into literacy guerrillas – protecting reading, writing and thinking from those who would sell the future of education as easily as they would market a database. Ann Sparanese has continued to ask questions and build alternatives. She has built collections in African American Studies, Hispanic Studies, World Music, and has won a grant to fund library services for Spanish-speaking citizens.[3] She demonstrates that an activist librarian can speak politics to ignorance, but also change the lives of disempowered citizens. New communities cannot only be served but created by intervening in assumptions about rights, responsibilities, literacy, community, nation and public service.

Michael Moore, reflecting upon how librarians protected his right to dissent, confirmed in the preface of his book that

> it should have come as no surprise that the librarians were leading the charge. Most people think of them as all mousy and quiet and telling everyone to 'SHHHHHH!' I'm now convinced that 'shush' is just the sound of the steam coming out of their ears as they sit there plotting the revolution.[4]

Ten years on from publishing this preface, I take Moore's commentary about librarians more literally. I am interested in the sound of, for and from librarians. Particularly, I want to investigate the activist podcasting librarian, to explore how the profession is using time and space shifting media to provide examples, opportunities and models for academics, university marketers, managers, students and citizens. Put another way, I am interested not in the 'shhhhh', but how and why librarians are using podcasts to deploy sound as both innovation and invention to solidify pathways for communication to users who may be reticent to use a library. Their quest for authenticity is built on a desire to improve information literacy. I begin this chapter with an introduction to iPod studies, showing how a small and mobile music device moved into higher education in the last decade, providing the platform for intellectual revelations through sound. While learners have gathered in classrooms, libraries and learning management systems, my chapter shows how communities of lifelong learners are assisted through the sounds – and more precisely the podcasts – of librarians.

But first I offer a statement of intent. The selection of delivery systems is a form of information management. However, the medium is not the message. Choosing a medium is the first moment – the first decision – in meaning, making and interpretation. When a platform is selected, producers make a decision about who they *will not* reach and the type of information they *will not* convey. It is ineffective to choose Twitter to convey complex ideas. However, as a pointer to richer information sources, it is excellent. Similarly if a librarian, teacher or writer wants to craft information that can be scanned at speed, sonic media is a mistake. For rapid searching on screens, visual literacy is efficient and appropriate. But for abstract ideas that slows the user's engagement with data and defamiliarises the relationship between readers and information, then sound is ideal. If reflection, imagination and creative thought are required, then sonic media is a strong option.[5] With such a caveat in place, this study of podcasting librarians can commence.

iPod studies

The 2000s emerged as the decade of gadgets. Some have succeeded. Others have failed. One of the fascinating success stories in the history of technology, as much as branding and marketing, is Apple's iPod suite. A decade on from the arrival of the first iPod, it is important to differentiate between Apple's public relations and the use of these platforms in private and public life. It is time to develop iPod studies as an important sub-component of sonic media, focusing on the mobility of sound. In the midst of accelerated change and obsolescence, teachers and librarians forget how recently the iPod and podcasts entered the language. Robin Mason and Frank Rennie's *Elearning: The Key Concepts* does not have an entry for podcasts.[6] That is no surprise. The book was published in 2006 only two years after podcasts moved from a *Guardian*-inspired neologism and into popular culture.[7] Since then, a range of websites[8] and guides have been produced to assist the movement into podcasting.[9]

The iPod has not only offered new ways of listening to music, but new ways of engaging with sonic media. Sound is a mode of communication that slows the interpretation of words and ideas, heightens awareness of an environment and encourages quiet interiority. It punctuates buildings, workplaces, leisure complexes and family life. The visual bias in theories of truth and authenticity means that sounds are often decentred or silenced in empowered knowledge systems.

Education rarely manages this sonic sophistication. Formal educational structures are geared to develop literacies in managing print. Too often, soundscapes are cheapened with monotone verbal deliveries in lectures, interjected with stammering and confusion, and do not open our ears to the other rhythms, melodies, intonations and textures in the sonic palette. The i-lecture rollout became commercially labelled as Lectopia and then, through a merger, it was known as EchoSystem 360.[10] This was an example of how an urgent – yet under-theorised – need to obtain 'online materials' from academic staff resulted in low quality sonic resources. The system was developed so that it could be automated and not subjected to the chance of academics 'ruining' the recording and distribution. This desire for standardisation rather than standards marginalised and undermined the complex relationship between media and education. Yet, as social media developed through the reduction in the price and complexity of hardware and software, new opportunities for sound and vision emerged.

Podcasts are simple to produce and receive and are suitable for distance education.[11] They also offer an intellectual opportunity for reflection on sound in learning. The most effectively branded platform for educational podcasts is iTunes U, which is part of the iTunes online store. The store's business model ensured that songs could be downloaded without a monthly or annual subscription fee. One-click purchasing led to impulse buying because of the relatively small costs and immediate desire for a track. Music videos, games, television programmes, films and apps were later sold. The arrival of the iPod Video, iPod Touch and the iPad also created and increased the value of video podcasts, or vodcasts, delivered through a larger screen.

The seamless integration of podcasts into the iTunes Music Store added another arm to the business model, with free materials available for downloading alongside commercial music. It is important to note that the proportion of users who download podcasts is much smaller than those who buy and download music.[12] It is part of the long tail[13] and is narrowcasting, rather than broadcasting. Communities not serviced by their local record store or radio station could – if digitally literate and prepared to enter a credit card number – find specialist content. It was in this context that iTunes U was developed. It was designed to be integrated into the iTunes Store but featuring university logos. Student content was not and is not the bulk of material situated in iTunes U. Instead, there are lectures, conference presentations, university alumni information and guides for students. In other words, most material is derived from staff in the form of teaching materials, promotional talks and corporate presentations of 'student life'.

The advantages of this educational material – for both enrolled students and lifelong learners outside schools, colleges and universities – are enormous. Sonic media offers a reflexive space for the teaching of abstract ideas.[14] Recognising this strength, it is important to log the weaknesses of post-visual (or blind) media. Not every subject is best learnt through digitised, mobile sound. Yet when podcasts and asynchronous sonic sessions are written and targeted for particular courses, approaches and student communities, the effects are powerful. For example, Jack Herrington outlines the importance of 'becoming a critical listener',[15] placing attention on structure, style, technical elements and content.

Initial leadership into iTunes U was derived from elite universities, including Duke, Stanford, the University of Michigan and the University of Missouri, but smaller institutions have increased their international corporate visibility through this relationship. Stanford has gained most from the publicly branded material. All of its podcasts are professionally produced and, while some of the sonic quality is variable, the tracks are introduced, advertised and mixed in a standardised and professional fashion. Stanford had a model to follow and improve, building on the high profile deployment of iPods by Duke University. In August 2004, Duke distributed 20 GB iPods to 1,600 first-year students. With enough space to store 5,000 songs, it was preloaded with orientation content in both spoken and written form, alongside information about Duke's academic environment and student activities. It was a US$500,000 investment from the University. The key element of the Duke story that is underplayed in the retelling is that the University also provided a Belkin bar microphone to attach to the iPod. Students used the microphone to record lectures and interviews for oral history and community media courses. Academics used the iPod to disseminate class content, record class based discussion and for file storage and transfer. It was aligned into the curriculum as a fieldwork recording tool.

At the end of the first year, Duke released its evaluative report of the iPod experiment:

> Initial planning for academic iPod use focused on audio playback; however, digital recording capabilities ultimately generated the highest level of student and faculty interest. Recording was the most widely used feature for academic purposes, with 60 per cent of first-year students reporting using the iPod's recording ability for academic purposes.[16]

The significance of 'the Duke moment' in the history of iPods in education was to recognise that much of the value of the unit was derived from the Belkin voice recorder. It meant that listening could – with technical ease – transform into recording. The 'what if' scenario is an enticing one. If Duke had distributed the iPods without the microphone, student behaviour may have drifted into listening to music. Instead, there was a more malleable and integrated relationship between listening and recording, downloading and uploading, the iPod and curriculum. If Duke's 2004 and 2005 'experiment' is assessed in terms of the wider iPod-owning constituency, then it is clear that most users mobilise the platform for listening rather than the production of material. Duke's story is different because, from the start of the unit's distribution with a microphone, there was an assumption of interactive production.

After two years of experimentation, the University moved away from providing iPods to students.[17] The iPod was treated, not as a branding or marketing device, not as a web 2.0 platform and the basis of social networking and collaboration, but as 'as a course supply, much like a textbook'.[18] In the space of two years, iPods went from the forefront of educational innovation to the basic kit of an undergraduate student. In reviewing this early history of both podcasts and iTunes U, three strategies emerged for their deployment in education:

- distribution of lectures for review;
- delivery of new educational materials (which may be termed 'supplemental materials'); and
- use for student assignments.[19]

Other functions started to develop in terms of branding and marketing, alongside the potential of developing a sonic archive for significant historical, theoretical and political moments. Tables 9.1 to 9.3 capture a sample of these podcasting possibilities that emerged during the decade of the iPod.

An increasing diversity of materials is distributed through podcasts, even though the lecture continues to dominate. Lecture recording is the simplest and least time-consuming way to create sonic material. Obviously, simply because lectures are syndicated to a student does not mean that they are heard. Still, a series of surprises have emerged in how students work with podcasts. Most significantly, it is believed that up to 80 per cent listen to podcasts at their computer rather than deploying the mobility of the iPod platform.[20] The potential of mobile education – delivering content anywhere and anytime – is distinct from the lived experience of students in learning by podcasts. But for librarians, mobile technology – like the old mobile library – has great potential in making traditional services relevant and useful for new users.[21]

As signified by Tables 9.1 to 9.3, the last five years have revealed strong uses of sonic media and podcasting, rather than as medication for

Table 9.1 **Examples of iTunes U podcasts – branding and marketing**

Name of sonic file	Department affiliation/ University	Comments
University of Warwick Podcasts	University of Warwick	The University of Warwick deploys an interview format of podcasts with featured academics on selected topics
Authors at MIT Series	MIT	Public speeches and podcasts from MIT authors and MIT Press authors
60 Seconds Lecture	School of Arts and Social Sciences/University of Pennsylvania	(Remarkably) short soapbox commentary from academics
Humanities Lectures	Humanities/University of Otago	Inaugural professorial address and significant keynote addresses
OU Life	Open University	Chancellery introduces students and iTunes users to the campus

Table 9.2 Examples of iTunes U podcasts – scholarly, professional development, archival and historical value

Name of sonic file	Department affiliation/University	Comments
CMS Colloquia Podcast	Comparative Media Studies/MIT	Guest speakers and diverse range of industry and fan based knowledge presented
Digital Campus	Centre for History and New Media/ George Mason University	How 'new media' have impacted on Universities, particularly in the United States
Research Channel	25 partner universities and research institutes	Integrated partnership of diverse universities
Journalism@ Stanford	Stanford University	Panels alongside keynote speeches
Town Meeting with Howard Zinn	WGBH	Vodcast with Zinn taking questions

Table 9.3 Examples of iTunes U podcasts – immediate educational use, student life and work

Name of sonic file	University	Course	Comments
Geography of Europe	University of Arizona	GUC325	Podcast lectures
Centre for Science Communication	University of Otago	Centre for Science Communication	Presentation of student films
Yale Athletics	Yale	University sports	Review of sporting successes and events
Student Voices	Arizona State University	N/A	Student podcasts on university news, global news and their experiences
Study Smarter Series	University of Western Australia	Various	Study skills programme

poor lecture attendance. As a teacher, I have located ten clear uses for podcasts in my practice.

1. Record a lecture to time and space shift its availability. This function is also useful to archive special events.
2. Record specific (and short) sonic sessions that convey specific and often abstract information for a targeted audience, to enable deeper learning.
3. Capture the student voice, constructing links between theory and practice, analysis and production.
4. Provide a way to present the student experience of a course, beyond surveys.
5. Provide audio feedback for assignments.
6. Provide sonic notes of supervisory sessions.
7. Generate new modes of supervision for off-campus students.
8. Disseminate student research and provide a show reel of student development.[22]
9. Create rich born digital data to embed within articles.
10. Record micro-interviews with staff and students on a Creative Commons licence that can be repurposed as Open Educational Resources.

For under-confident and inexperienced students, podcasts are an opportunity to connect theory and practice, thinking and doing. The advantages are clear: podcasts are inexpensive to produce. They build a community of learners and add emotion to education. They are successful, as assessed by A.W. Bates' early checklist that evaluated educational technology (set out in Text Box 9.1 below).[23]

While Bates assessed analogue education technology, the effectiveness of this checklist is still clear. Learning requires motivation, method, delivery and evaluation. Phrases like 'knowledge transfer' underestimate the planning required for learning. It suggests that ideas move between people as easily as a song is downloaded from iTunes. Dissemination, let alone learning, is much more complex. Sonic media performs this complexity, as they deliver information differently. Sound whispers its presence. When we share a sound, we share a story and a memory. However, because auditory literacies are under-researched, there is a tendency to underestimate the effectiveness of sound in learning. For example, Nandini Shastry and David Gillespie stated that

Text Box 9.1

Assessment of educational technology

- cost
- learning effectiveness
- availability to students
- user friendliness
- place in the organizational environment
- recognition of international technological inequalities

> [t]he popularity of podcasts has mostly to do with the fact that audio has become an easy way to consume information without much effort. Reading anything requires your complete attention; your eyes need to see the content, your mind needs to be involved in digesting it, and your attention must be fully focused on the visual matter to understand it. On the other hand, using audio allows you to multitask and does not require your eyes.[24]

Digestion is rarely an effective metaphor to understand the complex movement between information and knowledge, reading and understanding. Formulating binary oppositions of reading and listening, active and passive, attention and inattention, difficult and easy, is not capturing the complexities of learning through sound. However, Shastry and Gillespie do recognise the benefit of opening up new spaces and times while travelling, commuting or exercising to create new learning opportunities.[25] To transform the digestive metaphor into a culinary one, sound is the jelly of the media world. It fits into the spaces left by other responsibilities.

Listening is different from hearing. It is intentional, conscious and active. Listening is literacy for the ear. It is a social act and involves making choices in filtering and selecting sounds from our sonic environment. Listening is underestimated in our daily lives and undertheorised in academic literature. Jean-Luc Nancy confirmed that hearing is 'to understand the sense', while listening 'is to be straining towards a possible meaning'.[26] He argues that listening requires work, decoding the unknown and inaccessible into the realm of interpretation and understanding. The overwhelming majority of information we receive to understand the world emerges through our eyes. We believe what we see. Most of what constitutes knowledge and methods of study – like ethnography and participant observation – attach meanings to behaviour, derived primarily from the information we gather through vision. Differences between people are judged visually. Racism most frequently emerges from the differences we observe, rather than the diverse accents that we hear.

With this saturation of visuality, Michael Bull and Les Back probe 'the opportunities provided by thinking with our ears'.[27] We read sound through the ears as much as we read print on paper or text on a screen. Every act of listening is based on recalling a prior hearing experience. When we hear, we learn. Because we lack ear lids, we often accidentally and randomly build literacies, learning about ourselves through what we hear and how we evaluate it.

Listening is intensely personal and intimate. As Peter Szendy asks, 'what summons us to listen?'[28] For those involved in teaching and learning, our job is to connect the motivation for listening with a motivation for learning. Each new musical technology creates artificial ear lids to develop a new intimacy between the self and sound. The transistor radio in the 1960s disconnected teenagers from their family. The iPod has allowed diverse groups to claim space through sound, whether it is commuters, students or drivers. While hyper-personal, if teachers and librarians can find a way to share and enable sonic literacies and listening practices, then communities of interest – communities for learning – are built.

What if less is more? What if we gain more meaning from fewer media? Could there be positive consequences of using our senses in different ways to create fresh environments for listening, learning and thinking? Even if readers disagree with my assumption that fewer media may create more meaning by reducing the information choices we have to make, there is no doubt that fewer media – less sensory information – creates different types of learning. Educational technologies possess at least five functions:

- to provide a framework for the presentation of learning materials;
- to construct a space for the interaction between learner and an information environment;
- to offer a matrix of communication between learners and teachers;
- to offer a matrix of communication between learners and learners; and
- to offer a matrix of communication between teachers and teachers.

While it is easy in an era of digital convergence to align and conflate these roles – to combine presentation, engagement and communication into a synchronous bundle – there are advantages in the development of literacy and building an information scaffold to slow and differentiate these functions. Perhaps most importantly, podcasts return the emotion, connection and community to education. The next section of this chapter moves from investigating the role of the iPod in education to exploring the specific opportunities for librarians in building alternative learning communities.

Why should librarians use podcasts?

While the iPod has enlarged and enhanced auditory cultures and sonic literacies in education, there are specific and particular roles for librarians and information management professions in such a cultural shift. Librarians can instigate, develop, enhance, reflect upon and evaluate each of the five general functions of podcasts in universities that I have listed above. However, there are specific uses for podcasts developed by and for librarians that cannot be replicated by any other profession in higher education. Here are ten current uses of podcasts by librarians.

Returns the emotion to librarianship

The greatest gift derived from podcasts is to return the voice to education. Librarians and teachers can literally whisper their presence. Voices convey emotion, intensity, power, confusion, despair or interest. They transform public experiences into a private moment by moving complex ideas through the human voice and to the ear of another. Podcasts are a sonic hook that creates a relationship between a librarian and listeners. The medium for that connection is the voice. I conducted a project with the University of Brighton librarian, Sarah Ison. We constructed a basic 'what the library can do for you' session. I sent this as part of the orientation package to all students.[29] This meant that, right from the start of their education, a librarian was at the core of their teaching and learning. Because they heard her voice, it created a connection and relationship. They met her sonically before they saw her visually.

Podcasts make librarians more than the keepers of books. They have personality, lives, interests and enthusiasm. Plamen Miltenoff, Jo Flanders and Jennifer Hill recognised that 'the transition from bookworm to computer geek, from introvert pundit to outgoing public relations personality has been slow in coming and difficult to envision for some'.[30]

The conversational nature of podcasting has made such a transition easier. It has also enhanced the recognition that a librarian builds, and maintains the connection between information and citizens. Therefore, sound tailors particular sorts of information for new audiences. As an example, Sarah Long, Executive Director of the 650 North Suburban Chicago Libraries, interviewed interesting colleagues and authors, and aligned her region and staff. She provides a fascinating example of how a multi-campus library and librarians can form into a community.[31]

Podcasts are a pointer to resources

The characteristic of the read write web is a flattening of expertise and a confusion of popularity and relevance. This disintermediation is unhelpful in affirming the specific skills and knowledge of librarians. However, podcasts offer an opportunity for thought leadership from librarians, to intervene in the space between search and research and reintermediate the information landscape with regard to quality and relevance, rather than search engine optimisation and sponsored links. John Budd, in his fascinating book *Self-Examination: The present and future of librarianship*, explored the capacity of the profession not only in terms of facilitating access and enabling reading, but to shape ideas and form questions. He argued that 'people want to see, to read, to comprehend, to answer. With that information – and people's quest for it – as a beginning, the profession aims at giving people something they value'.[32]

He also asked the key question about a librarian's role in understanding the world. Do they follow the patterns of information generation and management or create those patterns? While Budd focused on the role of the profession in enabling new ways of seeing the world, librarians can create new methods for listening and creating a sonically rich architecture in our universities.

I am interested in how sound is used as a pointer and how podcasts can be deployed to direct students and citizens to better quality materials, while also providing scaffolding and a guide to and through this information. There is great potential in thinking about how sound can be used in a way that is disconnected from vision, enabling imagination, creativity and curiosity to re-enter education. Sound can enrich a visual media environment, but it can also be self-standing, independent and distinctive in guiding (re)searchers to new ways of thinking. The National Center for Accessible Media (NCAM) has shown great leadership in debates and discussions about how to create a media environment for a diversity of students and citizens.[33] With the eyes at rest, sound can be used to assist those confronting text based challenges.

In a seminar I conducted on sound in education at Middlesex University, Nazlin Bhimani revealed the potential of sound for international students studying by distance education.[34] She found that sound and sonic files carried via an email attachment provided an alternative to text based email instruction. The creation of reusable information that can be deployed through asynchronous media assists the management of unreliably supplied utilities such as electricity. It also creates a feedback loop – a dialogue – through asynchronous delivery of content.

Self-standing information literacy programmes

There are convincing arguments that the best information literacy programmes are integrated into the curriculum.[35] But there is a good case to be made about the value of just-in-time assistance from librarians before a semester starts or in recognition of challenges in skill development. Jaya Berk, Sonja Olsen, Jody Atkinson and Joanne Comerford described this as 'innovation in a podshell'.[36] They presented a pilot podcasting programme used at Curtin University in Western Australia to develop information literacy in the context of an academic library. They aimed for more than audio-blogging, but wanted to find new ways of delivering a programme to students. There are great advantages, including the ease of production and the capacity for materials to be reviewed and repeated until students are satisfied with their understanding. There is a wider recognition beyond librarianship that podcasting is an ideal mechanism to deliver training packages.[37] The great advantage of audio is that it can be a soundtrack while visual functions are undertaken. Students and staff can listen to a search technique or strategy from a librarian while performing it.

Specialist distance education training

Podcasts are ideal for distance education.[38] I have used podcasts with Sarah Ison in many ways. We have enacted a distance education orientation through podcasts, a virtual tour through library services and an introduction to Sarah's Twitter profile and blog.[39] The best use, however, was for the supervision of graduate students enrolled through distance education.

I initially became interested in how to use podcasts for the professional development of staff while supervising graduate students.[40] My original intention was to share supervisory practice with colleagues, but the unexpected impact of this recording and dissemination process actually became even more useful. First, students started to listen to each other's podcasts, helping each other as they moved through their research. Students who were disconnected geographically were connected sonically. However, the greatest advantage and surprise involved our librarian. She was able to hear in great detail the topics being researched by the students and customised advice and resources to them. This simply would not have been possible with geographically dispersed students. She could hear the development of the dissertation and offer strategic intervention and resources when required. Podcasting became a way to create a learning community, linking not only students and supervisors or students with each other, but students with their librarian. Significantly, every dissertation student thanked Sarah Ison in their acknowledgements. She was a librarian who became not only an information adviser, but a partner in research.

This community development strategy in supervision is both timely and important. In degrees like the Brighton based MA Creative Media, students can enrol full time or part time, distance education or on campus. Students complete one module at a time, or three modules a semester and a dissertation over the summer. One of the advantages of this flexibility is that students can complete a dissertation in each semester of the year rather than just during the summer. The consequence is that smaller cohorts complete their dissertation each semester when compared to the conventional summer enrolment. I was concerned that a community of learners would not be created. One particular semester really worried me. There were only four students completing the dissertation. Two were distance students: one in Blackburn, England; the other in Melbourne, Australia. My two on-campus students included a Brighton local and an international student from Cameroon, who had learnt English as a third language.

I wanted to find a way not only to bind the four students together, but also to create a postgraduate culture so that the much larger group of students completing the thesis over the summer would have a model for their dissertations. It was also necessary to show the relatively junior Media Studies staff how to supervise – so there was a training function as well. But I also wanted to involve our librarian, Sarah Ison, to enable her to help these diverse students who were literally all over the world.

It was probably the most successful intervention I have made in online learning. Every week I recorded a short session with the students, logging their progress. I then mixed and uploaded it to the Blackboard portal. I also released it to the public domain on the Internet Archive and via my Libsyn podcast so that the students could repurpose it for their professional show reels. This process continued throughout the entire semester. The students supported each other with references, advice and enthusiasm. It created an incredible sense of a group and a collective ownership of both the programme and the research being produced. Importantly, though, such a supervisory practice creates a significant feedback loop, allowing librarians and teachers to review their delivery pace and effectiveness.

English as second language students

Frequently the materials developed for distance education students improve the experience of on-campus scholars. Particularly, the capacity to move, review and repurpose information presents great opportunities for English for second language scholars. Jason Griffey's experience at the University of Tennessee made him realise that podcasts

> are asynchronous, allowing patrons to choose when they want library instruction; they teach to multiple learning styles; they allow for infinite review and reinforcement of skills; and they can be broken into smaller, more digestible chunks than the typical 50-minute instruction sessions in academic and public libraries.[41]

While podcasts offer rich content to distance education, Griffey realised that 'simply, many patrons can be better served with podcasts'.[42] There are multiple opportunities to review, pause, think and reconnect with information. Such a process creates an intellectual safety net for scholars developing both language skills and subject-specific knowledge.

Branding, marketing and awareness of services

Podcasting, particularly short sessions, are ideal for presenting library news. LibVibe is a great podcasting example of this function.[43] These specific presentations highlight new books, databases and new collections for specialist staff. Short, sharp, quirky and professional sessions gain an audience through a regularity of distribution. Students and staff anticipate the next instalment. Such a strategy creates what Angela Jowitt described as an 'alternative communication method',[44] with great value for geographically dispersed organisations and professions. The podcasts can be promoted on the library website, with specific episodes embedded into relevant pages. Arizona State University Library includes a range of functions in its podcasts, including tours, news, planning, subject-related material – but it binds this diversity through a Library Channel.[45]

Special collections

Regina Lee Roberts, at the World Library and Information Congress in 2007 in Durban, offered one of the most thorough reviews of the role of podcasting in information literacy.[46] As Curator of an African Collection, she argued that podcasts highlight special collections while building great links between librarians and academics. She recommended that librarians interview faculty members and present sonic book reviews of new monographs. Roberts found that podcasts were not only a way to repurpose data, but share it between institutions. As acquisition budgets collapse, it will be increasingly important to know the archival materials available, beyond a record in a library catalogue. With rich metadata and considered selection of creative commons licences,[47] the value of such podcasts in difficult economic times becomes clear. The usefulness of open education resources like podcasts is increasing, not only through iTunes U and the Internet Archive, but also with search engines like Podscope[48] which finds relevant words within podcasts.

Podcasting is narrowcasting. It targets content to less visible and financially viable audiences and offers an ideal platform to promote library resources. Newkirk Barnes reports that Mississippi State University uses podcasts to explore governmental documents and the microform department.[49] New media can create productive relationships with the old.

Professional development

As fewer staff will be completing more work in higher education in response to budget cuts, professional development may be neglected. There will always be more urgent, if not more important, tasks to complete. Yet, because of the timeshifting capacity of podcasts, they can fit into liminal moments of life that can become learning opportunities. For example, over one hundred Lunch 'n Learn Information Technology seminars at Princeton have been uploaded for timeshifting. The Joint Information Systems Committee (JISC) has made its podcasts available. Jenn Horwath realised that 'through podcasting, we aim to make our users aware of emerging technologies and help them become knowledgeable in their use'.[50] She argues that training can be completed not only just in time, but in good time and folded around other tasks. Podcasts fit into liminal spaces and times. While commuting, exercising, relaxing or completing low-level intellectual work, podcasts can weave around empty spaces. Handheld devices like the iPod and iPad are creating new relationships between librarianship, information literacy and mobility.[51]

Repackaging of content for different audiences

There has been much talk about digital natives and the Google Generation. I am not convinced.[52] However Berk, Olsen, Atkinson and Comerford argued that 'this generation has changed the way libraries need to package information literacy as we have to compete with divided attention spans. We recognised that podcasts give libraries one answer'.[53] However, for all communities of students – managing competing timetables and conflicts between family, work and study – the capacity to move quality information into the gaps of our lives is a powerful use of educational technology.

For example, the Seattle Public Library provides a podcast service for 'Teens'[54] and also a wide range of public events that are then re-packaged for new audiences, including seniors.[55] There have also been experiments in multicultural education, using podcasts to link universities with community agencies working with young people disconnected from learning environments.[56] For libraries and librarians, there is a range of functions that can be served through this repackaging of information.[57] An audio tour of the library not only can accompany new students while in the physical building, but can also prepare new students to understand the architecture of information. The London School of Economics (LSE) has a fine podcast audio tour, from an introduction and history through to the exit.[58] For distance education students, off-campus library services can be presented, along with detailed instruction on how to use a database. I have found that students use these podcasts in a loop to act as a soundtrack while searching and writing.

Building a better (not a beta) library

It has been a great decade in which to be working in communication, media and cultural studies. It has been a privilege to write, think and use our changing media environment in new ways. But the emerging and productive links between information studies and media studies have been the most pleasing. I was fortunate enough to complete a degree in internet studies in the late 1990s, during the period when librarians were teaching in this area. So the capacity of librarians to occupy positions of leadership in this field was clear to me, even before 2.0 started to be added to random nouns. But the partnerships between librarianship and media studies must continue to develop. Plamen Miltenoff, Jo Flanders and Jennifer Hill, from Learning Resources and Technology Services at St Cloud State University, showed the potential of such links in a 2008 conference paper, particularly with regard to podcasting.[59]

The University of California Santa Cruz is a great model for this best practice. They use podcasting and vodcasting for lecture series and also ensure that the library archives these sessions. Such a process ensures that the library remains the core, focus and hub of scholarship, communications and lifelong learning. By providing a home for disparate resources for academics, students and the wider community, there is a structural reminder of how librarians and libraries are integral to any teaching or research agenda.[60]

Questions of quality

Gilly Salmon and Ming Nie argued that ‘listening is easier than reading’.[61] While I respect both scholars and their work, they are not right. The literature on auditory cultures and sonic media is revealing complex, intricate and dynamic oscillations between hearing, listening and learning. In such a context, Nick Mount and Claire Chambers have provided us with a challenge. They realised that ‘more complex questions are being asked about how media should be used to influence learning for particular students, tasks and situations’.[62] One way to ask these new questions is to let our eyes rest and freshen the potential of sonic media.

Through the talk of social media and user-generated content, quality, professionalism and technical expertise are re-entering the discussion. While this last ten years in educational technology may be termed an 'iPod moment', teachers and librarians are moving away from the iPod as a recording device. The iPod is the symbol and activator of change, not the platform of change. One of the leadership roles that Media Studies scholars can offer to librarians and higher education more generally is a movement away from the iPod. Its use as a mobile platform for sonic files is clear. But its role as a recorder is limited. Its quality is reasonable for student work and software can clean up the sound, but reasonably cheap and powerful stereo recorders are now available. Flexible and useful recorders for a diversity of environments are the Zoom H2 and H4n Handy Recorders. They weigh 120 grams, have a power adapter or can use two AA standard batteries. They deploy a USB interface, permitting high quality recording with control over sound capture with four separate microphone capsules. The Zoom H4n also includes a small speaker to test the recordings.

The quality of the microphones does matter. While some information management scholars such as Berk et al. have stated that 'the difference in quality between a good microphone and a cheap one was minimal',[63] that is incorrect. If the initial recording is not adequate, then it is very difficult – indeed impossible – to boost, clean and enhance the file so that it is useable. These scholars do acknowledge that

> cheap microphones are more inclined to 'pop', which is an audible distortion on hard consonants such as 'p'. We reduced this problem by turning the microphone on an angle during recording and by using an iPod earbud cover as a make-shift pop-sock, which worked very well.[64]

Actually, a Zoom of either model – which offers easy connection to any computer via a USB – with a £5 pop screen, enables librarians to sit at a desk and record good quality sound.

Concurrently, editing software has also improved for podcasts and the construction of sonic files. While Audacity is a free and efficient open source software, it requires the installation of a LAME MP3 encoder to overcome software patents. It is not as intuitive as other recording and editing programmes. While the Adobe Audition 3 – which now enfolds the Cool Edit Pro editing suite – is arguably the best software on the market, its complexity and scale is beyond what is required for many educational productions. A more appropriate and available software at one tenth the price is Acoustica's Mixcraft, which is an intuitive multi-track audio recorder and remixer. While useful for musicians and remixers, it is also ideal for constructing podcasts and sonic material, composed of perhaps two or three tracks. It allows a simple mix down into MP3 files. There are now many intuitive and effective medium priced platforms and programmes available to improve the management of digital sonic files.

This is not 'living the beta' or Podcasting 2.0. Podcasting embodies the great paradox of social media. It appears to hyper-individualise, customise and tailor goods and services, delivering very specific material to consumers, students and citizens. At a time when state based public institutions and organisations are being abolished or underfunded, such a hyper-individualism cannot go without critique. John Maxymuk also questioned the value of podcasts and vodcasts because of 'the dry nature of the content generally on offer'.[65] But he noted exceptions when presenting information on special collections, music and art libraries. Maxymuk asked whether library materials can be made exciting, believing that they are 'more likely to be used by patrons desperately trying to cure insomnia than to find information'.[66]

While training in and for sonic media is helpful, any information is boring if presented in a monotone. The key area of improvement in delivery of the voice through media is to inject emotion into the words. A script must come to life, rather than be read as straight prose. Podcasts are not text-anchored, but start with a well drafted script. At their best, they are a conversation, triggering dialogue, action and transformation from the listener. Maxymuk recommends blogs, rather than podcasts, for librarians. Both can be used, but in different ways. The key decision is to think about the mobility of content, and the audience for it. Podcasts are like Google Goggles for the ear. They sort, point, recognise, emphasise and shape. Librarians can use them to initiate thought leadership, to correct the Google Effect, or the flattening of expertise.[67] They can reintermediate the information landscape. Perhaps most importantly, sonic media and podcasts build relationships. Podcasts can be sonic twitter for librarians, pointing to richer materials, sources and ideas.

The worry when recommending such postfordist strategies for a postfordist library is that already overworked librarians have even more responsibilities. This problem was revealed when I delivered a talk to school librarians in Portsmouth. They were an inspirational group: intelligent, caring and responsive to social change and challenges. One seemingly inexhaustible female librarian was blogging, podcasting, vodcasting, text messaging, and creating wiki-enabled book reviews and recommendations. She had just opened a Twitter account and asked me: 'Why the hell am I on Twitter?' I asked her what she was trying to achieve in 140 characters. She shook her head and replied: 'I have absolutely no idea. I'm closing it down when I get home.' Her moment of consciousness is important. Librarians cannot do everything. They should only use podcasts or any social media if it aligns with their learning and teaching goals. If it is not required or does not improve the effectiveness of a current media platform, then do not add one more responsibility on to staff. Select what is appropriate to a particular institution, collection and community. But if sound can enliven and renew, then podcasts provide not Library 2.0, but a restatement of the centrality of libraries as the core of our culture.

Notes

1. M. Moore, *Stupid White Men* (Camberwell: Penguin, 2002: 2001), p. xvii.
2. A fine example of the scale of these changes is J.C. Bertot, P.T. Jaeger, C.R. McClure, C.B. Wright and E. Jensen, 'Public Libraries and the Internet 2008–2009: Issues, implications, and challenges', *First Monday*, 14(11), 2 November 2009, *http://firstmonday.org/htbin/cgiwrap/bin/ojs/index.php/fm/article/viewArticle/2700/2351*
3. 'Small and Large Acts of Resistance – Ann Sparanese', *Library Journal*, 15 March 2003, *http://www.libraryjournal.com/article/CA281662.html*
4. Moore, above note 1, p. xviii.
5. The reason why sonic media creates this interpretative space is because of the gap between signifier (form) and signified (content). Printed signifiers, such as the word 'truth', offer a limited array of signifieds. While images offer an array of interpretative opportunities, the anchorage of the written word through such functions as captions to photographs restrict the available meaning systems. However, sound – along with smell, taste and touch – are senses that provide more ambiguous information to decode. The plurality of signifieds that emerge from such signifiers may not be useful in particular information systems, where definitive interpretations are required. However, if the goal is to encourage thought, questioning and critique, then receivers of sensory input that encourages ambiguity must work harder to connect signifiers and signified and build meaning.
6. R. Mason and F. Rennie, *Elearning: The key concepts* (New York: Routledge, 2006).
7. Podcasting is a portmanteau of 'iPod' and 'broadcast' and has stabilised its meaning to connote the online distribution of digitised media files and the

use of syndicated feeds. The feed and subscription model is like a sonic direct debit. It can be set, and files arrive without much thought. Playback is activated on portable media players and personal computers and timeshifted to suit the listening patterns of subscribers. The initial attraction to recording podcasts was that individuals beyond radio stations could deliver and distribute programmes, creating a diversity of content, voices, accents and programme length. Rapidly though, the early adopters who expressed their enthusiasm and interests were joined by empowered institutions like schools, universities, museums, government and corporate communications. A major area of success has been the deployment of podcasts in formal education.

8. 'How to Podcast Tutorial', *http://www.how-to-podcast-tutorial.com.*
9. M. Boyden, *The Greatest Podcasting Tips in the World* (Stratford-upon-Avon: The Greatest in the World Book, 2007); K. Islam, *Podcasting 101 for Training and Development* (San Francisco: John Wiley & Sons, 2007); M. Harnett, *A Quick Start Guide to Podcasting* (London: Kogan Page, 2010); S. Mack and M. Ratcliffe, *Podcasting Bible* (Indianapolis: Wiley, 2007); and J. Herrington, *Podcasting Hacks* (Sebastopol: O'Reilly Media, 2005).
10. Lectopia, *http://www.lectopia.com.au/ and Echo 360, http://www.echo360.com/*. Most amusingly, these organisations are part of the Lecture Capture Community, *http://www.lecturecapture.com/*.
11. A. Chan and C. McLoughlin disagreed with my argument here, reporting that 'although substantive data is not available at this stage, in a postgraduate distance education cohort consisting of mature age, working professionals, the students appeared to favour text based material in print or electronic (web based) form. In fact, some even asked for transcripts of the podcasts to be supplied so they could avoid having to listen to them' (p. 18). While I have found the opposite of their findings – with mature-aged female students using sonic media educational sessions in the car on a school run, for example – the assessment by Chan and McLoughlin of diverse learning communities requiring diverse media is an important corrective, particularly considering the title of their paper: 'Everyone's Learning with Podcasting: A Charles Sturt University experience', Proceedings of the 23rd Annual Ascilite Conference, 2006, *http://csusap.csu.edu.au/~achan/papers/2006_POD_ASCILITE.pdf*
12. The PEW Internet and American Life project conducted a study of podcast downloaders and configured a profile, finding them to be most frequently male and experienced internet users. Their first study was conducted at the end of 2006. See M. Madden, 'Podcast Downloading', 22 November 2006, *http://www.pewinternet.org/~/media//Files/Reports/2006/PIP_Podcasting_Nov06_Memo.pdf*. To monitor the changes in this profile two years later see M. Madden and S. Jones, 'Podcast Downloading', 2008, *http://www.pewinternet.org/Reports/2008/Podcast-Downloading-2008/Data-Memo/Findings.aspx*
13. C. Anderson, *The Long Tail* (New York: Hyperion, 2006).
14. T. Brabazon, 'Socrates in Earpods: The ipodification of education', *Fast Capitalism*, 2(1), 2006, *http://www.uta.edu/huma/agger/fastcapitalism/2_1/brabazon.htm*

15. Herrington, above note 9, p. 51.
16. Y. Belanger, *Duke iPod First Year Final Evaluation Report* (Durham: Duke University, 2005), *http://cit.duke.edu/pdf/reports/ipod_initiative_04_05.pdf*
17. B. Read, 'Lectures on the Go', *Chronicle of Higher Education*, 52(10), 2005, *http://chronicle.com/weekly/v52/i10/10a03901.htm*
18. S. Earp, Y. Belanger and L. O'Brien, *Duke Digital Initiative End of Year Report* (Durham, Duke University, 2006), *http://cit.duke.edu/pdf/reports/ddiEval0506_final.pdf*
19. Office of Technology for Education & Eberly Center for Teaching Excellence, 'Podcasting: A teaching with technology white paper', Carnegie Mellon University, 2007, *http://connect.educause.edu/files/CMU_Podcasting_Jun07.pdf*
20. *Ibid.*
21. Lilia Murray explored this process of innovation in 'Libraries "like to move it, move it"', *Reference Services Review*, 38(2), 2010, pp. 233–49.
22. A basic but clear guide to career building through podcasting is S. Sawyer, *Career Building Through Podcasting* (New York: Rosen Publishing Group, 2008).
23. A.W. Bates, 'Technology for Distance Education: A 10-year perspective', in A. Tait (ed.), *Key Issues in Open Learning – A reader: An anthology from the journal 'Open Learning' 1986–1992* (Harlow: Longman, 1993), p. 243.
24. N. Shastry and D. Gillespie, *Podcasting for Trainers and Educators* (Boston: Pearson Education, 2008), Kindle Edition, locations 88–96.
25. *Ibid.*, locations 438–437.
26. J. Nancy, *Listening* (New York: Fordham University Press, 2007), p. 6.
27. M. Bull and L. Back, 'Introduction: Into sound', from M. Bull and L. Back (eds.), *The Auditory Culture Reader* (Oxford: Berg, 2004), p. 3.
28. P. Szendy, *Listen: A history of our ears* (New York: Fordham University Press, 2008), p. 142.
29. T. Brabazon, 'Sarah Ison talks with Tara Brabazon about Libraries,' *Internet Archive, http://www.archive.org/details/SarahIsonTalksWithTaraBrabazonAboutLibraries*
30. P. Miltenoff, J. Flanders and J. Hill, 'Podcasting for School Media Specialists: A case study from Central Minnesota', TCC 2008 Proceedings, p. 21, *http://etec.hawaii.edu/proceedings/2008/Miltenoff2008.pdf*
31. S. Long, 'Longshots', *Library Beat, http://www.librarybeat.org/longshots*
32. J. Budd, *Self-Examination: The present and future of librarianship* (Westport: Beta Phi Mu Monograph Series, 2008), Kindle Edition, locations 38–42.
33. National Center for Accessible Media (NCAM), *http://ncam.wgbh.org*
34. N. Bhimani in T. Brabazon, 'The Sound of Education', *Internet Archive*, June 2010, *http://www.archive.org/details/TheSoundOfEducation*
35. S. Williams, 'New Tools for Online Information Literacy Instruction', *The Reference Librarian*, 51(2), April 2010, pp. 148–62.
36. J. Berk, S. Olsen, J. Atkinson and J. Comerford, 'Innovation in a Podshell: Bringing information literacy into the world of podcasting', *The Electronic Library*, 25(4), 2007, pp. 409–19.

37. K. Islam, *Podcasting 101 for Training and Development* (San Francisco: John Wiley, 2007).
38. J. Ralph and S. Olsen explore the role of podcasting for students located in 'off shore' campuses. See 'Podcasting as an Educational Building Block in Academic Libraries', *Australian Academic & Research Libraries*, 38(4), December 2007.
39. S. Ison and T. Brabazon, 'Twitter and Librarianship', *Internet Archive*, *http://www.archive.org/details/TwitterAndLibrarianship*
40. Examples of these supervisory sessions can be found in Tara Brabazon's Podcast, *http://tarabrabazon.libsyn.com/*. The initial experiment in sonic supervision was conducted with Abigail Edwards, Paul Nataraj, Venessa Paech and Maggie Wouapi.
41. J. Griffey, 'Podcast 1 2 3', *Library Journal*, 132(11), June 2007, p. 32.
42. *Ibid.*
43. LibVibe, *http://libvibe.blogspot.com/*
44. A. Jowitt, 'Creating Communities with Podcasting', *Computers in Libraries*, 28(4), April 2008, p. 54.
45. Library Channel, Arizona State University, *http://lib.asu.edu/librarychannel*
46. R. Roberts, 'Podcasting for Information Literacy', World Library and Information Congress, 19–23 August 2007, Durban, South Africa.
47. Podcasting Legal Guide, *http://wiki.creativecommons.org/Podcasting_Legal_Guide*
48. Podscope, *http://www.podscope.com*
49. N. Barnes, 'Using Podcasts to Promote Government Documents Collections', *Library Hi Tech*, 25(2), 2007, pp. 220–30.
50. J. Horwath, 'Social Tools: More than just a good time?' *Partnership: the Canadian Journal of Library and Information Practice and Research*, 2(1), 2007, pp. 1–7.
51. S. Foo and J. Ng, 'Library 2.0, Libraries and Library School', Proceedings of the Library Association of Singapore Conference, Singapore, May 2008, pp. 8–9.
52. G. Lorenzo, D. Oblinger and C. Dziuban, in 'How Choice, Co-creation, and Culture are Changing what it means to be Net Savvy', ELI Paper 4, October 2006, also questioned the technological ability of the Google Generation.
53. Berk et al., above note 36, p. 411.
54. Teens Podcast from the Seattle Public Library, *http://itunes.apple.com/gb/podcast/teens-podcast-from-the-seattle/id267257330*
55. Seattle Public Library, Events, *http://itunes.apple.com/gb/podcast/the-seattle-public-library/id191495727*
56. J. Beilke, M. Stuve and M. Williams-Hawkins, 'Clubcasting: Educational uses of podcasting in multicultural settings', *Multicultural Education & Technology Journal*, 2(2), 2008, pp. 107–17.
57. Meg Atwater-Singer and Kate Sherrill recommend a careful discussion about the best functions of podcasting and Web 2.0 tools before producing these materials: see 'Social Software, Web 2.0, Library 2.0, & You: A practical guide for using technology @ your library', *Indiana Libraries*, 26(3), 2007, pp. 48–52.

58. LSE Library Tour, *http://itunes.apple.com/gb/podcast/lse-library-tour/id 278972091*
59. Miltenoff, Flanders and Hill, above note 30.
60. To review how this process can be undertaken, see Sarah Cohen, 'Taking 2.0 to the Faculty', *C&RL News*, September 2008.
61. G. Salmon and M. Nie, 'Doubling the Life of iPods', in G. Salmon and P. Edirisingha (eds.), *Podcasting for Learning in Universities* (Maidenhead: Open University Press, 2008), p. 10.
62. N. Mount and C. Chambers, 'Podcasts and Practicals', *ibid.*, p. 45.
63. Berk et al., above note 36, p. 414.
64. *Ibid.*
65. J. Maxymuk, 'Online Communities', *The Bottom Line: Managing Library Finances*, 20(1), 2007, p. 55.
66. *Ibid.*
67. T. Brabazon, 'The Google Effect', *Libri*, vol. 56, 2006, pp. 157–67, *http://www.librijournal.org/pdf/2006-3pp157-167.pdf*

10

The invisible (wo)man

Tara Brabazon and Nazlin Bhimani

Abstract: This chapter presents an interview with the librarian, Nazlin Bhimani. She presents her models and strategies for academics and students to improve their engagement with online resources.

Key words: libraries, librarians, information literacy, information management, new media

Most work in universities is invisible. A good undergraduate lecture takes many hours to transform a drab monologue into the foundation for student learning, combining relevant scholarly literature and appropriate media. A considered postgraduate seminar requires continual reflection about group dynamics and the integration of each week's topic into the arc of the course. Distance education demands labour-intensive preparation before the semester commences. The micro-teaching moments via email, messaging and Skype are unrecognised in workload calculations.

One of the consequences of budget cuts is that this unseen work has increased. But academics are like icebergs: some of our efforts remain visible in classrooms, journals and books, even if the preparation remains below the surface. For librarians, almost all of their work is invisible. They run orientation sessions. They (wo)man information desks. Like the Wizard of Oz and his curtain, they wait behind online query screens.

It is difficult to log the scale and breadth of their role. To offer one example, when Tara was writing the introduction to this chapter you are now reading, she was marking the first cycle of assignments in her first-year course. Each semester, the hope is that students implement correct referencing styles, enact careful editing of their prose and read sources at the level required for a degree. Four or five outstanding submissions shine from every pile of papers. There are also thirty or forty that require immediate assistance in the most basic of scholarly protocols. Academics may complain about dumbing down or the declining standards in schools. There is, however, an alternative way of thinking. We can ensure that struggling students gain information literacy skills so that discipline-specific knowledge may emerge. Such a strategy is based on a solid, honest and open partnership between academics and librarians. Fine librarians remain in universities. It is important to value their words and contribution to higher education. As an example of the work that remains invisible in staff development reviews and job specifications, Tara interviewed one extraordinary librarian to explore information, digitisation, community and learning.

Introducing Nazlin

Nazlin Bhimani was born in Uganda. She completed her education in Canada, graduating with a BA in Music and an MA in Musicology at the University of British Columbia and a Master of Library Science at the University of Western Ontario. When appointed to Middlesex University, she became a Teaching Fellow and attained a Post Graduate Certificate in Higher Education. She started as the Campus Library and Information Manager for Art and Design and the Subject Librarian for Film, Video and Interactive Art. She then assumed the role of School Liaison Manager for Engineering and Information Science, and the Institute for Work Based Learning. In late 2010, she began a new post as Christ's College's Librarian at the University of Cambridge.

Nazlin holds international experience, more qualifications than many academics, and has moved between the arts and sciences and the new and old university sector. When assuming her new appointment, it was timely to create a conversation about information, knowledge, librarians and academics.

TB: *Do you believe that information literacy should be taught as a self-standing topic or subject or embedded in curriculum?*

NB: Information Research Skills (also referred to as 'information literacy' and 'information fluency') is one of several key areas of learning skills development that need to be addressed across all sectors of the twenty-first century education system. This bundle of inter-related skills (searching, finding quality and appropriate information sources, and the ethical use of information) cannot stand on its own without the other related skills, especially those of advanced critical reading and IT proficiency. Together these stand at the heart of the process of becoming educated and learned (the original meaning of 'literate'). JISC has been advocating a platform of essential literacies since 2008, as is evidenced in the *Learning Literacies in the Digital Age* report.[1] Yet, despite the growing familiarity of the skills and literacies agenda, with its requirement for joined-up thinking within the academy, the rolling out of this agenda across higher education institutions has been surprisingly – and damagingly – tentative. For example, one very basic challenge that is not being adequately met is how to get a disparate group of specialist educators within an institution (librarian, language support, e-learning and teaching staff) to work together in partnership to deliver a learning programme fit for purpose in a world which will become increasingly dominated by new technologies and behaviours consequent upon their wide and disparate application.

Teaching information research skills in isolation from the curriculum is a bit like providing a manual called *Cyberspace for Independent Travellers* and saying to the student 'You can stand on your own two feet now, so off you go. It's all a bit scary and won't make much sense, and you'll spend many light years in the wrong galaxies, but enjoy the ride!' It is important to take an embedded approach because information research skills need to be seen as part of a developmental process over time and meaningful in context. For an embedded approach to work, librarians need the active participation of university teaching staff. To be frank, some academics have a very old-fashioned understanding of libraries and librarians and this understanding has not changed despite the revolution in the information landscape and advances in the way academic library services are being provided. In contrast, many of those academics who have opened the door to collaborative working with library staff have begun to see the major benefits, rethinking their teaching and learning methods, and giving much more significance in assessment to the evaluation and use of online resources.

My feeling is that the professional divide between librarians as information resource experts and university teaching staff has to break down. The university is changing out of recognition but we still have these old divides which, to be honest, are often really discouraging. But I'm optimistic and believe that at some point all the digital literacies, including information literacy, will be integral to the curriculum, and some of the terrific collaborative pilot projects I have been fortunate enough to work on will become the norm.

It is worth noting that librarians in the United States and Canada often are given faculty status and are in tenure track positions. They are expected to publish in their discipline and many do. If librarians in the UK were also given faculty status, the perceived division between them and academic teaching staff may be reduced. This would enable a more equitable working environment – one in which academic teaching staff may be more willing to include librarians in programme planning and curriculum design, as well as in research.

TB: ***What can teachers do to help librarians in their role? How can we support your work?***

NB: Collaborate! Take librarians more fully on board and give us recognition as key staff in supporting teaching and learning, and in helping to drive forward a productive engagement with new learning technologies. Also, teachers often don't realise how much face-to-face support for students is provided by the librarian – both on the enquiry desk and in one-to-ones – and the more the librarian is part of an academic team, the more joined-up can be their contribution. The role of the librarian in supporting research students is becoming particularly significant as information on the internet created by experts becomes more widespread and the benefits of teaching researchers how to stay current and utilise networking opportunities with experts in their fields of study become more important. Also of significance is the fact that librarians – who are usually adaptable to using new technologies, including social networking tools – provide a 'blended support service', especially for the distant, work based or part-time student. This is usually a combination of a wide variety of methods including face-to-face tuition, online enquiry services and Skype.

Participate! When you ask for a library workshop, do not assume that it is a couple of hours off to catch up on your administrative work or research. Work together with the librarian to plan and deliver workshops based on live issues in the curriculum. Then follow up the workshop with developmental tasks and, most importantly, use the assessment process to measure the progress of the student in managing and utilising more complex resources.

Advocate! Promote the importance of information literacy and the role of the librarian in the student's learning experience. Include the librarian in your course team, list the workshops in the course handbook and ensure that students attend the workshops.

Successful integration therefore includes collaboration, participation and advocacy by both librarian and teaching staff.

TB: ***What do you see as the library of the future?***

NB: The library of the future needs to be as inspiring as the old libraries. A place and a space that fills you with wonderment, one that motivates learning, encourages inquisitiveness, and yet feels homely. Will it be? I'm not so sure. There can be something very clinical and cold about the high-tech learning resource centre and sometimes redesigns of libraries try a bit too hard to look like shopping malls or trendy internet cafes. Of course, this library of the future, at least in the developed world, is going to be governed by the digital landscape. Learners will want to be able to access information as quickly and efficiently as possible on a myriad of platforms – both static and mobile. There will be an increase in shared learning activities.

There will be a more fluid feel to a library and there will be more flexible spaces. But I would like to think there will still be books – and lots of them. I would like to think that the core of the library will still be a beautiful harmonious space in which to lose yourself as a student or researcher.

The virtual library of the future is another issue. I would like to imagine some virtual space which is as distinctive to the web as the physical space of my ideal library. Certainly, with the development of the semantic web or web 3.0, the library of the future will look very different. The focus will be on semantically linked content, enabling users to find the root and permutations of the information in various formats and media. This, in turn, will affect the information seeking behaviours and workflows of users, and we need to understand these to design this virtual library that is available seamlessly on multiple platforms.

TB: ***You have been a major supporter of emerging technologies in and for librarians. In your experience what web 2.0 tools have proven most useful for your work?***

NB: The web 2.0 social networking tools allow us to disseminate information in 'bite-size' chunks more quickly and easily, and to share and gather opinions, ideas and feedback on our services and resources. The opportunities these emerging technologies also present for collaboration with like-minded colleagues are fantastic. So, with web 2.0, we are now not only consumers of information but also producers of information. With web 2.0 technology the information finds its way to us, rather than us having to find it. User-generated content can be problematic in an academic environment and so, again, information literacy or the evaluation of information sources becomes so much more important.

In terms of the selective dissemination of information, researchers are now able to keep updated and current on their research topics by simply subscribing to RSS feeds from databases, journals and websites – and this is sent directly to their desktops (either via email or RSS readers). The Research Information Network (RIN) commissioned a study on the use of web 2.0 tools by researchers in different disciplines and found that, if used effectively, the use of these tools can allow for the wider and more rapid communication of research.[2] These technologies create different workflows from those that librarians have been used to and it is therefore important for librarians to understand these changes in order to ensure that their service provision is aligned appropriately. For instance, while selective dissemination of information was very much the realm of the librarian, researchers are now encouraged to do this for themselves in order to benefit in other ways, for example, by making the most of the inherent networking opportunities that these tools provide.

My experience of using web 2.0 tools has been positive. We can now have an open dialogue with our users, sharing views and stories in an informal voice on our library blogs and on our Facebook site. We also use wikis and other interactive software (such as our 'Library 2.0' subject guides[3]) to engage with our users in the teaching of information/research skills. Social bookmarking and referencing tools – such as Delicious, Zotero and Mendeley – allow for the sharing of links and bibliographies. Linkedin and Facebook enable dialogue with other individuals, institutions and groups and therefore provide further networking potential with researchers and/or experts in industry. The potential benefit of establishing research networks by using these technologies to share and collaborate in scholarship is wonderful. I use Twitter for networking with other librarians;[4] I find it to be extremely useful in that it enables me to keep current in the area of information science and it allows me to be aware of 'conversations' taking place on different professional topics in the 'Twittersphere' – whether it's information literacy, the future of libraries, teaching and learning, or issues in higher education.

The bigger challenge is to ensure that the web 2.0 services used by librarians are easily visible to users in their preferred online territory.

Some libraries have been successful in aggregating these tools alongside traditional access points to create portals offering a 'mash-up' of sorts.

TB: *What do you think is the great gift or potential that librarians can give to teachers, students and the higher education sector?*

NB: Librarians bring to the table their expertise and, believe me, this expertise is absolutely on the frontline as universities engage in massive changes that the twenty-first century is continuing to bring. But I want to emphasise something else. Librarians will continue to be, very literally, the interface between, on the one hand, resources and systems for accessing these resources and, on the other, individuals and groups in pursuit of information and eager to transform that information into knowledge that is meaningful and useful to them. Librarians may work in large facilities in even larger institutions, but our work is to help individuals in their quest. Certainly the greatest professional satisfaction comes from helping individuals open those doors and, where necessary, climb through those windows.

I fear that we may lose this personal contact. Indeed, it is my one great fear. Without doubt, we need to ride on the back of this amazing technical revolution, but technological 'solutions' in the library of the future may significantly reduce the number of highly skilled librarians, often with specialist subject knowledge, who are available to support and encourage the very special learning experience that the library offers. Why is the human element so important? Well, not only do students find it difficult to use these multifarious and disjointed solutions, but worse they are wrongly perceived as being adequate and sufficient for learning. The various studies on the information-seeking behaviour of library users by the Pew Foundation, the Online Computer Library Center (OCLC), the Research International Network (RIN) and the Joint Information Systems Committee (JISC)[5] contest this, of course. Librarians are succeeding in bringing clarity and focus to information searching and evaluation through their teaching of information/research skills.

TB: *What do you think is the greatest challenge facing the library profession right now?*

NB: There are at least seven things that I can identify as important challenges to the library profession right now:

- the financial challenge of demonstrating value for money and the tangible impact of library services on the institution;

- changes in the information landscape (the digitisation of information resources and the availability of open access resources via institutional repositories);
- changing information-seeking behaviour of library users;
- the need for these users to learn the skills necessary to navigate this digital landscape;
- the proliferation of data generated by modern technological tools in all disciplines and its further proliferation through re-use;
- the advances being made in the development of a semantic web; and
- the increased pressure to think through a vast range of legal and ethical issues raised by new ways of working with information.

However, as I see it, by far the biggest challenge is preparing the necessary multi-skilled librarian of the future: the librarian as technology expert, as teacher and as bona fide member of a research team. This means, in my view, that library schools need to make a root and branch review of their curriculum in order to ensure that professional academic librarians are being provided with the appropriate skill-set. In particular, I believe that the teacher–librarian role should be addressed, while the librarian's own skills as a researcher – contributing as an equal within multi-disciplinary teams – need to be developed. Within a research team, the librarian, appropriately trained, will be able to make a unique contribution in ensuring that data is expertly described, archived and curated so that it can be made available for use by the wider research community.

As a profession, we have a mountain to climb and, though we have made advances in terms of provision of resources and study environments, we have hardly started. The constant evolution of technological solutions, the pressures of the current economic climate and the changes in the information environment will mean a continuing need to innovate and adapt how we work to provide appropriate support to our institutions and students, and to survive as a profession.

Going back to the point I made at the beginning concerning the difficulty in joining up the work of different kinds of educator within the academy, it is clear that we have to rethink institutional structures so that they adapt to the changing nature of information, knowledge and learning. As I have already said, the library is the front line in an ongoing operation to rethink and redefine the nature of a university in the twenty-first century.

Endings

Too often in university meetings, librarians are absent. They are frequently not welcomed or included as part of the committee. While Groucho Marx joked about refusing to join any club that would have him as a member, such platitudes do not address the consequences of librarians remaining invisible when discussing the core business of universities. Nazlin is right: libraries are 'the front line' in rethinking the purpose of universities. With leadership from librarians like Nazlin, this reflection on our past and revisioning of our future remains productive and empowering.

Notes

1. See JISC, 'Learning Literacies for the Digital Age', 2009, *http://www.jisc.ac.uk/publications/briefingpapers/2009/learningliteraciesbp.aspx.*
2. See C. Gray, 'If You Build It, Will They Come? How researchers perceive and use web 2.0', Research Information Network, 2010, *http://www.rin.ac.uk/our-work/communicating-and-disseminating-research/use-and-relevance-web-20-researchers.*
3. 'Library 2.0' refers to the use of collaborative, social and multimedia web based technologies in a library. See, for example, the Library 2.0 Subject Guides portal which we developed at Middlesex University at 'Library Subject Guides', *http://libguides.mdx.ac.uk.*
4. Twitter has been useful to obtain immediate feedback from librarian colleagues on many occasions. On one occasion, my request for thoughts on whether food should be allowed in libraries elicited 124 responses from librarians, students and library users; the topic was so popular that it became a 'trending topic' on Twitter in the UK. See 'Food in Libraries', *http://twapperkeeper.com/hashtag/foodinlibraries.*
5. See L. Connaway and T. Dickey, 'The Digital Information Seeker: Findings from selected OCLC, RON and JISC user behaviour projects', OCLC Research, 2010, *http://www.jisc.ac.uk/publications/reports/2010/digital information seekers.aspx*

11

The impact of the video-equipped DSLR

Matthew Ingram

Abstract: Many areas of the media have been transformed through digitisation. Photography was one of the earliest and most startling. This chapter investigates the relationship between the digital single lens reflex camera (DSLR) and the prosumer (the professional consumer). Now that the quality of hardware has improved and the amateur has access to it, what is the future for the professional photographer?

Key words: digital single lens reflex camera (DSLR), prosumer, Facebook, Flickr

The advent of the digital single lens reflex camera (DSLR) in the 1990s allowed professionals to incorporate the digital dark room into their repertoire. These benefits were later disseminated to amateurs with the introduction of cameras such as the Canon EOS 300D. One of the principle advantages of the DSLR and the film based models that preceded it is the ability to change the lens. Professionals and amateurs alike had access to a wide variety of creative possibilities by the use of interchangeable lenses, ranging from the ultra-wide angle shot to the long telephoto zoom lens.

The creative control afforded with a DSLR is found in two key areas. The first is the ability to freeze motion, ensuring that a fast-moving object is in focus. The second creative control is the ability to adjust the depth of field; if an image has a deep depth of field, this means generally that most parts of the photo are in focus. This is especially applicable in landscape photography where the scene ranging from the foreground to the background may be of interest. An application of depth of field within portrait photography is where the photographer wants the subject to be in focus and the background to be out of focus, thereby making the subject stand out. These options are not available to users of compact cameras. They have limited controls – hence the phrase 'point and shoot'. Owning a DSLR does not necessarily mean that great photography is generated through automated functions. This creative control is useful only if the photographer has the ability to implement these possibilities in his or her photography. The DSLR can still take a poor picture in untrained hands.

Users of compact digital cameras have also seen much technical advancement during the same period and some compact cameras now have creative abilities that go some way to mimic the effects of the DSLR. The compact digital camera, quite early in its life cycle, could shoot video, but often of very low quality. Now most mobile phones also have this ability. The most modest technology gives users the ability to shoot, edit and upload their creations in some format. In 2008, with the introduction of the Nikon D90 and the Canon 5D Mark II, high-level functionality was incorporated. Now that this functionality is present, a wide range of users and uses can emerge. This chapter investigates the communities built around the proliferation of the DSLR beyond professional photographers. It is an example of 'prosumer' (the professional consumer) in action.

The video DSLR

The video DSLR has the potential to offer cinematic quality at a fraction of the cost. The creative control in video is as important as it is in photography, the principle creative control being the ability to have that shallow depth of field and an interchangeable lens system with large maximum apertures. In 2010, broadcast quality camcorders were available to purchase for between £5,000 and £10,000. In comparison, similar quality from the video-equipped DSLR might cost £700 for a Canon EOS 550D. The video DSLR has been used by mainstream productions such as *Iron Man 2*, and was used as the only type of camera on the final series of *House*.[1] This episode of *House* is typical of the capabilities of the video DSLR, using very shallow depth of field to draw the viewer's attention to the actor. Producers have talked about the advantages of the video DSLR, such as its smaller size compared with traditional broadcast camcorders and the creative control of the shallow depth of field, but the mainstream is probably not where the video DSLR will have its greatest use.

The independent and home film-makers are the major beneficiaries of the video DSLR, which has the ability to shoot at 1920 × 1080 (currently the highest domestic HD resolution available) and vary the frame rate from 24 to 30 frames per second (fps). The latest generation is equipped with external microphone sockets and can provide excellent quality when combined with a shotgun microphone or equivalent.

The video DSLR does, however, fall down in one key area as the current autofocus system relies upon contrast focusing, which means there is a limited ability to keep up with fast-moving objects – so it would not be suitable for a *Blair Witch*-type project. In most applications, the camera operator would have to resort to using traditional follow focus techniques (which, basically, is manual focusing) rather than autofocus. The video DSLR can also suffer from what is known as the 'jello effect' – when the camera is moved rapidly it can appear that the footage is wobbling. Slow panning or using the camera in one position can eliminate this unwanted effect. For the independent film-maker, being able to shoot at this quality for this price would overcome these considerations. For the home cinematographer, these disadvantages will be minimal but the ability to shoot high-quality stills and video in one package is attractive.

A community of video cinematographers

In the space of the three years since the launch of the video DLSR, a community of video cinematographers has emerged.[2] They disseminate media through normal social media network services, such as YouTube, Facebook groups, and Libsyn for podcasts. There are examples of people's cinematography, tutorials, reviews and much more diverse uses. The cinematography takes a variety of formats, such as art-enabled video, short pop videos, basic home movie footage, commercials and adult movies of both amateur and professional quality. The 'art' video allows the cinematographer the opportunity to showcase his or her talent as a film-maker, although the high-end results may result in high-end employment, as there will be many more cinematographers than actual jobs available. The 'pop video' probably serves a dual purpose for promoting the musician as both an artist and a film-maker. The traditional type of 'home movie' material that is being shared is usually very personal to the film-makers and their friends and is circulated for pleasure and entertainment. The commercial work available is varied – for example, the simple sales video with sellers demonstrating the effectiveness of their products. There are also the wedding photographers and cinematographers selling their services, demonstrating their product through a video presentation.

Pornography remains an innovator in the uses of new technologies and this is true in the use of the video DSLR. The impact of this new technology might be having its least impact. The amateur scene does not often require high quality and, in fact, the amateur approach to the work is more characteristic of that genre. For high-end work, the price or type of camera is a very small proportion of the total budget required, so the video DLSR has little impact. With these points in mind, there are examples in the adult film industry that have used the video DSLR to source footage that would have been challenging with a more traditional set up. A diversity of communities is sharing their sound and vision. The rationale for this sharing is varied.

Many do it for the accolade of people looking at their media, which may be termed 'ideas leadership' or brand management; others would like to secure work. The numerous Facebook/Flickr groups that are focused around the video DSLR provide a guide to communities that exist, from amateur techniques through to professional/business approaches to social media. These groups often use Facebook as a mechanism to sell their merchandise. The growth area is between these two extremes where cinematographers are changing their approaches based upon the flexibility of the video DSLR. The key is that people are sharing their media and generating commentary for both profit and non profit-making reasons. As with every community, there is a spectrum of activity and quality. The assessment of quality will always attract attention and be open to debate but, even when deploying a basic search of the social media network, something of interest will be available to the seeker.

The future

The areas of advancement are clear. First, there will be improvement in autofocus technology. These will take the format of cameras that resemble the DSLR.[3] If there is an increase from 1080 to a higher resolution HD format then it is likely that these cameras will reflect this. If 3D use continues to increase through the use of specialist lenses or cameras, this capability will need to be incorporated. These new generations of video DSLR are likely to possess the ability to shoot video in a raw format that contains no compression, so editing exposure can be achieved easily and superior quality obtained. There will be greater editing capabilities within the camera, incorporating many of the functions that are used after the media is transferred to the computer. The media generated from these new cameras will have wifi resident on the platform, rather than relying upon a computer, and the capacity to upload movies direct from the camera to social media networks. The companies that make accessories will invent new devices that attempt to give the impression to the user that they cannot live without them. Yet, through the technological change sharing communities will proliferate, providing information, support, tutorials and insight.

Notes

1. 'House', Season Finale Teaser, *YouTube*, *http://www.youtube.com/watch?v=yAaZZQhuyMo*
2. For example, DSLR Video Shooters, *http://www.facebook.com/#!/DSLRVideoShooters*
3. Sony have released the NEX VG-10 which has the large sensor associated with video DLSR, but its footprint this that of a camcorder, Sony.co.uk, *http://www.sony.co.uk/product/cam-high-definition-on-memory-stick/nexvg10ebdi.yg*

12

Why media literacy is transformative of the Irish education system: a statement in advocacy

Laura Kinsella

Abstract: Is it a 'right' to understand and participate in media? Is it a 'right' to be able to access and use online functions, tools and platforms? This chapter assumes a position of advocacy. With specific attention to Ireland, the importance of media literacy is outlined as an enabler of the other functions of citizenship.

Key words: media literacy, media education, Ireland, interactivity, information society, imagined communities, multiliteracies

> *It is the entitlement and birthright of every person born in the island of Ireland, which includes its islands and seas, to be part of the Irish Nation. That is also the entitlement of all persons otherwise qualified in accordance with law to be citizens of Ireland. Furthermore, the Irish nation cherishes its special affinity with people of Irish ancestry living abroad who share its cultural identity and heritage.*[1]
>
> Article 2 of the Irish Constitution

In the era of globalised information, Ireland plays on a global field economically, socially and culturally. Innovations in information communication technology facilitate daily interactions in digitised networks. The dramatic penetration of information communication technology has resulted in the most significant shift in information circulation since the progression from oral communication to print and text based books.[2] This has given rise to what some refer to as the 'information society'. Webster refers to the information society as 'an apparently new way of conceiving contemporary societies. Commentators have increasingly begun to talk about "information" as a defining feature of the modern world'.[3] The 'information society' is the term used to capture a feeling of change and to identify a shift that involves an increased creation, distribution and use of information, which becomes the 'pervasive commodity'.[4] Despite conceptual contentions surrounding the definition of the information society, there is a communal agreement amongst theorists that there is a significant change occurring.

New literacies

The changing dimensions of interactivity require new literacies to participate in this global arena. In this chapter I argue that a robust media education module must be implemented into the Irish education system in order to equip students to engage fully in the information society. If we are to move beyond avatars, trolls and puppets, then media literacy is the pathway to this goal.

In recent years, media literacy has received international attention; indeed, the European Commission has identified it as being equivalent in significance to reading, writing and numeracy skills.[5] While the imperative of media literacy is undisputed, there is no agreed definition of it. In a response to a wide-ranging stakeholder consultation in 2004, Ofcom's working definition of media literacy is '[t]he ability to access, understand and create communications in a variety of contexts'.[6] Despite this diversity of function and definition, media literacy is still not given an enabling, facilitative or credible role in the formal Irish education system.[7] While one could argue that media literacy should be embedded into all aspects of formal education, I focus on the Senior Cycle of Irish secondary level education. Recent efforts[8] to incorporate media education into primary schools have gained momentum; within the Senior Cycle, however, media studies is not an option.

Since the 1970s, efforts have been made to promote and implement media education within the Irish national curriculum. Collaborative campaign efforts from the Curriculum Development Unit of the City of Dublin Vocational Education Committee (CDVEC), based in Trinity College, were influential in developing teaching resources, in-service training and educational initiatives that incorporated media studies. Similarly, the Teachers Association for Media Education (TAME) – initiated and supported by the Irish Film Institute and Radio Telefis

Eireann, the national service broadcast provider – have collectively succeeded in inserting aspects of media studies at intermittent stages throughout the mainstream education system. Aspects of media studies are adopted into the primary education curriculum. Also, in the Junior Cycle of secondary school, film has been incorporated into the English syllabus, and the recently introduced Civic, Social and Political Education also touches on media studies.[9] An attendant discipline, Communications Studies, is included in the Leaving Certificate Applied, which aims to broaden the scope of education to facilitate a wider breadth of learners. Media Studies is also offered in a transition year, a non-compulsory year, between the Junior and Senior Cycles; this, however, is largely a voluntary initiative and there is no national curriculum. Despite the efforts made by TAME and its success in raising the profile of media education in Ireland, since 2007 it has not been active. Thus media education in Ireland no longer has a nationally coherent focal point or established support network.[10]

In a 2007 report entitled 'Critical Media Literacy in Ireland',[11] published by the Radharc Trust, Ireland's shortcomings in providing critical media literacy to Irish citizens is highlighted, alongside calls for the establishment of a national group to focus on media education. The Report states that the lack of such an organisation has led to a problem of national coherence, consistency and unequal access. There are uneven and disparate initiatives throughout the country which rely on the enthusiasm and expertise of individual teachers, which means that some schools will provide aspects of media education, while other students will not have this opportunity. The work of many teachers is not supported by a localised or dedicated resource for media education, and this undermines the development of this subject. While there are opportunities to engage with elements of media education within the national curriculum, it is not formally tested and it is not compulsory. This indicates that, in spite of the recommendations from the European Commission, it is not equivalent in significance to reading, writing and numeracy skills.

Ireland falls behind other media literacy initiatives in international education. In Australia, media education is compulsory in public schools. While many countries such as Canada, the United Kingdom (UK) and the United States (US) are updating their media studies curriculum, there is currently no separate media literacy curriculum at either Junior or Senior Cycle in the Irish education system.[12] In recent years, experts have called for the consideration of the position and role of media studies within Irish education. Media scholar Brian O'Neil stated that 'it is felt by advocates, media education offers a paradigm of what education should be like in today's complex society'.[13] He notes the positive reception for principles of media education by educationalists and principle stakeholders in Irish education.[14] This was further reinforced by the European 2002 Action Plan,[15] which noted that curricula must meet the needs of the knowledge society. Indeed, the Irish Leaving Certificate is undergoing a review, and critical thinking and information processing are amongst these skills which correlate directly with a media literacy agenda.

While formal education encourages students to access information, it falls short in teaching students how to be critical of that information and how to produce media content. Instead of promoting a critical analysis of message consumption, the Irish education system teaches rote memorisation akin to what Freire describes as the 'banking concept'.[16] Educational theorist Douglas Kellner explains that this model is based on the argument that 'learned teachers deposit knowledge into passive students, inculcating conformity, subordination and normalisation'.[17] The banking system encourages students to consume and memorise knowledge without encouraging them to critique or challenge it – a method of teaching that stems from the industrial era. A dated literacy curriculum and methods of assessment fail to teach critical thinking skills. In an age marked by information saturation, media literacy skills are essential to enable students to be selective and question the information that they consume. Definitions of what it means to be literate in the information society and knowledge economy have changed. Pedagogies must meet these challenges.

Managing disadvantage

Those who are unable to navigate new media platforms, access information and then critically use it fall into the disadvantaged component of the participation gap. The participation gap is 'the unequal access to the opportunities, experiences, skills, and knowledge that will prepare youth for full participation in the world of tomorrow'.[18] The participation gap is a concept which aims to address issues of 'social inclusion through knowledge equity'.[19] A social divide exists between those who can participate in the information society and those who lack the necessary literacies. Coiro, Cammack, Kinzer and Leu illustrate how the US has already developed trends of two classes of learner: those who have sufficient literacy skills and those who do not.[20] Students who lack literacy skills tend to be from minority backgrounds. By grade four, students from white, wealthier backgrounds score twice the literacy levels than those students from minority backgrounds, and this discrepancy is widening. Class, education, race and gender are the key indicators that sustain this divide.[21] The participation gap exasperates existing inequities and presents fundamental challenges to a society that claims to be democratic and aims to provide equal opportunities for all its citizens. This growing inequality can be readily translated into an Irish context with parallel trends emerging from a similar media environment to that of the US. Therefore, as technology continues to become more sophisticated, a child who fails to acquire information literacy is further disadvantaged.

Bundy develops this point, noting that information literacy enables students to negotiate messages and information on multimodal platforms, which facilitates life-long learning, a key characteristic of many careers within the information society.[22] As technology continues to develop at a rapid pace, students who are taught to be information literate can scaffold literacies from one platform to another.[23] This scaffolding approach to problem solving will allay technophobia and provide an awareness of the limitations of technology.

Media literacy theorists stress the importance of recognising the difference between the participation gap and the digital divide. The digital divide addresses the issues of access to information communication technologies. While this is still a large concern, as one fifth of the world does not have access to adequate telephony, access to information technology is not enough to participate in the information society.[24] This is particularly pertinent as in 2009 the 'Smart Schools = Smart Economy'[25] plan to invest €1.5m was unveiled. The strategy by the Department of Education and Science aims to put a laptop and software in the hands of every teacher in the country. The rationale for this is that it will reduce the information divide when, in reality, it will reduce the digital divide, both of which are considered by many blinkered policy-makers to be synonymous. At the local, national and global levels the information divide is much more complex and runs deeper than can be resolved with just an information and communications technology (ICT) remedy.[26]

Tara Brabazon highlights the ramifications of students remaining operationally literate in describing the 'Fordist essays' that she receives from students; by 'Fordist essays' is meant the 'copy and paste' approach to regurgitating information accessed from Google and similar search engines.[27] This indicates that while many students have competent operational literacy skills, they lack the ability to critically engage with this information: just being able to operate Google does not mean that the student can understand, evaluate and critique the information so acquired, or understand who and what Google is. This was highlighted in a report issued by the Joint Information Systems Committee (JISC) in January 2010, which noted that, despite increased access to web 2.0 technology, the information literacy of young people had not improved.[28] Educators must therefore meet the challenges presented by digital environments and scaffold literacy skills to bridge the gulf that lies between students' experience of formal education and their everyday lives outside school.[29] Brabazon notes that 'scaffolding may be the most important term, concept and idea to create media literacy'.[30] Thus incorporating media education into the curricula enables educators to engage with the everyday experiences of students, draw from their enthusiasm for popular culture, and facilitate the literacies to critically engage with their media environment.

Following this trajectory, Kellner calls for a more dialectical approach to teaching media literacy, as students often know more about various media domains and artefacts than teachers.[31] A more participative, student-centred approach to learning can engage students and encourage them to think critically about the media that they consume. This can be used to address issues of prejudice, bias and misrepresentation in the media that students may encounter in their daily lives. In Ireland, for example, tensions arise as it becomes a more multicultural society. Many of these tensions are exacerbated by xenophobic or racist media sensationalism. Media education can provide a platform to address topics of current concern and counter the negative effects associated with media consumption. Rob Watling's proposal for a 'curriculum of the future'[32] connects media education with wider social change, focusing on the correlation between media literacy, participation and citizenship. Watling calls for a flexible and experimental approach to teaching media literacy that draws from students' own experiences of media engagement and reflects a wider social project.

Similarly, Kellner asserts that the promotion of multiliteracies is part of a wider multicultural project and encourages a more egalitarian and progressive society.[33] Multiliteracies are the arsenal to negotiate different social contexts in both a physical and digital domain. Similarly, Castells explains how technology has linked economies and cultures together in what he describes as a 'network society' resulting in 'networks of production, power and experience'.[34] Information communication technologies enable a world wide web of economic and cultural networks. Furthermore, as knowledge transfers and communities merge online, immigration and emigration patterns around the globe also affect communities offline. Immigration and emigration patterns throughout the world and in Ireland have created the challenge of providing people from diverse backgrounds with the necessary skills to enable them to participate in a multicultural society. Castells[35] continues this trajectory, adding that these networks and economies in the Information Age allow new forms of identity to flourish.

Multiliteracy for an Information Age

Multiliteracies can be viewed as a dialogical language between socio-cultural changes and information communication technological innovations. This is particularly prominent in an Irish context as the rise of the information society coincided with Ireland's economic boom or 'Celtic Tiger', albeit all but devastated now. However, the cultural revitalisation of Ireland continues to thrive despite the economic collapse and Ireland has taken centre place on the global stage.[36] Fagan notes how, in the information society, Irish culture progressed to internationally acclaimed status. The popularity of Irish culture is testament in the success of shows such as *Riverdance* and *St Patrick's Day Parades*. Cultural products, such as *Riverdance*, U2 and the Irish Pub are, to a large extent, manufactured by the global cultural industry. The information society has circulated concepts of Irish identity within a global terrain. Media education can teach Irish students the literacies to engage with the Irish Diaspora, which presents a wealth of economic and cultural resources. Historically, emigration trends have meant that Irish identity has always been a 'globalised identity'.[37] The famine, British rule and unemployment forced millions of Irish people to emigrate and form communities throughout the world. Therefore Irish culture and identity have national roots that are inseparable from the trauma of mass emigration. Any notion of an Irish identity in a global context is fluid, hybrid and complex. This pattern continues. Figures show that in the year to April 2010, 65,300 people left Irish shores,[38] about the same in 2009, and this trend is predicted to continue. Media literacy is the key to strengthening and maintaining these links with communities abroad.

Benedict Anderson's concept of 'imagined communities' provides a useful understanding of communities manifesting in a globalising environment.[39] He argues that 'all communities larger than primordial villages of face to face contact are imagined. Communities are to be distinguished, not by their falsity or genuineness, but by the style in which they are imagined'.[40] A romantic notion of 'Irishness', expressed and circulated in cultural products such as songs and poetry, and manifest in celebrations of St Patrick's Day in cities such as New York and Chicago, are a testament to this desire for an 'imagined community' beyond traditional communities.

New communication platforms present new opportunities to harness and optimise on the Irish Diaspora, but Irish government must equip citizens with the literacies to participate fully in this global community. Web 2.0 plays an integral role in harnessing the Diaspora and developing this concept of Irish identity. Harnessing the notion of a global identity, which – as Kitchen and Boyle point out – amounts to a connected nation of 70 million people, presents a powerful way to proceed and address Ireland's current economic crisis.[41] Multiliteracies allow citizens to galvanise these global relationships and networks. The need to create new strategies to enrich relations with the Irish Diaspora has been noted by key figures in the Irish government. In April 2007, the then Minister for Foreign Affairs, Dermot Ahern TD, called for a review to our approach

> to our community across the globe and to develop a strategy for the years ahead. Maintaining and enhancing our links with our communities abroad has been a particular priority for the government. Just as the nature of our diaspora has never been fixed, our attitudes and our capacity to engage with the Irish abroad have changed with our nation's fortunes. We need to regularly reshape our policies in this key area.[42]

Similarly, the Irish economist, David McWilliams, has argued that Ireland should 'exploit the demographic potential of the Diaspora'.[43] Amongst the Irish communities abroad there is a wealth of skills, networks, business acumen and financial and political resources that could help Ireland as it tries to rebuild its economy.[44]

The Irish Diaspora presents potential relationships of trade and business, connecting international organisations and facilitating cultural collaboration. Multiliteracies enable Irish citizens to capitalise on the talent, success and support of their fellow citizens abroad. Kitchen and Boyle point to another potential diaspora: roughly 10 per cent of the Irish population is made up of foreign nationals. During Ireland's economic success, many eastern European and Asian nationals immigrated to Ireland and formed an 'affinity diaspora' that could open new markets abroad as they return to their home countries.[45] Multiliteracies provide students with a better understanding of migration and ease the tensions that arise from immigration and emigration which, in turn, enables Irish citizens to build relationships and affinity with the Irish Diaspora, strengthening and developing on what it means to be Irish in the Information Age.

To communicate and critically engage in the information society one must be media literate. Media education can have a transformative effect on Irish education and I have outlined only some of the benefits of introducing a more sophisticated contemporary approach to education. Media education offers a platform to embrace diverse cultural identities, strengthen curriculum and improve democratic citizen participation. The Information Age has presented unprecedented changes and challenges for Ireland in a local and global context. Technological innovations, coupled with progressive ideologies and information transfers, present an opportunity and impetus to restructure education. By neglecting a robust media education module in formal education, the Irish government is limiting the opportunity for Irish students to participant fully in the world of tomorrow. While other countries throughout Europe and worldwide present media education as a fundamental part of a contemporary curriculum, Ireland negates this. The omission of media literacies fundamentally hinders the ability of the Irish citizen to succeed, compete and develop in the global arena, economically and socially. Alan Bundy[46] focuses our attention on the most pressing global issues of geopolitical, democratic, sustainability and health and adds that none of these can be addressed unless citizens are information literate and act both locally and globally. Citizens must build a global community to address such issues, but governments need to equip citizens at the national level.

Notes

1. Constitution of Ireland, *Bunreacht na hEíreann*, 1 July 1937, *http://www.taoiseach.gov.ie/attached_files/Pdf%20files/Constitution%20of%20Ireland.pdf*
2. D. Kellner, 'Media Literacies and Critical Pedagogy in a Multicultural Society', online course materials for 253A Education, Technology and Society, UCLA, 2007, *http://www.gseis.ucla.edu/courses/ed253a/newDK/medlit.htm*

3. F. Webster, *Theories of the Information Society* (London: Routledge, 2006).
4. A. Bundy, 'One Essential Direction: Information literacy, information technology fluency', *Journal of eLiteracy,* vol. 1, 2004, *http://www.jelit.org/6/01/JeLit_Paper_1.pdf*
5. European Union Directorate, 'Factsheet on Media Literacy', General Information, Society and Media, 2010, *http://ec.europa.eu/culture/media/literacy/docs/factsheet_media_literacy.pdf*
6. S. Livingstone, E. Van Couvering and N. Thumin, 'Adult Media Literacy: A review of the research literature on behalf of Ofcom', Media@LSE, *http://stakeholders.ofcom.org.uk/binaries/research/media-literacy/aml.pdf*
7. B. O'Neil, 'Media Education in Ireland: An overview', *Irish Communications Review*, vol. 8, 2000, pp. 57–64.
8. FÍS (meaning 'Vision') is a film project for primary schools that started in 2000. Its aim is to explore film as a medium of expression in the arts and to introduce children to aspects of the film-making process. FÍS is based at the National Film School at IADT, *http://www.fis.ie*
9. O'Neil, above note 7.
10. *Ibid.*
11. C. Barnes, B. Flanagan, F. Corcoran and B. O'Neill. 'Final Report: Critical Media Literacy in Ireland', Radharc Media Trust, Dublin, 2007, *http://arrow.dit.ie/cgi/viewcontent.cgi?article=1019&context=cserrep*
12. *Ibid.*
13. O'Neil, above note 7, p. 57.
14. *Ibid.*, p. 58.
15. Council of the European Union and Commission of the European Communities, 'eEurope 2002: An Information Society for all', Brussels, 14 June 2002, p. 14, *http://ec.europa.eu/information_society/eeurope/2002/action_plan/pdf/actionplan_en.pdf*
16. P. Freire, *Pedagogies of the Oppressed,* Myra Bergan Ramos (trans) (London: The Continuum Maiden, 2006).
17. D. Kellner, 'New Technologies/New Literacies: Reconstructing education for the new millennium', *Teaching Education,* 11(3), 2000, p. 246.
18. H. Jenkins, R. Purushotma, K. Clinton, M. Weigel and A. Robinson, 'Confronting the Challenges of Participatory Culture Media Education for the 21st Century', MacArthur Foundation, 2006, p. 5, *http://digitallearning.macfound.org/atf/cf/%7B7E45C7E0-A3E0-4B89-AC9C-E807E1B0AE4E%7D/JENKINS_WHITE_PAPER.PDF*
19. D. Kellner, 'Technological Transformation, Multiple Literacies, and the Re-visioning of Education,' *E-Learning and Digital Media,* 1(1), 2004, pp. 9–37, *http://www.wwwords.co.uk/rss/abstract.asp?j=elea&aid=1771*
20. D.J. Leu, C.K. Kinzer, J.L. Coiro and D.W. Cammack, 'Towards a Theory of New Literacies Emerging from the Internet and Other Information and Communication Technologies', in R.B. Ruddell and N.J. Unrau (eds), *Theoretical Models and Processes of Reading* (5th edn, Newark, DE: International Reading Association, 2004), p. 1570.
21. Kellner, above note 19, p. 12.
22. Bundy, above note 4.

23. T. Brabazon, 'I'm not Going to be Your Monkey', *Times Higher Education,* 22 April 2009, *http://timeshighereducation.co.uk/story.asp?sectioncode=26&storycode=406259*
24. T. Brabazon, 'Teaching Learning and Writing through Popular Culture Module', Study Guide, University of Brighton, 2010.
25. ICT Ireland, 'Smart Schools = Smart Economy', Report of the ICT in Schools Joint Advisory Group to the Minister for Education and Science, Department of Education and Science, Dublin, 2009, *http://www.into.ie/ROI/Publications/OtherPublications/OtherPublicationsDownloads/SmartSchools=SmartEconomy.pdf*
26. Bundy, above note 4.
27. T. Brabazon, 'BA (Google): Graduating to information literacy', IDATER online conference, Loughborough University, 2005, p. 8, *https://dspace.lboro.ac.uk/dspace-jspui/bitstream/2134/2485/4/Brabazon.pdf*
28. JISC Technology and Standards Watch, 'Information Behaviour of the Researcher of the Future', CIBER briefing paper, UCL, 11 January 2008, *http://www.jisc.ac.uk/media/documents/programmes/reppres/gg_final_keynote_11012008.pdf*
29. Brabazon, above note 27.
30. *Ibid.*
31. Kellner, above note 2.
32. R. Watling, 'Practical Media Work and the Curriculum of the Future', *The Curriculum Journal,* 12(2), July 2001, pp. 207–24.
33. Kellner, above note 19.
34. M. Castells, *The Information Age: Economy, society and culture* (Oxford: Blackwell Publishing, 2000), Vol. 1, The Rise of the Network Society.
35. *Ibid.*
36. C. Fagan, 'Globalization and Culture: Placing Ireland', *The ANNALS of the American Academy of Political and Social Science*, 581(1), 2002, pp. 133–43.
37. *Ibid.*
38. N. Stanage, 'Emigration: The next generation', *The Irish Times,* 8 January 2011.
39. B. Anderson, *Imagined Communities: Reflections on the origin and spread of nationalism* (London: Verso. 1991).
40. *Ibid.*, p. 6.
41. M. Boyle and R. Kitchen, 'New Strategy can Enrich Relations with Irish Diaspora', *The Irish Times*, 1 January 2009, *http://www.irishtimes.com/newspaper/opinion/2009/0127/1232923366914.html*
42. M. Boyle and R. Kitchen, 'Towards an Irish Diaspora Strategy: A position paper', National Institute for Regional and Spatial Analysis Working Paper, No. 37, National University of Ireland, Maynooth, 2008, p. 1.
43. Boyle and Kitchen, above note 41.
44. *Ibid.*
45. *Ibid.*
46. Bundy, above note 4.

13

YouTube Academy

Tara Brabazon

Abstract: YouTube's slogan is 'Broadcast Yourself'. But how does such a statement transform when the 'you' is an academic? This chapter explores the specific functions that YouTube can hold for academics, with specific attention to best practice and innovative deployments for both corporate and professional purposes.

Key words: YouTube, social media, online lectures, research dissemination, participatory culture

One source of strange stories and even stranger behaviour is the academic conference. This chapter commences with the tale from one such event, during morning tea. The coffee had the quality of milky dishwater that had lost the battle with a macaroni cheese dish. The biscuits were so hard that a dental appointment was required after consumption. The conversations emerging from such culinary disappointments were lively. Delegates revelled in the technological transformations punctuating our professional lives. After discussing a provocative point with one delegate, I asked if he had elaborated on the idea in a refereed article. He replied with a windscreen wiper gesture – part hypnotist and part drag queen – that he had not presented the concept in a journal because all his dissemination is via lectures uploaded to YouTube.

Quiet pause from huddled group of caffeine-starved academics.

The gathered scholars looked at our YouTubing colleague. He was a late fifty-something bloke, wearing a shiny grey suit with just a little bit too much polyester to gain managerial credibility. Not a great voice. No charisma. Nothing marked him as distinct from any other fifty-something academic in the crowd. Yet he had decided that not only was YouTube signalling a new age of broadcasting, but that uploaded lectures were the future of the academy.

Scanning YouTube at the conclusion of the conference, the suited scholar was true to his word. Every lecture delivered in the past three years had been recorded and uploaded. The value of the sessions was dubious. Watching academics lecture is as exciting as changing the time on the microwave oven. The idea that under-prepared powerpointed lectures are then uploaded so that even more people can feel the draining of their higher intellectual functions is a decision worthy of some attention.

Doing 'everything' with YouTube

The relationship between universities and social media is now mature enough to track trends, best practices and structural errors. Writers such as Jean Burgess and Joshua Green confirm that YouTube is 'useful for understanding the evolving relationships between new media technologies, the creative industries, and the politics of popular culture'.[1] Even with this wider media attention, its role in the contemporary academy is underwritten. There are many 'stories' of how companies like YouTube were created.[2] There are several guides on how to use social media or, as one title affirms, *How to do Everything with* YouTube.[3] Some offer a pathway to 'business success'.[4] Others assist readers to become 'a star' on YouTube.[5]

The public relations narrative is well worn. YouTube is a company founded by Chad Hurley, Steve Chen and Jawed Karim. Launched in June 2005 and now owned by Google, users upload content that is watched by digitally literate audiences who occasionally comment on it. While there is much discussion in the research literature about how 'participatory culture' and 'democracy' are enabled through affordable software and hardware,[6] the characteristic of YouTube is uneven involvement. Most users are casual, watching an occasional video and exiting the portal. As with all social media, a small group of core users comment, critique, rank and respond. However, and like the best 2.0 platforms, YouTube is easy to use, with a clean interface assisting intuitive uploading of videos, quick access and simple structures for interaction. As an aggregator of content – rather than a producer of content – YouTube facilitates searching and embedding of files. David Weinberger termed it a 'meta business'.[7] As a metaphor for our era, YouTube is better than most: it produces nothing, but gathers, frames and enhances what already exists.

Video capture has been possible for some time. As Matthew Ingram and Mick Winter discussed in their chapters, mobile phones, webcams and stand-alone cameras are small and cheap. Editing software is easy to deploy. Amateurs not only gather footage of their friends and families but also tumultuous events like tsunamis and the Virginia Tech shooting. YouTube solved the problem of video sharing by automating uploading so that most users only press play to see footage. With free sign-up and no software to install, YouTube facilitates a culture of connectivity via streaming, not downloading. The site's great benefit for web designers and educators is the simplest: the ease of embedding video into other websites. This means, with minimal knowledge of html, visual content can be integrated into personal and professional portals.

Broadcasting academics

YouTube has many uses for academics. The first function is signalled by the original description of the website before the now famous 'Broadcast Yourself'. The site's previous byline was 'Your Digital Video Repository'. It was not as catchy. While academics earnestly contribute to institutional repositories, YouTube's original purpose was to store video for reuse. It still has – even through the copyright breaches – great power as a gateway to popular culture. Digital rights management and copyright violation fears have made it risky and inefficient to use commercial videos in our classroom teaching. In such an environment, YouTube is an easy and accessible method to share popular culture. Clips may be played in lectures and tutorials or embedded in online learning environments.

The second use of YouTube for academics is as an archive of non-commercial material. Video blogs present commentaries and testimonies from web-literate users. Before web streaming, it was necessary for researchers to travel to specialist archives to see amateur video of family life. Currently, thousands of individual cataloguers capture, upload, view and comment on an array of experiences, stories, narratives and struggles.

Obviously, this do-it-yourself initiative activates a key critique of the YouTube discourse. Digitally literate and broadband-enabled consumers gain another avenue to express their 'creativity' and 'voice'. The digitally excluded lose the opportunity to see alternative views and present their own. In other words, the impact of digital exclusion in a 2.0 environment is much more serious and expansive than a disconnection from the read-only web. In logging these silences and absences in the read write web, the third great use of YouTube for academics, who are both highly literate and empowered users, is as an intellectual repository – a visual archive for precious and rare scholarly moments. Five examples convey this value.

- a discussion between Noam Chomsky and Michel Foucault on the nature of humanity, creativity, freedom, governmentality and anarcho-syndicalism;[8]
- an interview with David Harvey, via the University of California channel, UCTV;[9]
- the urbane and sophisticated Hélène Cixous questioning the nature of intellectual life;[10]
- a shuffling and brilliant Slavoj Zizek improvises when a mobile telephone rings during his presentation – in response, he takes a phone call from God;[11]
- a Cornel West interview with Tavis Smiley reveals his commitment to a wide dissemination of ideas; the phrases 'bling bling' and 'vanilla suburbs' have never been used as effectively in the one sentence.[12]

As an archival record of academic life, such footage is evocative, influential, revelatory and irreplaceable. While the quality of video capture may not be high, some events are so startling and important that any record is beneficial.

A fourth use of YouTube is for university marketing. Many institutions have a channel where they upload promotional videos and advertisements. As an exercise in disintermediation, university marketers drop links in the media supply chain so that they are not reliant on paying for newspaper, radio or television coverage. A convincing model of this process is the University of Auckland's YouTube commercial, featuring Dr Elana Curtis.[13] If students are interested in an institution, they can go to the university's channel to find material and assess the comments in response to the footage. Another example of this use is Massey University's film, which followed two students – Stuart and Lana – through their day.[14]

A fifth deployment of YouTube for academics is to offer a review function and 'how to' guide for users of software and hardware. In an act of participatory reintermediation – replacing institutional gatekeepers for a consumer's perspective – viewers create or see reviews of hardware, software, books, music or films. The Royal Melbourne Institute of Technology (RMIT), for example, presents a guide to Blackboard.[15] Another example of online skill development is a user demonstrating the Acoustica Mixcraft track-building process.[16] Instead of journalistic or corporate advertising, we can learn how users understand and operate software and hardware.

A sixth use of the portal for academics is as a mode of dissemination for new strategies in teaching and learning. So much of our teaching lives are isolated in classrooms, lecture theatres and seminar rooms. The chance to watch and understand other teacher's choices improves our professional lives. The University of Utah's 'Best Practices for Teaching in a Video Environment' is professionally produced and can be the basis of future development by other institutions.[17]

For students, seeing how peers learn and construct assignments provides vicarious mentoring, intellectual scaffolding and motivation. YouTube is a great portal for – and about – our students' work. An example of this use is the University of Hull's School of Arts and New Media animation show reel.[18] Employers can access the footage and it provides a trajectory of student development through a degree.

One final application of YouTube for academics is the use of the portal to disseminate research. YouTube provides a space to repackage findings for different audiences, updating results and generating tailored video to embed in online-refereed articles. These alternative modes of dissemination can link to an article lodged in an institutional repository. It can also provide a record – a visual abstract – of a conference presentation.[19]

Vodcasting, like podcasting, is cheap to produce and disseminate.[20] While the production values may not be high, the spontaneity and speed of response is a great advantage. Through YouTube, there is a chance to remake an old institution into a new university. This is not (only) about brand management, but a chance for universities to (re)claim a position of thought leadership. While 'new media' is maturing and developing into a more complex, intricate and diverse environment than any of us could have imagined a decade ago, there are still too many commentators who frame the 2.0 community as composed of benevolent, anti-corporate vegan hippies, continuing the summer of love in digital form.

Certainly, there is much nonsense online. There are also gems of revelation. In recognising the consequences of these two statements, our task in universities is clear. At every opportunity, we should embed media literacy theory into our curriculum. We have a chance and a responsibility to teach generations of students the skills to sort and sift online data into a workable shape for analysis and evaluation. It is also our responsibility to improve the calibre of online information. One strategy to enact this goal is to add a step to the dissemination of research. In the analogue age, a refereed article and a couple of conference appearances satisfied funding agencies and research managers. Now we have an opportunity and an imperative to repurpose our scholarship for audiences who would never read an academic article or an annual report on university research. Creating effective video is more difficult than producing strong audio content. Innovative attempts should be acknowledged that trial new modes of dissemination, beyond recording or videoing lectures or conference presentations.

Richard Harrington and Mark Weiser stated that 'consumers want video content'.[21] They may be right. However, academics and students have a key role in such an environment: to increase the quality of media, information and debate. YouTube has suffered through the reputation of featuring too many videos of cats/children/brides jumping/dancing/falling awkwardly. It is used for – and has the potential to offer – much more than footage of a tipsy wedding party behaving badly. It may transform from 'consumer-controlled video' into a new opportunity for learning.

Notes

1. J. Burgess and J. Green, *YouTube: Online video and participatory culture* (Cambridge: Polity, 2009), p. vii.
2. S. Lacy, *The Stories of Facebook, YouTube and Myspace* (Richmond: Crimson, 2008).
3. C. Fahs, *How to do Everything with YouTube* (New York: McGraw Hill, 2008).
4. G. Clapperton, *This is Social Media: Tweet, blog, link and post your way to business success* (Chichester: Capstone, 2009).
5. F. Levy, *15 Minutes of Fame: Becoming a star in the YouTube revolution* (New York: Penguin, 2008).
6. For example, see Henry Jenkins' chapter 'What happened before YouTube', in Burgess and Green, above note 1, pp. 109–25, and John Hartley's chapter 'Uses of YouTube – Digital Literacy and the Growth of Knowledge', in Burgess and Green, above note 1, pp. 126–43.
7. D. Weinberger, *Everything is Miscellaneous* (New York: Henry Holt & Co, 2007).
8. 'Noam Chomsky – Noam vs. Michel Foucault' (Eng. subs), *YouTube*, *http://www.youtube.com/watch?v=kawGakdNoT0*
9. 'Conversations with History: David Harvey', *YouTube*, *http://www.youtube.com/watch?v=02eskyHJY_4&feature=related*

10. 'Hélène Cixous', *YouTube*, *http://www.youtube.com/watch?v=ZKUQWv0irVw*
11. 'Zizek Receives a Phonecall From God', *YouTube*, *http://www.youtube.com/watch?v=sKvcN9CVFec&feature=related*
12. 'Cornel West Interview', *YouTube*, *http://www.youtube.com/watch?v=PMhya8SIWmY*; *http://www.youtube.com/watch?v=5kJpk60rFh4*
13. 'The University of Auckland Commercial – Dr Elana Curtis', *YouTube*, *http://www.youtube.com/watch?v=ajosnJqsQMs*
14. 'A Day in the Life of a Massey University Student', *YouTube*, *http://www.youtube.com/watch?v=p-TrlvsRToU*
15. 'How to Use the Discussion Forum in Blackboard – RMIT University', *YouTube*, *http://www.youtube.com/watch?v=MJjLRShTpz0*
16. 'Mixcraft 5 Tutorials – Mixcraft 5 Windows Part 1: Launching Mixcraft and Arrangement Window', *YouTube*, *http://www.youtube.com/watch?v=CCr5WFGDQNg*
17. 'Best Practices for Teaching in a Video Environment', *YouTube*, *http://www.youtube.com/watch?v=u-zvPLluOgM*
18. 'University of Hull @ Scarborough Student Animation', *YouTube*, *http://www.youtube.com/watch?v=F1lnqqDVNKI&feature=PlayList&p=D61587798BB1F95D&index=5*
19. For an example of my use of this function, please refer to 'Digital Dieting: A Keynote Presentation', *YouTube*, 2010, *http://www.youtube.com/watch?v=BU46mF89z0Q*
20. R. Harrington and M. Weiser, *Producing Video Podcasts* (Amsterdam: Focal Press, 2008).
21. *Ibid.*, p. 2.

Part 4
Fandom, Consumption and Community

14

Live fast, die young, become immortal

Katie Ellis

Abstract: There are many ways in which to mark death, particularly the death of a celebrity. However, social media and the capacities of the read write web have enabled fans to memorialise and remember dead celebrities in new and often strange ways. This chapter explores the online response to the unexpected death of Heath Ledger. Although pre-dating the online frenzy created from Michael Jackson's death, the way in which fans eulogise and create e-memorials remains an area to monitor and research.

Key words: online fandom, celebrity, popular culture, death, Heath Ledger

> *The thing I remember the most about Heath is that he was so alive.*[1]
>
> Ann Hathaway to Barbara Walters
> (at the 2009 Academy Awards)

> *I'm not sure I put thought into how I want to be perceived and how I come across. I've never really concentrated on that. All my effort goes in between the time of action and cut.*[2]
>
> Heath Ledger to contactmusic.com

On 22 January 2008, when actor Heath Ledger died of an accidental drug overdose in his Manhattan apartment, celebrity internet culture commenced a new era. His sudden and unexpected death immediately became major news with predictions circulating about the longevity of his fame. *Time* described him as 'reminiscent of James Dean, a Hollywood legend who also died young and famous'.[3] In the following days, internet searches for various permutations of 'Heath Ledger' caused an 'internet meltdown'.[4] The anniversary of his death was marked with an Oscar nomination. He subsequently won the award.

Death is not enough to enable celebrity cult figure status. Other factors – including talent, eccentricity, personal demons (such as drugs), and a passionate following before death – shape the potential for a cult following.[5] The building of a myth and cult status in the internet era can result in a potential lack of mystique. With tweets, thousands of photographs at various and often unflattering angles, and shaky mobile phone footage uploaded to YouTube, the specialness of celebrity is often tarnished. Yet Ledger, who appeared in generation-defining films, behaved in often eccentric ways. He maintained a passionate following and shunned unprecedented internet access throughout his life. These characteristics combined to define a new trajectory for achieving cult figure status after death in the post-internet era.

Prescience

What makes Ledger important in the history of celebrity deaths and fandom, though, is that he was prescient for what would emerge months after his overdose. The death of Michael Jackson was of a scale and scope that not only confirmed his self-anointed status as the King of Pop but that Twitter, in particular, had entangled with other social and popular media. By focusing on Ledger's – rather than Jackson's – death, a particular moment in celebrity, fandom, media and community can be captured.

The legacies attributed to celebrities who die young reveal more about living fans than the celebrity in question, especially when rebel iconography is attached.[6] Warner Bros created a public persona of James Dean that tapped into the contempt for respectability emerging in 1950s America.[7] Successive generations are attracted to this perceived rejection of institutional authority. A common theme throughout Dean's television, theatre and film roles was teenage alienation and assimilation.[8] Although similar to Dean in many ways, the internet era has shaped Ledger into a different type of enigma. Web 2.0 allows fans an outlet to communicate their appreciation of talent and express passionate following, while internet gossip sites exploit celebrities' eccentricities and personal demons for profit.

Like Dean, Ledger often played outsiders who find belonging in unconventional ways, including the famous Australian outlaw in *Ned Kelly*, a heroin addict in *Candy*, and a high school social misfit in *10 Things I Hate About You*. Ledger achieved most accolades for his performances in *Brokeback Mountain*, where he portrayed a cowboy unable to reveal his true sexuality. In *The Dark Knight* he became the homicidal Joker. By introducing gay themes to the popular zeitgeist, *Brokeback Mountain* was a generation-defining film.[9] Judell aligns Ledger's performance in this film with Dean's *Rebel Without a Cause*, describing the film as being 'to homosexuals and single women what *Rebel Without a Cause* once was to rebellious adolescents'.[10] In 2007, the respected scholarly film journal, *Film Quarterly*, issued a special edition on *Brokeback Mountain*, describing it as having a major impact on public opinion and mainstreaming homosexuality.[11] Yet Ledger was not recognised with an Oscar for his performance. David Carr of the *New York Times*, who observed Ledger on the promotional trail for this film, described his campaigning skills as lacking: '[H]e had little aptitude or appetite for trite talk at parties or events.'[12] His posthumous presence on the 2009 circuit was more successful.

Mediated grief

As technology strives for transcendence, grief is mediated through email, blog comments and Facebook groups. The pain his death caused to his passionate followers can be seen in the number of online tributes to Ledger. In both life and death, he exists in the 'universe of simulation'. For Baudrillard, simulation 'is the generation of models of a real without origin or reality: a hyperreal'.[13] Celebrity is a simulation, fixing individuals as an image vastly different from an actual identity. As Cary Grant famously commented, 'everybody wants to be Cary Grant. Even *I* want to be Cary Grant'.[14] A sense of self is often distinct from the celebrity image created. The internet mediation of celebrity creation has exacerbated the simulacra. Internet celebrity gossip is a simulation of a reality that does not exist. Web 2.0 has contributed to a rise in celebrity obsession, particularly in the macabre and specifically in death.[15] Following Ledger's death, the outpouring of emotion, both in terms of internet searches and then the creation of dedicated sites and Facebook groups, is an example of hyperreal grief for a hyperreal personality. Some see the intense focus on Ledger as evidence of a temporary mini-cult status, believing that the pace of internet celebrity gossip will prevent Ledger from entering the permanent pop-culture pantheon.[16]

The internet is an aestheticised, post-metaphysical environment where web-literate consumers go for information and to experience human emotion. Celebrity seduces web users to experience the simulacrum.[17] If fandom is simply a community surrounding a particular person, character or text, then web based fandom is able to align these communities of typically disparate members. The immediacy and accessibility of online communities allows fans to engage in the creation of the image of particular celebrities. Bloggers are now instrumental in the shaping of celebrity and, significantly, whether a celebrity will be successful.[18] Although Ledger died, his image lives on in another medium: the internet. His community of fans was instrumental in shaping this simulacrum memory and memorial.

The internet has created a new mode of celebrity gossip characterised by aggression with little to no referent in reality. Celebrity internet gossip has accelerated, with the material effect on both the creation and continued success of celebrities. A recurring theme throughout many of Ledger's interviews was his unwillingness to create an off-screen tabloid persona, preferring to put his efforts into acting. Celebrity gossip creates a persona that sells films or products. Throughout his life, Ledger oscillated between ignoring the paparazzi and tormenting them. They were his 'demon'. The aggression, spread and power of internet celebrity gossip is exemplified by reports that Ledger's family in Australia learned of his passing along with the rest of the world.[19]

Ledger reportedly spat at journalists on the set of *Candy*, causing the paparazzi to seek revenge with water pistols at the Sydney premiere of *Brokeback Mountain*. Although intrigued by his life and relationships with many of Hollywood's most beautiful actresses, the Australian public turned its collective back on Ledger when he ate an orange during an interview with entertainment reporter, Katherine Tulich, who was interviewing him for the popular television breakfast show, *Sunrise*. Breakfast audiences were *personally* insulted and Ledger issued an apology which, in turn, was picked up by celebrity gossip sites across the internet.[20] While inexperience and hunger was a convenient excuse, a line in the sand had been drawn. Ledger felt no responsibility to share his life with people (strangers) who were under the impression they had a right to this kind of access. Tulich was most exasperated because she was not even asking hard questions.[21] Yet the day after he died, *Sunrise* dedicated the entire program in tribute to the Australian star.

Living digital death

Historically the celebrity apparatus has maintained an illusion of invisibility. But the internet is changing the relationship that fans have with celebrities.[22] The unprecedented access channelled via the internet is diminishing the 'untouchable icon' status of celebrities. Lynn Bartholome questions whether Ledger's cult status will continue because 'very few [celebrities] would make the pantheon now, and it's because of the media and because of the internet – we just know too much about too many people'.[23] The constant reworking of Ledger's life and death in the days, months and years following his overdose demonstrates the accelerated pace of celebrity news on the internet. Arguably, in the constant reworking of Ledger's death, consumers were receiving what 'we' wanted: celebrity gossip. Or is it more complex? Death is now mediated by the internet.[24] New stories emerged as media outlets aggressively competed with each other for a different angle on the causes and consequences of the death. The iconography of the dead celebrity in combination with a 24-hour news cycle creates techno-fuelled transcendence, even of death.

The Ledger story persisted as a result of the characteristics that Puente argues lead to cult status, which include talent, passionate fans, eccentricity and personal demons.[25] In addition to these more traditional reasons for longevity, celebrity gossip sites utilising web 2.0 technologies were able to capitalise on the uncertainty surrounding his death, allowing users to generate their own content to mediate his death. His talent and young daughter have been a recurring concern. Finally, Ledger's ability to exclude, ignore and torment the paparazzi during his life has fuelled, rather than inhibited, a prolonged interest. As the event descended further into mediation and simulation, other iconic internet generation celebrities were dragged into the story.

Facebook groups and keyword searches continued to grow as the print media competed with blogs to package the story in a different way. The media played an instrumental role in the grieving process, surrounding and shaping celebrities who have died. Media coverage has traditionally acted as an extension of the public grieving process that took place in town squares and churches.[26] However, with the increasing democratisation of the media on the internet, mediation is minimised.[27] This is especially true of the celebrity death grieving process in which user-generated content reinforces the view that fans somehow intimately know the celebrity. Facebook groups allow fans to talk to others who feel connected to Ledger in the same way. Although many ridicule the intense grief felt by some over the death of their favourite celebrity, the grief can be intense because fans feel they do know the celebrity through the consumption of hours of media.[28]

On the day he died two 'RIP Heath Ledger' Facebook groups were immediately established and members began to post tributes, pictures and reflections on what his death meant to them. Although the sites are dwindling, they offer a space where fans return to post comments and reflections after they re-watch a Ledger film, for example, or mark an anniversary of birth or death. The messages left by these groups represent a purer outpouring of grief than the speculation offered on internet gossip sites. On one Heath Ledger Facebook fan page with almost 200,000 members, a comment posted in January 2011 describes Ledger as 'the best actor of my generation'.[29]

Although comments sections on sites such as ninemsn and the *Sydney Morning Herald* attracted tributes and expressions of sympathy towards the family, the articles themselves engaged in the intense and aggressive speculation that characterises internet celebrity gossip. This marks a radical difference in the treatment of other celebrity deaths such as James Dean. While there is no mystery in the way in which Dean died, Ledger's death, reported early and without much detail, seemed to drag on its narrative possibilities. The accelerated pace of internet celebrity gossip is a self-generating information machine that requires an intense focus on celebrity to exacerbate and excuse obsessional behaviour and maintain interest.

Ledger's life and death became a simulation of every conceivable Hollywood genre: will disputes, possible love child at 17, Academy Award, beautiful ex-lovers attending his funeral, drugs, psychotic thoughts, declarations of immortality, drug binges, police/FBI investigations, and claims and rejections of suicide. The story did not end when Ledger was awarded a posthumous Academy Award. Christmas 2010 saw reports of an ongoing feud between his family and former fiancée, Michelle Williams.[30] Early 2011 saw the announcement of an art exhibition of his work and costumes in the Western Australian Art Gallery in his home city of Perth, Western Australia.[31]

Heath Ledger is one of the first major celebrities to die young in the internet era. Michael Jackson would follow and accentuate the trend. While initial reports[32] predicted that the fast-paced celebrity-obsessed internet news culture would prevent him from achieving the iconic status of James Dean, one year later the circumstances surrounding his death were still major news on the internet. As I am writing this chapter in 2011, it is not uncommon for Heath Ledger stories to lead on the popular Australian News Limited website, www.news.com.au.[33] Although similar to Dean in terms of his participation in generation-defining films, his leaving home to find fame and fortune as a teenager, and his eccentricity and personal demons, Ledger's 'cool' is of a different brand. In a generation of product placement, being famous for being famous and outrageous photographs on the internet, he refused to participate. While it may be too early to tell with any great certainty, Ledger *could* enter the pantheon. Like Dean, he was talented, had a passionate following already, behaved in eccentric ways and wrestled with personal demons. His death brought the criteria for achieving cult status into a new era as his passionate fan base and the celebrity apparatus used web 2.0 to mediate his death.

Notes

1. M. Zeidman, 'Anne Hathaway Discusses Oscars, Heath Ledger and Life', *Hollywood Today*, 22 February 2009, *http://www.hollywoodtoday.net/2009/02/22/anne-hathaway-discusses-oscars-heath-ledger-and-life/*
2. 'Heath Ledger – Ledger Blasts Advertising Actors', *Contact Music*, 25 August 2005, *http://www.contactmusic.com/new/xmlfeed.nsf/mndwebpages/ledger%20blasts%20advertising%20actors*
3. A. Altman, 'The Clues in Heath Ledger's Death', *Time*, 23 January 2008, *http://www.time.com/time/arts/article/0,8599,1706361,00.html*
4. A. Moses, 'Heath Ledger's Death Triggers Net Meltdown', *Sydney Morning Herald*, 24 January 2008, *http://www.smh.com.au/news/web/net-meltdown/2008/01/24/1201025052926.html*
5. M. Puente. 'Dying Young is No Guarantee of Icon Status in the Internet Age', *USA Today*, 30 January 2008, *http://www.usatoday.com/life/people/2008-01-29-iconic-by-death_N.htm*
6. C. Springer, *James Dean Transfigured* (Texas: University of Texas Press, 2007), p. 98.
7. *Ibid.*, p. 26.
8. M. DeAngelis, *Gay Fandom and Crossover Stardom* (Durham: Duke University Press, 2001), p. 73.
9. R. White, 'Special Feature on Brokeback Mountain: Introduction', *Film Quarterly*, 60(3), Spring 2007, p. 20.
10. B. Judell, 'Heath Ledger: The next James Dean?', *Culture Catch*, 5 February 2008, *http://www.culturecatch.com/film/heath_ledger_james_dean*
11. *White, above note 9.*
12. D. Carr, 'Delicately Campaigning for a Star Now Departed', *The New York Times*, 5 February 2009, *http://www.nytimes.com/2009/02/06/movies/awardsseason/06carr.html*
13. J. Baudrillard, *Simulacra and Simulation* (Ann Arbor: University of Michigan Press, 1994), p. 1.
14. F. Inglis, *A Short History of Celebrity* (Princeton: Princeton University Press, 2010), p. 187.
15. 'Web 2.0 Driving Addictive Celebrity Worship Disorder', *The Age*, 25 February 2009, *http://www.theage.com.au/world/web-20-driving-addictive-celebrity-worship-disorder-20090224-8gpc.html?page=3*

16. Puente, above note 5.
17. D. Weinstein, 'Celebrity as Simulacrum', *CTheory*, 28 June 1994, *http://www.ctheory.net/articles.aspx?id=244#text%201*
18. A. Petersen, 'Celebrity Juice, not from Concentrate: Perez Hilton, gossip blogs, and the new star production', *Jump Cut*, No. 49, Spring 2007, *http://www.ejumpcut.org/archive/jc49.2007/PerezHilton/index.html*
19. Puente, above note 5.
20. 'Heath Says Sorry', *The Age*, 26 August 2005, *http://www.theage.com.au/news/people/heath-says-sorry/2005/08/26/1124563022449.html*
21. *Ibid.*
22. T. Mole. 'Hypertrophic Celebrity', *Media Culture*, 7(5), 2004, *http://journal.media-culture.org.au/0411/08-mole.php*
23. Puente, above note 5.
24. M. Gibson, 'Death and Mourning in Technologically Mediated Culture', *Health Sociology Review*, 16(5), 2007, pp. 415–24.
25. Puente, above note 5.
26. S. Gordon, 'Star Sorrow: Coping with celebrity grief', *AOL Health*, 26 July 2010, *http://www.michaeljacksonmemorialconcert.com/star-sorrow-coping-with-celebrity-grief-aol-health-blog.html*
27. G. Turner, *Ordinary People and the Media: The demotic turn* (Thousand Oaks: Sage, 2009), p. 72
28. Gordon, above note 26.
29. 'Heath Ledger', *Facebook*, *http://www.facebook.com/#!/pages/Heath-Ledger/25514023521*
30. C. White, 'Michelle Williams will not take Daughter Matilda to see Heath Ledger's Family this Christmas', 22 December 2010, *Perth Now*, *http://www.perthnow.com.au/entertainment/michelle-williams-will-not-take-daughter-matilda-to-see-heath-ledgers-family-this-christmas/story-e6frg30c-1225974830404*
31. 'WA Museum to Honour Heath Ledger', *ABC News*, 25 January 2011, *http://www.abc.net.au/news/stories/2011/01/25/3121011.htm*
32. Puente, above note 5.
33. See White, above note 30; 'Ledger's Uncle Blames His Crimes on Grief', *News.com.au*, 5 February 2010, *http://www.news.com.au/breaking-news/ledgers-uncle-blames-his-crimes-on-grief/story-e6frfku0-1225827263474*; B. Rule, 'Gemma Ward Opens up about her Life with Heath Ledger', *Sydney Herald Sun*, 30 January 2011, *http://www.news.com.au/entertainment/movies/gemma-ward-opens-up-about-her-life-with-heath-ledger/story-e6frfmvr-1225996813206#ixzz1DVnxAWcZ*

15

All we hear is Lady-o Gaga: Popular Culture 2.0

Alexander Cameron

Abstract: Many celebrities have used the read write web to build their fame. Few have used Twitter, Facebook or YouTube as effectively as Lady Gaga. She mobilises her fans – the monsters – in a way that transcends comparisons with earlier singers such as Madonna, Britney Spears or Cher. Most importantly, she uses social media to integrate music, fashion, photography and fandom to create a hyper-reflexive popular culture.

Key words: Lady Gaga, monsters, interactivity, popular culture, fandom, Twitter

Stefani Joanne Angelina Germanotta was born on 28 March 1986 in New York City. Within less than a quarter of a decade, she has ascended popular culture. By 2010, she was positioned at number seven in the World's 100 Most Powerful Women and second in the list of the Most Powerful Musicians in the World.[1] She has sold more than fifteen million albums and fifty one million singles worldwide. She is not known as Stefani. She is Lady Gaga.

Building on Katie Ellis's chapter on celebrity death mediated by social media,[2] I investigate a living celebrity and her fans. This chapter examines Lady Gaga as a digitised popular culture figure, in particular looking at her roles in music, fashion, gender, sexuality, and fandom. What makes Gaga interesting in popular culture is that her entire career was framed by the read write web. Interactivity with an audience is not abstract for this performer. She deploys Twitter, Facebook and YouTube – amateur platforms – with resilient professionalism. Further, she has used the read write web to move beyond the music industry and into fashion and photography. For such a chameleon, she is not an 'invented' popular culture figure in old media such as television. She remains clear in her project:

> For some of us it's a much more innate gift, a much more spiritual experience. We don't have to be plugged in to a particular movement in order to be a part of it. It's transcendent, it's an inspiration that we're born with.[3]

Her self-belief becomes a gift shared with her audience. In an era of sharing, she has managed the media with resilience and excellence.

Gaga transcends popular culture. She is a creative industries hub. She aligns music, fashion and digitised design under a platinum hair-bow. While successful proto-Gaga musicians such as Madonna took nearly two decades to enforce their influence on popular culture, Gaga shot from zero to hero in two years. She was literate in Madonna's sign system and transcended her. In Gaga's second music video, she wore electronic glasses that flashed to her audience 'GAGA. POP. CULTURE'.[4] Gaga has made pop popular again, moving innovative ideas to new audiences through digitisation.

Music

Gaga is a pioneering force in the music industry and has managed to embrace the shift from compact disc to digital download. In 2009, Gaga helped to boost UK download sales by 50 per cent.[5] She uses YouTube to enhance her popularity. With 1,160,812,509 upload views as of February 2011, she is listed as the '20th Most Subscribed (All Time) – Musicians – Global'.[6] This makes Gaga the first ever music artist to reach over one billion views online. Her most popular video, which is the most watched video online, is 'Bad Romance' which, as of February 2011 had 343,630,478 views.[7] Gaga has her own interpretation for this online success:

> I must create music, and if you must, what is it that you have to say? Why make it at all? So I resigned myself to make the kind of music that I wanted to listen to – not what I thought anyone wanted to hear or what would be most credible or notable, I just created what I wanted to listen to, what I thought was great, what I thought could be groundbreaking where I was living which was an area where indie was much more popular, and pop music was considered to be annoying, corporate and unimportant. So I decided in true gaga fashion to be revolutionary and go against the grain, and make pop music in a town where there was none.[8]

Of course, being so visible and experimental with the read write web has consequences. She has confronted critique from journalists and other performers. Gaga has remained resilient amid the attacks and commentary:

> Criticism can be wonderful if you have a strong sense about what you're creating, but if you have an incessant need for validation from an outside place, then that is not yourself. Then criticism can be detrimental and completely life changing. You don't want the world to dictate what you create; you want to be a funnel. It must always come from you.[9]

The negative criticism that Gaga receives is riddled with comparisons with fellow artists, including Christina Aguilera, Gwen Stefani and Madonna. Gaga has been accused of copying Madonna's style in terms of persona, attitude and music videos. She has been deemed unoriginal in her music and an 'asexual, confected copycat'.[10] In an article for *The Sunday Times*, Camille Paglia, Professor of Humanities and Media Studies at the University of the Arts in Philadelphia, states: 'Gaga has borrowed so heavily from Madonna (as in her latest video – Alejandro) that it must be asked, at what point does homage become theft?'[11] However Gaga feels differently about her 'theft' from previous musical icons:

> I'm still working on it [her originality]. I reference constantly but I have most recently felt that I have had some truly original moments and if you get one really good original moment in your career you're solid.[12]

In public, Gaga has a hateful, competitive relationship with Madonna, as shown when they appeared in a sketch on *Saturday Night Live*, pulling hair and fighting, with Madonna comically adding 'What the hell is a disco-stick?'. However, in a live interview with SHOWstudio, Gaga talks in depth about her relationship with Madonna and how she feels about the musical legends that preceded her:

> Madonna is a wonderful person, she is so full of the most wonderful freedom and spirit and she is so kind and working with her has always been very exciting and very fun and we have shared some wonderful honest moments together. I ask her questions, and she's given me advice. It's been through my experience in the industry that

> I have connected on a much deeper level with the most iconic and legendary people that I have admired, and yet have not connected with any of my contemporaries. But I would say the one thing that they all have in common, the legends that is, is that they are the nicest most wonderful human beings you have ever met in your life and that has freed me, I used to be quite guarded in interviews thinking that the media was trying to destroy me, and I let it go. I let it go much more when I got to meet all these people that I worshipped.[13]

It seems that Gaga is already considering herself to be significant in popular culture and differentiating herself from her fellow contemporary pop-artists.

Another area of the music industry that Gaga has pioneered is that of the 'music movie'. She takes the industry standard three-minute-thirty-seconds single, and transforms it into a seven- to ten-minute mini-movie. This music movie brings together conventions from both movies and music. Her first single to feature this was 'Paparazzi',[14] which begins with ambient music and title credits, listing the production company, stars and director. The music movie then starts with dialogue. Gaga is in bed with a male acquaintance. They embrace and share a kiss. They move to the balcony where the male acquaintance pushes Gaga over the railing. The song now commences with Gaga in a wheelchair, and concludes when Gaga poisons her boyfriend as revenge and ends with a call to the emergency services stating, 'I just killed my boyfriend'. Using conventions from movies and plaiting them with music have made her videos distinctive and they gain attention in the media. The music video for her single 'Telephone'[15] follows the same structure as 'Paparazzi', except that the song is broken into segments, separated by dialogue. Gaga continues to incorporate new ideas into the music that she creates, and this is what keeps her music fresh and contemporary, and allows it to continue to shock audiences.

Gender and fashion

Gaga first came under attack from the media about her sexuality after her performance at the Glastonbury Festival in the UK in 2009. Photos surfaced that appeared to show a phallus between her legs. A media storm surfaced, throwing accusations around about the performer's gender and sexuality. Gaga responded a few days later by posting a sarcastic comment through her Twitter account: 'I just had to go home and suck my own hermie dick, suckka'.[16] Through social media, Gaga can literally answer back to her critics. Indeed, Gaga embraced the critics' opinion of her when she posed on the cover of *Q* magazine. In the photo shoot she poses topless, wearing tight black trousers with the clear outline of a large phallus showing through, all under the article title 'She's the Man'.[17] The article claims Gaga to have been active in determining the photo shoot, stating that she wanted to 'strap a dildo to my vagina'.[18] Unlike other figures of popular culture who release press statements from their agents when under fire from the media about their sexuality/gender, Gaga goes on Twitter and feeds the media cycles.

Gaga is an avid supporter of women's rights and equality in both sexes. She is also known for her androgynous appearance.

> I reject wholeheartedly the way we are taught to perceive women, the beauty of women, how a woman should act or behave. Women are strong and fragile, women are beautiful and ugly, we are soft spoken and loud, all at once. There is something mind controlling about the way we are taught to view women and my work is both visually and musically a rejection of both of those things but more importantly a quest and its exciting because all of the avant garde clothing and the lyrics and music style which was at a certain time and at once weird and odd or unattractive, uncomfortable, shocking. It's now trendy. So perhaps we can make woman's rights trendy, make feminism, strength, and security, the power of the wisdom of the woman – let's make that trendy.[19]

In another interview with Norwegian journalist Gjermund Jappee, Gaga tackles inequality in the music industry:

> If I was a guy and I was sitting here with a cigarette in my hand grabbing my crotch and talking about how I make music because I love fast cars and f****** girls, you'd call me a rock star. But when I do it in my music and in my videos, because I'm a female, because I make pop music, you're judgmental. And you say that it is distracting. I'm just a rockstar.[20]

Gaga is not a manufactured pop star who makes music, poses for the paparazzi and signs autographs for her fans. She challenges the way in which media report on musicians through her use of web 2.0 platforms. Another key way in which she troubles her critics is through the way she dresses. Gaga is known for her outrageous dress sense, from wearing an outfit made entirely from Kermit the Frog puppets to a dress composed of cuts of meat. She stands by the fact that fashion and music are entwined.

> On a cultural level I feel that music and fashion have always mirrored one another. There's a creative consciousness, a trend that is part of the way people think about art and colours and patterns and music and fashion. Music and visuals are connected. I guess I could say that they cannot be separate, I need fashion for my music and I need music for my fashion.[21]

Gaga's dress sense completes the package. She uses it to augment her music and musical performances, as well as to boost her influence over the industry.

Fandom

Gaga's relationship with her fans is unique. She does not refer to them as fans; they are her 'monsters'. The reason for this is that she believes her fans are the outcasts of society, in particular the LGBT community of whom she is a key supporter. During the first five minutes of her concert, Gaga tells the audience that whilst at her show, they can be whoever and whatever they want to be. She tells them that they are in a safe and loving place. She even shouts out at one point that everyone should '[c]elebrate your gay pride!'[22] It is therefore clear that Gaga embraces her fans as social outcasts. It is important to note that Gaga is also being very clever. She is using the fans' insecurities to target them and make them feel part of a community, transcending popular culture.

Many music artists view their fans through a one-way window. The artist communicates with fans through music, but the fans cannot communicate with the artist. Gaga is different in the sense that she turns this window into a two-way view, through which she utilises new media such as Twitter and Facebook to directly inform and communicate with her fans. Through these new media platforms, she has managed to create what seems to be a very personal relationship with each of her fans. Twitter is a social networking application created for people to share their thoughts in updates of 140 characters. Celebrities immediately started using it to keep their fans updated with their everyday movements. Fans loved this because it gave them a voyeuristic view of an artist. Suddenly the celebrity was not a mystical and elusive creature.

Gaga, however, has taken the use of Twitter to a different level. She believes that other celebrities are not using it for the right reasons:

> I actually think it's part of why Twitter is so great is because for me you can build trust with your fans if you use it for the right reasons. People that argue on twitter or are just using it as a celebrity networking device – it's boring and it has nothing to do with your fans or your vocational purpose. I use the internet. I've embraced the internet in a pop cultural kind of way. I think about what a pop artist would have done in the 80s if the internet were what it is today, and they would have embraced it. I think it's wonderful to embrace that there's now two windows. Embracing the internet is what a pop artist should do, it's the new era, it's the way we live, and we are wired.[23]

The fact that Gaga sees Twitter differently from other celebrities has boosted her career and popularity among fans: she uses Twitter to invite the fans to communicate with her, rather than Gaga just communicating to her fans. Gaga is constantly inundated with videos and letters and tweets from her fans:

> I feel so blessed, it's so unexplainable, the love that I feel for my fans and how they treat me. All of the videos that they create and the lovely notes and the artwork. Just the other day I spent a few hours reading through all this fan mail, and I sat with Haus of Gaga and people that I work with and we all rave about how talented and lovely my fans are. I guess all I would say is I think love is a symbiotic thing – especially when it's real. So perhaps it's just very real and I put love into my fans and they put love into me and we just continue to give love back and forth to each other – forever.[24]

Gaga confirms a connection with her fans, enhanced through the use of Twitter. Gaga also understands the power that comes through Twitter. Simply by sending a tweet to a fan she can make someone's day and make them feel an explosion of emotions – be it excitement, tears of joy, or love. However, it is not only Gaga who is given power by the means of Twitter: her fans can also use this platform in force to communicate with their favourite artist.

> Just the other day I revealed to my fans that my grandpa is sick, and it's very difficult for me because I'm away and I want to be home but I don't want to disappoint my fans because so many of them spent money on tickets for my shows. So I sat down at my piano and I said to them, 'I had a bad day, my grandpa is sick.' The next day I went to say hello to my fans on Twitter and I had seen that there were all these lovely messages from them and that worldwide they had trended 'get well grandpa gaga.' That has nothing to do with my music or my clothes or making an album number one or a song number one.[25]

This type of allegiance promotes Gaga as a popular artist and makes her a 'Madonna 2.0'. I am not arguing that if Madonna had been given the tool of social networking in the peak of her career she would not have used it, but because Gaga has utilised what the read write web is offering her, she has achieved accelerated success.

Gaga also augments her relationship with her fans by defending and supporting them. Most celebrities would stick to their management and bodyguards. However, when a die-hard Gaga fan turned up at the Manchester Evening News Arena with Coke cans in her hair (an ode to Gaga's 'Telephone' video), she was asked to remove them by security. Gaga instantly tweeted to her fans: 'Outraged ... Staff at the MEN aren't letting people into the arena with cans in their hair. So many sad Little Monsters.'[26] Gaga then later tweeted: 'All is well at MEN Arena, feel free to wear your coke cans proud in hair. Security has been reprimanded for censoring Little Monster freedoms.'[27] Another occasion when Gaga defended her fans was when Cole Goforth, a 15-year-old from Tennessee, was sent home from school for wearing a T-shirt emblazoned with 'I (Heart) Lady Gay Gay'. When Gaga found out what had happened, she sent a tweet to Cole stating: 'I love you cole, just be yourself. You're perfect the way God made you.'[28] She therefore builds community by mobilising the individualising capacity of the hash tag. Through social networking applications, such as Twitter and Facebook, Gaga inverts conventional celebrity relations. Whilst other celebrities use these devices to place themselves on a pedestal for all their fans to see, Gaga gives fans value, worth and belonging.

This chapter has explored Gaga as a popular culture icon. Even in the short space of time between this chapter being written and published, the University of Carolina has opened a course entitled 'Lady Gaga and the Sociology of Fame'.[29] Professor Mathieu Deflem explains that the course is not about Lady Gaga in particular: 'It's not the person, and it's not the music. It's more this thing out there in society that has 10 million followers on Facebook and six million on Twitter. I mean, that's a social phenomenon.'[30] Deflem also states that the course will 'unravel some of the sociologically relevant dimensions of the fame of Lady Gaga with respect to her music, videos, fashion, and other artistic endeavours'.[31] The course recognises the journey presented in this chapter. It is impossible to predict where Lady Gaga will go or what she will do in the next week, let alone the next decade. She has achieved in a few years what many musical legends call their 'life-work'. Gaga is pioneering. Gaga is a catalyst. Gaga is popular culture. Gaga is digital.

Notes

1. Forbes, 'The World's 100 Most Powerful Women', 2010, *http://www.forbes.com/wealth/power-women*
2. Chapter 4.
3. Lady Gaga, 'In Camera: Lady Gaga', interview by Alexander Fury, *SHOWstudio*, 2010, *http://showstudio.com/project/in_camera/lady_gaga*
4. LadyGagaVEVO, 'Pokerface', *YouTube*, 2009, *http://www.youtube.com/watch?v=bESGLojNYSo*
5. Music News, 'Lady Gaga Helps Download Sales in UK Rise more than 50pc', *The Telegraph*, 2010, *http://www.telegraph.co.uk/culture/music/music-news/7634463/Lady-Gaga-helps-download-sales-in-UK-rise-more-than-50pc.html*
6. LadyGagaVEVO, *YouTube*, 2011, *http://www.youtube.com/user/LadyGagaVEVO*
7. *Ibid.*
8. Lady Gaga, 'In Camera: Lady Gaga', above note 3.
9. *Ibid.*
10. C. Paglia, 'Lady Gaga and the Death of Sex', *The Sunday Times*, 2010, *http://www.thesundaytimes.co.uk/sto/public/magazine/article389697.ece*
11. *Ibid.*
12. Lady Gaga, 'In Camera: Lady Gaga', above note 3.
13. *Ibid.*
14. LadyGagaVEVO, 'Paparazzi', *YouTube*, 2009, *http://www.youtube.com/watch?v=d2smz_1L2_0*
15. LadyGagaVEVO, 'Telephone', *YouTube*, 2010, *http://www.youtube.com/watch?v=EVBsypHzF3U*
16. Lady Gaga, 'I just had to go home and suck my own hermie dick, suckka,' *Twitter*, 2009, *http://www.twitter.com/ladygaga*
17. Q4Music.com, 'Lady Gaga for Q', *Q Magazine*, 2010, *http://covers.q4music.com/Item.aspx?pageNo=6150&year=2010*
18. *Ibid.*
19. Lady Gaga, 'In Camera: Lady Gaga', above note 3.

20. Lady Gaga for ladygaga.net
21. Lady Gaga, 'In Camera: Lady Gaga', above note 3.
22. R Allen, 'A Night at the Monster Ball: The Lady Gaga experience', *SheWired*, 2010, *http://www.shewired.com/Article.cfm?ID=25421*
23. Lady Gaga, 'In Camera: Lady Gaga', above note 3.
24. *Ibid.*
25. *Ibid.*
26. Lady Gaga, 'Outraged ... Staff at the MEN aren't letting people into the arena with cans in their hair. So many sad Little Monsters', *Twitter*, 2010, *http://www.twitter.com/ladygaga*
27. Lady Gaga, 'All is well at MEN Arena, feel free to wear your coke cans proud in hair. Security has been reprimanded for censoring Little Monster freedoms', *Twitter*, 2010, *http://www.twitter.com/ladygaga*
28. Lady Gaga, 'I love you cole, just be yourself. You're perfect the way God made you', *Twitter*, 2010, *http://www.twitter.com/ladygaga*
29. M. Deflem, 'University offers Lady Gaga Sociology Course', *BBC*, 2010, *http://www.bbc.co.uk/news/education-11672679*
30. *Ibid.*
31. *Ibid.*

16

Copyright and couture: the Comme il Faut experience

Leanne McRae

Abstract: Tango is serviced by a range of businesses. Yet Comme il Faut remains the most famous shoe designer for the dance. However, how the company has managed and negotiated the relationship between product and consumer is unusual. Controlling its intellectual property while expanding its business, this study of Comme il Faut enables researchers to track the complex relationship between dancers, dancing and e-commerce.

Key words: tango, fashion, online shopping, e-commerce, intellectual property, Comme il Faut

Popular imaginings of tango often involve darkened cafes and backrooms in Buenos Aires, seductive women and Latin lotharios meeting and moving in passionate embraces as a prelude to tumultuous romances and mesmerising one-night stands. This myth is popularised in film via images of Rudolph Valentino in *Four Horsemen of the Apocalypse*, and even Arnold Schwarzenegger in *True Lies*, dancing with red roses clutched between teeth. Elegant women drape the chests of their partners. While all archetypes hail half-truths, the realities of dance, intimacy and gender find complicated activations within tango. It is these spaces where the improvisation and inspiration of tango reveal dynamic dialogues of leading and following that ultimately manifest the cliché 'it takes two to tango'. This dance is a conversation that is challenging and unpredictable.

Tango has changed over time. It once provided a proactive framework for male heterosexuality to demonstrate masculine competencies in order to attract women. The men would practise together to refine their skills in order to show off to the women in the dance halls and bordellos.

Women would select their partners and decorate or adorn the male's movements with her feet and legs, entangling him as a seductive prelude. The women were not passive or submissive, but were instead the focus of male presentation of their prowess on the dance floor. As a result, there was less emphasis on females following than there was on males leading. Indeed, to this day there remain popular perceptions among some tango communities that a woman's (or follower's) primary responsibility within the dance is to decorate or adorn.

As tango music changed, new ideas about dancing emerged. A greater role for followers was imagined. There has since become a greater emphasis on following technique and the sophistication of what they allow within the dance. Following technique is as complex and rich as leading in the range of skills, abilities and masteries required. Yet the mystique of tango remains and the role of femininity as an equal to the masculine takes on new appearances in the dance. Followers still adorn, but they embellish in a variety of ways that complement and highlight their physical skills within the embrace.

In the tango world, the choice of shoe for followers becomes a source of debate, conversation and interrogation between women. Different shoes serve as a marker of tango heritage and the role of embellishment, femininity and fetishisation within the dance. But finding the right shoe that also deploys correct balance, weight and functionality – along with attractiveness and design – can be problematic. Until relatively recent times, followers danced in regular street shoes. As the dance became more popular and was deployed in instructional environments, footwear was limited to the classic ballroom T-strap model that was supportive while allowing optimal function in the dance. Dancers usually had the choice of either black or red, depending on the colour of their outfit.

But tango has specific movements and methods that are not easily facilitated in shoes designed for ballroom dancing. Shoe designers had to think about the specific needs of tango dancers. Newer designs activate fresh ways of thinking about fashion, dance and desire. A company that has effectively integrated cutting-edge design in the arch and functionality of the shoe, with focused attention to style, is Comme il Faut. This company operates out of a small shop in Buenos Aires and is owned and operated by Raquel Coltrinari and Alicia Muñiz. It features high-end haute couture footwear specifically crafted to emphasise and facilitate the follower's role within the dance.

These shoes have become highly sought-after signifiers for elite tango aficionados. This desirability has been constructed by Comme il Faut in its operational protocols. It fiercely guards its intellectual property. This results in a culture of secrecy that adds cultural capital to the purchase and wearing of these shoes. Consumers must hunt down the few agents worldwide that sell these shoes either at tango events or online. If purchasing online, they must then deploy a whole range of abstract and highly literate fitting and fabric knowledge in order to decode the web protocols of Comme il Faut that limit the display of shoe images. Then there is also a whole range of fashion and dancing enlightenment that must be activated in order to select correct sizing among different fabrics, toe-box and heel designs that all influence the performance of the shoe on the foot and on the floor.

This chapter decodes the intricate choreography of Comme il Faut as a company and consumer interface. Initially, the place and role of intellectual property relationships with fashion and shoes is explored to provide a rationale for Comme il Faut and the culture it has created. The discussion then expands to explore the special place Comme il Faut occupies in the online world through an examination of the web protocols that are expected of distributors and the cognizance they encode within consumers in their online adventures. Finally I examine more deeply the consequences and innovations of Comme il Faut in its deployment of controlled and contained intellectual property along with an expanding consumer base through web 2.0 literacies. The place and role of Comme il Faut as a tango shoe company is explored along with its operational protocols and attitudes to selling that mobilise a culture of haute couture. Dancing, design and drama interface through this company to reveal a complex interaction between dancers, their dancing equipment and the social acumen that influences and contains tango on and off the dance floor.

Intellectual property: copyrighting couture

In the age of the information economy and creative industries, intellectual property laws have become the terrain on which struggles over meaning, culture and consumption are being waged. Within this environment, the ability to protect creativity, knowledge, information generation and a range of abstract and intangible post-industrial manufacturing processes highlights the perceived importance of patents, copyrights and trade marks in the twenty-first century. Fashion designers and couturiers face particular challenges in this environment. For Comme il Faut, these difficulties are shown through its obvious protocols designed to protect the intellectual property of its product in an environment where the plagiarism and copying of artefacts is rendered increasingly easy with the use of streamlined production techniques, digital technologies and cheap labour.

Fashion pirating costs the clothing industry 'an estimated $12 billion'[1] and manifests in unofficial and illegal fashion houses producing fraudulent material and designs. The reason for this inflated plagiarism predicament is that fashion falls into the 'negative space'[2] of intellectual property law. Fashionable items struggle to conform with the intellectual property categories of patents, copyrights and trade marks. This anxiety is further compounded by inconsistencies in international intellectual property law which, until 1994, did not have any cohesive global regulation. It was not until the Uruguayan round of the General Agreement on Tariffs and Trade (GATT) negotiations that an agreement emerged on 'Trade-Related Aspects of Intellectual Property Rights (TRIPS), which lays out a set of minimum standards for all the members of the World Trade Organization (WTO) to adopt'.[3] Despite these agreements, it remains a truism that what protects designers in one national context may not translate into another.

Much of the difficulty in protecting fashion designers from pirating comes from the ambiguities surrounding definitions. Hedrick realised that 'the specialized nature of fashion design protection requires clear definitions of "fashion design", "design", and "apparel"'.[4] Within these categories, it is difficult to determine in what way fashionable items can be protected. Current intellectual property law is not nuanced enough to cater for ambiguous values of cultural capital and ephemera deployed within legal definitions.

The tenses, syntax and grammar of fashion are confusing and contradictory. As Barnard has affirmed,

> like the word 'fashion', the words 'adornment', 'style', 'dress' and 'clothing' can also be used as either verbs or nouns. They refer both to an activity and to either the items used in an activity or to the products of that activity.[5]

These conflicts result in 'the most complex of social systems'[6] within fashion knowledge, definitions and practices. Contradictory and fluid meanings generate instabilities in ideas and ideologies that are attached to cloth to create a highly contentious system of flexible fabric frameworks. Llewellyn Negrin argues for the ambiguities of fashion by outlining the spaces in which consumers activate these juxtaposing possibilities:

> At any one point in time, a particular item of dress can simultaneously signify several different meanings, some of them directly contradictory to each other ... in fact the most successful fashion items are those which have the capacity to signify several contradictory meanings at the same time ... since they enable the wearer to feel that s/he is defining his/her own individuality because of the range of possible meanings which they offer, while at the same time s/he is in fact conforming with the prevailing modes of fashionable dress.[7]

These multiple meanings provide unclear spaces for definitions when intellectual property law is applied to fashion. These definitional insecurities are also compounded by the nature of the fashion industry which relies heavily on borrowing, hybridising and the hijacking of past designs. Alec Balasescu argues that 'among fashion designers in Paris, copying is a matter-of-fact issue, it is something that exists and one has to deal with it. For many, counterfeiting is an engine of creativity'.[8] Coco Chanel stated that she was 'delighted if her models were copied, because it was a measure of her prestige'.[9] For her, copying was part of the cultural capital attached to haute couture design.

While many fashion designers remain resigned to the appropriation of their designs and the borrowing of their material for the purposes of inspiration, the activity of counterfeiting does also operate on a fraudulent and financially damaging level. Balasescu has confirmed that 'in legal language, a counterfeit is an object that "does not differ in a significant manner" from another product, already registered'.[10] This style of blatant plagiarism – of appropriating and replicating an exact design for profit – equates to theft and directly impacts on the capacity for designers to capitalise on their own intellectual property. For designers, concerns also emerge when an inferior product is produced and sold to consumers under the guise of an authentic item. This practice has the potential to damage the reputation of designers in an industry where notability is a currency. Some legal protection is offered under trade mark law where designers may register their brand or label. Any item bearing the trade-marked logo not produced by the designer can result in prosecution under trade mark law. However, this does not extend to the design itself, but rather the illegal use of the brand label. In the UK, these laws tend to be extensive and cohesive.

> The Trade Marks Act established criminal offences relating to the unauthorized use of a trade mark. The provisions are wide and cover importation of counterfeits, labelling, packaging, warehousing, production, distribution, retailing, advertising, promotion and production of the means to produce counterfeit goods and labels and so on.[11]

These laws can be enforced to prosecute in the specific conditions of branding and labelling theft. If a design is registered, the Trade Marks Act can prosecute those offenders. However, it is very difficult to have a design registered under either trade mark or patent legislation, because the courts are unable to distinguish functional from design elements within fashionable items.

> Courts categorically treat clothing as functional, thereby precluding trade mark. The possibility still exists that a portion of a design could be eligible for trade mark protection; however ... courts struggle to separate non-functional design elements eligible for protection from the overall functional apparel design.[12]

Fashionable items are also precluded from copyright law because of the required definitions of usefulness. These requirements state that 'copyright protection ... does not extend to "useful articles", which are defined as those "having an intrinsic utilitarian function that is not merely to portray the appearance of the article or to convey information"'.[13] Fashion, as an idea conflated with clothing and apparel, is fundamentally encoded as 'useful' within this language. However, sections of the design can be separated and copyrighted. For example, 'fabric patterns can be copyrighted'.[14] However, this distinction provides limited protection in a copy-rampant industry.

Patent law also provides little protection for fashionable apparel primarily because of the length of time required to fulfil the patenting process, which can be five years or more. By the time a patent may be granted, the accelerated fashion industry has moved onto other designs, trends and styles, making the patent obsolete. Any legal avenue to pursue counterfeiters requires fashionable items and designs to be 'registered', categorised and defined through available legal categories, which appear to be woefully inadequate even for 'real world' or offline conditions. In the online environment, fashionable items – their images and designs – can be transmitted and translated at speed, making the offline patenting procedures poorly equipped to deal with web based crime. The comparably slow offline legalities that operate through the torts and laws written on paper and with pen cannot match the digitised domains of data transfer and downloading where the spaces between legal and illegal use are increasingly blurred.

Each of these examples demonstrates the extent to which intellectual property law fails the fashion industry. Balmer has correctly affirmed that, in the US,

> the patent statute has been called upon to address technologies that could not have been even fathomed in 1790, such as iPhones and instant mashed potatoes. Yet today's patent statute does not differ substantially from the first patent statue enacted in 1793.[15]

This means that there is a systemic failure to address the specific and nuanced needs of creative industries such as fashion and similar industries like 'furniture, food, and automobile industries',[16] as they move into the highly accelerated and fragmented economic, social and cultural conditions of the twenty-first century.

Online retailers and the long tail of e-commerce

The expansion of the world wide web has made copyright violation and intellectual property a key issue for designers, writers, policy-makers, theorists, consumers and retailers. In the 2000s, the concern over copyright infringement on social networking and web 2.0 interfaces like YouTube has stimulated social debates and policy interventions designed to protect producers and authors of material, and account for a consumer desire to view, produce and consume artefacts in violation but without exploitation of the author's copyright. In *Remix,*[17] Lawrence Lessig recounts the story of Stephanie Lenz who was pursued by the Universal Music Group for posting a video of her 13-month-old son dancing to Prince's 'Let's go Crazy'. Examples such as this, which presented no clear intent by the creator of the clip to violate Prince's copyright or the capacity for the company to make profit from music sales, demonstrate the tenuous terrain for copyright entered into with the proliferation of digital technologies. Even though the digital divide still remains a serious and significant issue for policy-makers to address and ensure more equitable distribution of these technologies, the attendant concerns over creativity and copyright within this realm have generated inadequate attempts to police and provide equitable interactions between copyright holders and consumers. A key issue is the unruly and unconfined nature of digitisation, which presents specific and difficult consequences to overcome.

> Due to the transnational nature of ICTs, the internet is not subject to national and international law; rather it is governed by a set of international agreements, all feebly enforceable, and negotiated among the heterogeneous group of stakeholders.[18]

Ambiguity within digital regulations has meant an uneven and unclear activation of online copyright and intellectual property protection. The consequences can be catastrophic, as is indicated in the case where 'Viacom sued YouTube for copyright infringement seeking injunctive relief and $1 billion in damages for showing 150,000 of its copyrighted clips illegally 1.5 billion times'.[19] On YouTube, where it is believed 'approximately 100 million videos are watched every day',[20] these issues become amplified. For fashion designers, the proliferation of online technologies has its own specific set of complexities and conflictions. Hedrick realised that 'design pirates have the ability to mix and match portions of designs without coming close to infringement',[21] showing that 'clothing ... can be copied by pirates based on a photograph'.[22] Therefore, the decision to make couture available online through e-commerce channels must be carefully made.

E-commerce or online shopping has grown exponentially in the last decade: 'According to the US Department of Commerce, online retail sales were $108.7 billion for 2005.'[23] In 2007, 'US e-commerce sales ... reached $251 billion'.[24] This type of buying and selling is characterised by particular factors, namely that consumers do not experience the product directly and need 'the unconventional method of payment where the buyer and seller never meet face-to-face'.[25] In order to participate in this type of consumption, customers must have access to effective online hardware and software, such as a high-speed internet connection as well as specific online literacies to navigate, decode and understand online shopping websites and procedures. These literacies straddle the online and offline worlds where information must be combined, remixed and reshuffled for the consumer to make smart and effective online choices.

Buyers must have key understandings of website layout and structure so they can navigate the physicalities of the e-shopping universe with confidence.

However, functional skills are not enough. They must also have a series of confluent and competing capabilities in expanding and developing their awareness of online shopping procedures and pitfalls. One example is an awareness of the need to seek out non-obvious information about shipping and returns policies. Consumers also need a detailed image literacy to decode the signs and codes of photographic material provided for products. Coupling this information, they also require an ability to translate descriptive text into visual imagery. Customers must possess or develop research skills and keyword mastery to assist in gathering product information, and they must have a highly reflexive understanding of product language. This knowledge is essential as it assists in reducing the insecurities created when shopping online. The anxieties that need placating for e-shoppers range from the 'leading perceived risks involve[ing] the loss of credit card and other personal information'[26] to 'concerns over delivery and return ... or exposure to a computer virus'[27] and 'various transaction costs'.[28] Consumers seek to allay these fears through strategies designed to increase surety with the vendor and safety of the exchange. Retailers also deploy a range of website design factors and information protocols in order to overcome the ideologies and expectations of traditional shopping experiences:

> e-marketing vendors have to provide a secure channel for not only monetary transactions, but to logistical solutions to overcome one of the most powerful assets of traditional bricks-and-mortar businesses: the possibility for the customer to walk out with the purchased product in hand. Virtual businesses have to convince the customer that the product can easily be returned if it is not satisfactory. The warranty and customer support must work despite different geographical locations and the customer has to be convinced to make the purchase without the actual physical product in front of them.[29]

These conditions create complexity in the online buying and selling process. For these reasons fashionable items such as clothing and apparel have not been a staple of online retailers. Purchasing these items requires specific and tactile literacies from the consumer. It is only recently that vendors have become more successful in selling clothing and apparel as experienced shoppers have gained the skills to understand and decode the strengths and pitfalls of shopping online. These consumers tend to possess high levels of internet usage and have developed the expertise to reduce the perceived and real risks of buying online.

When buying fashion, the key risks also involve the performance of the product 'best described as disappointment that the product did not perform as well as the customer thought it would'.[30] It is only through trial and error that consumers learn the skills to select the right item and reduce the potential for disappointment. By choosing reliable vendors and by deploying functional and reflexive literacies in clothing, fitting and fabric, customers are able to reduce the risks of buying a product that conventionally 'require[s] a "multisensory" or "tactile" experience prior to purchase decision'.[31] The purchase of 'standardised products such as airline tickets, videos and DVDs'[32] does not require this level of interaction with the product. Therefore, buying clothing online is a special and multiliterate experience.

Angela Thomas-Jones has demonstrated, in her evocative work on eBay, the stringent and staunch protocols that buyers and sellers negotiate with as they interact on and through the site. Thomas-Jones argues that not only do buyers have basic knowledge of clothing and their differences but they also function to regulate sellers through ranking and review mechanisms. These tools are crucial for the functioning of the eBay site 'along with eBay's clothing buying guide, [and the] high level fashion and specific body literacies ... required to sell and buy articles accurately'.[33] It is also a 'system built on trust and feedback'[34] so that 'if a seller betrays their trust, then they are given negative feedback',[35] which other buyers use as guides to assess the reliability of the seller in making their risk assessments. This feedback system is effective for eBay because 'online apparel shoppers have difficulty assessing products and tend to easily abandon the purchasing process'.[36] The reviews provided by other shoppers are judged as authentic assessments of the reliability, quality and service systems of the seller. As a result, online shoppers tend to be rigorous comparers and use the digital format to save time on purchases by accessing the information available to contrast and examine similar or competing products. In doing so, they learn specific web literacies and deploy a range of highly nuanced understandings of products, service, buying and selling in their interpretations.

While customers may 'differ in their rules and strategies when they access or analyze information',[37] they are gathering experiences that build into an online shopping oeuvre that serves to assist consumers in their ability to deploy a diversity of meanings while they shop. These meanings are complex and contradictory, and sellers must be able to provide an effective 'balance of offline/online provision'.[38] For virtual retailers, this means providing an essential interface for the exchange of email so that consumers can have their questions about a product answered in a timely and responsive manner. It requires the construction of integrated and intuitive websites that enable access to the specific information of value to an online shopper – which may differ dramatically from that of a customer in a bricks-and-mortar store. Li argues that these design elements are crucial to effective online selling:

> How information is displayed and presented may also influence consumer decision-making. Intuitively, some information formats help consumers to facilitate choices while others might increase the cognitive effort of consumers to process information.[39]

Sellers need to understand the different motivations of online shoppers. Lieberman and Stashevsky, for example, argue that online 'consumers are likely to collect information before making a purchase'[40] and that 'product categories that are more accessible in terms of obtaining product information enjoy higher rates of preference for shopping online'.[41] Therefore, supporting text and information may be required for online shoppers to assess and interpret the product effectively before making the purchasing decision. This crucial intervention by sellers is ranked by Lieberman and Stashevsky as being fundamental to successful online selling because 'doubts about quality of information concerning the purchasing choices and reliability of internet vendors were even more inhibiting than security issues'[42] when making a buying choice. Consumers want to know that what they are seeing online is replicated in the product that arrives at their door. Within this rationale, their inability to try the product first – particularly when it comes to clothing and apparel – means that vendors must be rigorous and diligent in assuring that the product information is detailed, accurate and easily accessible on websites. Consumers do not have the opportunity to have a tactile and intimate experience with the item of clothing or footwear they wish to purchase. This lack of sensory interaction means that other methods of assessment must be activated by the customer.

Fashion and failure

The tactile and sometimes sensual interfaces with fashion make it a unique buying experience located in the unruly and intimate imaginings of customers. In describing her occupation of being a fashion buyer for a department store Joanne Entwistle argues that assessing and selecting clothing is fundamentally emotional and often unpredictable:

> This encounter is, first and foremost, a sensual one. Buyers set about examining the garment's features – its shape, colour and other tactile qualities, the testing can take numerous forms – touching, feeling, and examining the sample on a hanger, observing it on a fit model, or indeed by actually trying the garment on if no model is available.[43]

The intimacy of this relationship to clothing is embedded in the buying process and in the trying on of items to see how they fit and feel on the body. Through this sensory experience customers gain an insight into the form, fit and function of the item that cannot be gauged by observing it on a hanger or on another individual. In fashion 'there is no substitute for this direct encounter with the product'.[44] Online items therefore present a series of difficulties to consumers that are challenging to surmount. Entwistle recounts the experience 'when, after September 11 [2001], buyers were unable to go to New York, as Fashion Week was cancelled, a whole collection was bought on CDRom and proved to be a total failure'.[45] Therefore, it would seem that by comparison, buying apparel online is not an effective method of shopping. Yet consumers are, in increasing numbers, making these purchases by developing the online and offline literacies required to make informed and careful choices. They are also developing the high levels of literacy to move between the spaces of offline and online worlds to translate the experiences of each environment in order to provide a cohesive shopping milieu in their digital spheres.

Despite the perceived need for online retailers to provide detailed and precise descriptions, images and ideas about their products in order to substitute for the lack of interaction with the item online, in some circumstances different literacies need to be activated by consumers. Desire is a key trope for the creation of optimal online shopping conditions. The strategies deployed by buyers when balancing risks in online versus offline shopping contexts are often swayed by desiring tropes embodied by consumers in their imaginings of their selves, the product, and their relationships to consumption. In the age of copyright challenges and intellectual property concerns, designers and creators – as well as sellers and distributors – need to balance the desires of the customer with the concerns of the creator. Comme il Faut presents an evocative case study of a reinscription of the protocols and expectations of both online and offline shopping experiences where consumers respond favourably to a distinct and precise lack of product visibility. Comme il Faut specifically encodes its company to create a culture of exclusivity and its online vendors provide the key interface into and through this exclusive sphere.

Comme il Faut couture

Comme il Faut in Buenos Aires is a unique store. Upon entry, there are no displays of the shoes on shelves. Instead, a shopper is confronted with black and leopard-print sofas in an elegantly designed room attended by helpful staff. Upon introduction, the prospective purchaser describes the type of desired shoe. The consumer must hold enough knowledge so that this product can be described with accuracy. Shop assistants scurry out to the back and retrieve a series of samples. This process continues until the shopper is satisfied.

The company has a total of 15 agents who sell their shoes worldwide. These organisations are located across Europe, Hong Kong, Canada and the United States. Some sell online, others only at their dance studios or tango events. In the online environment, a peculiar modality of engaging with the consumption process is activated. Because Comme il Faut is particularly protective of its intellectual property, no pictures of the shoes are allowed online. Instead, only partial images are permitted along with a short description of the shoe, usually supported by a glossary of terms. This relationship presents a curious interface between a series of known factors being activated by Comme il Faut. Its concern with copyright is manifested along with the specific knowledge and literacy required of its consumers to engage in this selecting and buying process. These understandings are highly ambivalent and Comme il Faut relies on its vendors creating an intimate relationship with consumers to ensure adequate customer service to reduce the variables for purchasing error. However, this process is also supported by the culture of exclusivity surrounding these shoes, cultivated by the haute couture manufacturing processes of Comme il Faut. Consumers are usually willing to deploy higher levels of cognitive engagement despite the barriers confronting the online experience because of the special nature of these shoes, and despite the difficulty of the purchase. The complexities of the engagements in and around Comme il Faut present a unique set of conditions by which to understand the relationships between intellectual property, popular culture, dancing, design, and desire.

This process is often so complex that some customers prefer the experience of shopping online because they actually obtain more information from the online vendors than the shop assistants in the bricks-and-mortar store. The following transcript of an interview with a buyer of Comme il Faut describes the competing ideas encircling the company and its ideologies.

In this example, the customer displays an intricately detailed knowledge of shoe design, fabric functions and product language. The communication is highlighted between women and the knowledge that they possess about their dancing needs. The interface between ideologies of style and function are present as the sensuousness of the product creates the motivation to pursue the purchase. Yet, as the buyer extends her

Text Box 16.1

Interview with a buyer of Comme il Faut products

1. How long have you been dancing tango?

Commenced tango lessons in September 2003 (I don't consider I was dancing tango for at least the first three years).

2. Thinking back over your tango experience, at what point did you hear about CiF shoes and how were they characterised to you?

In October 2006 I attended Cecilia Gonzalez and Donato Jurez workshops in Sydney. Cecilia wore a pair of black and silver CiF shoes at a practice (open-toe with a single band of black suede, the heel cage had silver leather cut out detail – they were lovely). I asked ******** about the shoes at a milonga associated with the workshops. **** advised she had a couple (I think – could have been more) of pairs of CiF and that they were better quality Argentinean tango shoes; they were more expensive but had superior designs and balance, and could only be purchased in BsAs or on the internet.

3. What made you decide to buy CiF shoes?

The designs and exclusivity – in that order. Plus I wanted to see if they were as well balanced as **** professed.

4. Have you more than one pair? Why? What do you enjoy about these shoes?

I have four pairs of CiF. I had six pairs but was unhappy with the fit of two, which I no longer have. I bought my first pair in November 2006 – a black suede sling-back, and purchased another two pairs online and two in Argentina (different material, heel cage and strap combinations), searching for the 'best' ankle stability for my foot – I have thin narrow ankles relative to the ball of my foot. I love all of the shoes and enjoy wearing them for their look and fit. For dancing, I adore the Mary Jane style, but unfortunately it has the highest heel and I am still getting used to them.

5. Have you been to the CiF store in Argentina? Can you describe the experience?

Yes, I purchased two pairs from the store in February 2008. I did not enjoy the experience. There are no shoes on show; instead you have to describe the shoe(s) you are interested in buying to sales assistants who bring stock for you to try in a fitting room. I visited on two occasions and noticed that, despite what you described, the same shoes are brought out – to other tourists and locals.

The range (styles and colours) of shoes that were offered was limited and I got the impression there were more shoes and that they were trying to shift shoes that hadn't been selling. The sizing and fit were varied, which also concerned me – were they seconds? I hadn't packed my current CiF shoes as I was confident of buying a pair in BsAs to dance that evening. I finally found a pair of sandals that I thought would be OK. I mentioned to the manager/owner as I paid that I was disappointed they didn't have styles I was looking for. She looked concerned and said it must have been a language breakdown and she had the style I was chasing. She located two pair of Mary Janes; I selected one and included them with the other pair I had selected.

6. Did you enjoy shopping this way?

No, I didn't enjoy shopping at the CiF store in Argentina – I bought a style of shoe (sandal) I wouldn't have considered buying online.

7. Have you bought CiF online? If so, from which site?

Yes: *http://www.malevashoes.com*

8. What was this experience like? Did you find it easy or difficult to decide which shoes to purchase? What kind of assistance was provided by the seller?

Shopping at Maleva shoes was enjoyable. The site is straightforward and provides a detailed glossary, which I found helpful. Email updates every four to six weeks advise when new stock has been added to the online boutique. Generally my selection is narrowed to two to three pairs of shoes as I am not interested in approximately 75 per cent of the shoes uploaded due to heel size or heel cage style. Photos (of part of the shoe) are now included, which provides useful information on colour and material. Now that I have a number of CiF shoes I am familiar with the styles and can quickly assess if a particular pair may suit my requirements. The seller responded to email questions quickly and provided good advice, being more concerned that the appropriate footwear was purchased rather than closing the sale.

9. What was your greatest concern with this purchase? Getting the right size? Using Paypal or some other online payment system? Receiving the goods in a timely fashion and intact? Or anything else?

My concern at the time of my first purchase from Maleva shoes was the method of shipment and if the goods would arrive, as tracking wasn't offered. I have now met the seller and feel less concerned. Sizing was also an issue as I fall between the straight sizes offered (I am a size 37.5).

10. Did what you thought you were buying match with the actual product when it arrived? What were the differences – if any?

On both occasions, shoes purchased from Maleva shoes were accurately described with regard to colour, style and material. Sizing was an issue. I was advised by the seller that I would have to change sizes depending on the material – suede shoes would stretch and I should buy a pair that was a half size smaller (37), and some leathers have less stretch and I should purchase a 38. This was good advice for suede but I was disappointed with a fabric shoe (bought in a size 38) as it was too big.

11. What did you do if you found the shoe did not match your imagining? Were you disappointed? Did you just deal with it? Did you pass on your purchase to another dancer? Were you even happily surprised with the difference?

I sold the fabric shoe in size 38 to another dancer after wearing for an hour. I wore the sandals bought at the CiF store in Argentina on my holiday. The strapping became painful and the shoes had poor balance so I gave them to another dancer to try/keep.

12. Which CiF buying experience is your preferred – online or offline – and for what reasons?

I prefer shopping online as I have the convenience of shopping when I want to. The email updates from Maleva shoes make it a fun experience to see the new styles, as well as which shoes haven't sold and are on sale. Also, it's a time efficient way to shop as a result of the criteria I have compiled from the sample of CiF (and other brand) shoes I have purchased.

experience of this product, she must develop the literacies to assess, interpret and understand her choices. This is achieved through trial and error, email conversation with the vendor, mobilising a network of sub-consumers (those to whom she can on-sell or pass on shoes that are not suitable), and deploying highly literate understandings of heel height, fabric, toe box and ankle strap parameters and performances. These engagements of consumers are hidden in the online shopping oeuvre where concerns about privacy and securing payment systems are most often spotlighted to the detriment of the more mundane mobilisations of authenticity and functionality in the product itself. The interviewee demonstrates and deploys the complex meaning systems that motivate the purchase. These are wide-ranging, personal and public, in the interface between customers, their dance and the company.

Comme il Faut is an Argentine shoe company, yet its name summons very different connotations for the product. The French name firmly encodes the company within the traditions of haute couture and Parisian design. The history of French fashion can be traced back to the seventeenth century when European taste elevated French clothing and apparel as being elite and elegant. As Stewart suggests, 'French manufacturers and exporters have traded on their reputation for tasteful luxury products and have represented the French as possessing a more refined taste than other nations'.[46] This ideology has percolated through time during which archetypal French designers have been held up as quintessential arbiters of taste, style and fashion – Dior and Chanel being leaders within this cohort in terms of marketing their cultural capital. Despite the exclusive ideologies of French design and the narrowing of the market to upper-class clientele, who did not demand styles to wear but were guided by the superior taste of the designer who created particular items of clothing for them, the deployment of taste categories was assisted by the effective marketing of these products. The interface with the creation of fashion as a category is mobilised when advertisers seek to market products to clients. In order to make items special, elite and unique – not simply clothing that is functional for weather, occupation or status – ideals about wealth and poverty, privilege and entitlement, and style and taste need to be activated. As a result, there has always been a close but conflicting relationship between advertising and fashion.

> Paris first set trends in the seventeenth century, certainly because of the political predominance of the French state and cultural ascendancy of the Court of Versailles, but also because Lyonnais silk manufacturers pioneered national and international advertising.[47]

Importantly, the ideas about France and Paris as the heart of fashion and stylish apparel were effectively marketed to other nations and consumers. This is instructional in contextualising the relationship of Argentina with these ideas. By the twentieth century, the institutions of Paris couture were well embedded in fashionable literacies.

> While Great Britain continued to be the largest foreign market for French clothing, the United States had taken second place by the mid-1920s. Western European countries came in third through seventh place in these boom years, but the New World countries of Canada and Argentina moved up to eighth and ninth places.[48]

Argentina's connections with haute couture have been firmly established since the early twentieth century. This influence can be seen in the filtering of designs by Comme il Faut to embody and embrace the ideologies of French fashion design. It makes its products to conform to French copyright law, 'based on the "unity of art"'[49] – thereby not distinguishing between art and commerce and activating the ethics contained within Parisian design of 'using "exclusive" fabrics, rich trim, careful fitting, and fine hand-sewing'.[50] Buyers of Comme il Faut are encoded into this culture and seek out the difficult consumption process in order to possess an item of haute couture that mobilises elite style and function.

Comme il Faut relies on its customers to develop their own highly literate understanding of design, dancing and desire. It does not allow full images of its shoes to be displayed by the online vendors. In order to purchase the shoes, shoppers often need to enrol in a mailing list to receive full images, either in a special 'member section' (as is available through Lisadore[51] and Diva Boutique[52]) or receive email notifications with image files attached. In protecting its intellectual property, the company has created an added layer of exclusivity by treating its product and its design as if it is not a copyright concern, but rather a trade secret – that is, the design and function of these shoes contains 'information that is not publicly disclosed, that is valuable, and that provides economic advantage to a business or other enterprise because it is not publicly known'.[53] This secrecy creates desirability. These ideas are aligned with tango as a dance invoking an intimate and secret communication between partners. Dancers seeking these shoes are embracing complex ideas about themselves, their dance and their desires – to be stylish, sexualised and sensuous.

It is also intimately connected with the histories of fashion availability, marketing and monitoring the high levels of copying occurring within the industry. Originally, 'fashion illustrations commissioned by couturiers or by editors, evoked elegance and revealed obvious features, like the silhouette, but obscured subtle design features'.[54] Designers have always been aware of the high levels of copying of their designs. The online environment may offer a new set of difficulties and strategies, but these are not significantly separate from their experiences in the offline world where 'suppliers can and do limit the flow of their products, developing exclusive arrangements with some stores ... to protect the value of their products'.[55] Comme il Faut continues the history of fashion design and distribution in the online environment that has always existed offline. Key differences are embodied in the way in which Comme il Faut manages its bricks-and-mortar store in contrast to its online vendors.

Online sellers provide an intersecting network of illicit and approved knowledge about Comme il Faut shoes. Their inability to show images of the shoes means that they must construct an interface of images, texts and imaginings to facilitate the buying process. A glossary of style can be tracked through these sites where 'taste ... [as] a dynamic force ... [is] forged out of the ongoing relationships and encounters with product markets'.[56] Consumers interact with and create taste based literacies as they embody their role as stylish consumer. They create an imaginary map drawn between the product, its description and the understanding that the consumer possesses about the language in the text deployed and its application to dancing. Women who consume Comme il Faut are activating complex awareness, demonstrating a control and mastery over their dancing and consuming practices.

The success of Comme il Faut is bound up in the way in which the company encodes itself as high-end fashion coupled with the limited consumer access to its product. This intersection creates a convoluted axis of information literacy on behalf of consumers who need to have a diverse digital, design and dancing background. These processes reveal the highly nuanced relationships and ideas that consumers deploy in their purchasing procedures. It also points to the manner in which ideologies of consumption are unevenly mobilised in these spheres. Despite the concerns with consumer motivation for online buying and the claims of more information being desirable for effective consumer engagement, Comme il Faut demonstrates that the online shopping environment is far more complex. Shoppers tend to buy online when they cannot find what they want through other means. It is no accident that 'the majority of virtual stores sell new or hard-to-get articles'.[57] This means that creating a culture of exclusivity creates the conditions most suitable for online buying. Fashion sellers need to find a balance between the information a customer requires to make an informed choice and constructing the couture as unique, special and desirable. Comme il Faut has created an effective intersection between these ideas.

For Comme il Faut, the history of counterfeiting and inadequate copyright protection for fashion has assisted in its approach to production and sales. It has made the failures of intellectual property and the high levels of copying within fashion work for it by configuring itself as haute couture, thereby normalising the secrecy surrounding its product and lack of information at the point of purchase. Reducing availability has created demand. Each shoe design is produced only in batches of thirty. This elevates the shoe into an exclusive product. Consumers are encoded to feel as though they are purchasing a limited edition item. Within the discourses of haute couture in which the elite ideologies of quality are promoted, Comme il Faut embodies the process and procedures of scarcity. Its French name elucidates the Parisian couturiers, signifying an intimacy with European fashion. The contradictions and confluences with tango reveal the complexities in meaning systems being deployed. For women this is significant. Tango was a dance of the street and in bordellos. Women who danced tango were not reputable women. Even though tango has evolved far from these origins, the myths remain. As a result, women who dance tango today not only seek to distance themselves from these origins of harlots and seductresses, but also to maintain the discourses of femininity within the dance that is positioned as opposite but equal to the men. Comme il Faut provides an effective mechanism for women followers to activate these contradictory meanings. The shoes are ultra-feminine in their designs to signify the flirtatiousness of women on the dance floor. But they are also high fashion and deploy the meanings of class and sophistication, removing these women from the street-urchin origins and styles of femininity that once danced the tango.

In an age of online buying and selling, new consumer literacies are emerging against a backdrop of copying, borrowing and reinscribing fashion designs. However, within these literacies are some older notions about desirability, fashionability and style that are being activated and rejuvenated in this environment. Instead of reducing the risks, some vendors are cultivating reputations for providing elite, hard-to-get goods that embody an attractive risk balance ethic at the heart of online buying. Consumers often buy items online that they cannot get locally. The risk associated with not being able to experience the product directly is what motivates the online sojourn. Comme il Faut uses its couture origins and ethics to translate and transgress the boundaries of fashion for its consumers. The literacies needed to decode its product are nuanced and precise, making the company an archetype of online buying. Indeed, its online oeuvre appears to operate more effectively than its offline bricks-and-mortar store because online the spaces between consumption, couture and consciousness reveal the contradictions in which purchasing decisions are made, thereby enabling them to be reified, visualised and resolved.

Notes

1. L. Hedrick, 'Tearing Fashion Design Protection Apart at the Seams', *Washington and Lee Law Review*, 65(1), 2008, p. 218.
2. *Ibid.*, p. 217.
3. A.A. Andolsen, 'Get Smart! About Intellectual Property', *Information Management Journal*, January/February, 2006, p. 37.
4. Hedrick, above note 1, p. 220.
5. M. Barnard, *Fashion as Communication* (London: Routledge, 1996), pp. 8–9.
6. T. Brabazon, *Ladies who Lunge: Celebrating difficult women* (Sydney: UNSW Press, 2002), p. 36.
7. L. Negrin, 'The Meaning of Dress', *Arena Journal*, No. 7, 1996, pp. 132–33.
8. A. Balasescu, 'After Authors: Sign(ify)ing fashion from Paris to Tehran', *Journal of Material Culture*, 10(3), 2005, p. 290.
9. *Ibid.*, p. 294.
10. *Ibid.*, p. 290.
11. L. Alcock, P. Chen, H.M. Ch'ng and S. Hobson, 'Criminal Remedies against Counterfeiting', *Journal of Brand Management*, 11(2), 2003, p. 138.
12. Hedrick, above note 1, p. 227.
13. *Ibid.*, p. 228.
14. B. Scruggs, 'Should Fashion Design be Copyrightable?' *Northwestern Journal of Technology and Intellectual Property*, 6(1), 2007, p. 129.
15. N.L. Balmer, 'Fashionable IP or IP for Fashion?' *Washington and Lee Law Review*, 61(1), 2008, p. 277.
16. Hedrick, above note 1, p. 263.
17. L. Lessig, *Remix* (London: Bloomsbury, 2008).
18. G.S. Drori, 'Information Society as a Global Policy Agenda: What does it tell us about the age of globalization?' *International Journal of Comparative Sociology*, 48(4), 2007, p. 309.
19. J.J. Darrow and G.R. Ferrera, 'Social Networking Websites and the DMCA: A safe-harbor from copyright infringement liability or the perfect storm', *Northwestern Journal of Technology and Intellectual Property*, 6(1), 2007, p. 1.

20. *Ibid.*
21. Hedrick, above note 1, p. 262.
22. *Ibid.*, p. 243.
23. Y. Lieberman and S. Stashevsky, 'Determinants of Online Shopping: Examination of an early-stage online market', *Canadian Journal of Administrative Sciences*, 26(4), 2009, p. 316.
24. M. Park and S.J. Lennon, 'Brand Name and Promotion in Online Shopping Contexts', *Journal of Fashion Marketing and Management*, 13(2), 2009, p. 149.
25. C. Comegys, M. Hannula and J. Vaisanen, 'Effects of Consumer Trust and Risk on Online Purchase Decision-making: A comparison of Finnish and United States students', *International Journal of Management*, 26(2), 2009, p. 296.
26. Lieberman and Stashevsky, above note 23, p. 320.
27. Comegys, Hannula and Vaisanen, above note 25.
28. Lieberman and Stashevsky, above note 23.
29. Comegys, Hannula, and Vaisanen, above note 25.
30. *Ibid.*, p. 297.
31. F. Dall'Olmo Riley, D. Scarpi and A. Manaresi, 'Purchasing Services Online: A two-country generalization of possible influences', *Journal of Services Marketing*, 23(3), 2009, p. 93.
32. *Ibid.*
33. A.Thomas-Jones, 'eBay: Marketing the real body in the virtual world', in T. Brabazon, (ed.), *The Revolution will not be Downloaded: Dissent in the digital age* (Oxford: Chandos, 2008), p. 169.
34. *Ibid.*, p. 167.
35. *Ibid.*
36. Park and Lennon, above note 24, p. 149.
37. P.F. Li, 'Effects of Individual Difference on Choice Strategy in Goal-Directed Online Shopping', *Journal of American Academy of Business*, 15(2), 2010, p. 187.
38. Dall'Olmo Riley, Scarpi and Manaresi, above note 31, p. 94.
39. Li, above note 37, p. 187.
40. Lieberman and Stashevsky, above note 23, p. 319.
41. *Ibid.*
42. *Ibid.*, p. 320.
43. J. Entwistle, 'The Cultural Economy of Fashion Buying', *Current Sociology*, 54(5), 2006, p. 711.
44. *Ibid.*, p. 713.
45. *Ibid.*
46. M.L. Stewart, 'Copying and Copyrighting Haute Couture: Democratizing fashion, 1900–1930s', *French Historical Studies*, 28(1), 2005, p. 103.
47. *Ibid.*, p. 113.
48. *Ibid.*, p. 109.
49. Balasescu, above note 8, p. 291.
50. Stewart, above note 46, p. 106.
51. Lisadore, accessed online, 19 October 2011, *https://www.lisadore.com*

52. Diva Boutique, accessed 19 October, 2011, *http://www.diva-boutique.com/women_welcome.aspx*
53. Andolsen, above note 3, p. 41.
54. Stewart, above note 46, pp. 114–15.
55. Entwistle, above note 43, p. 717.
56. *Ibid.*, p. 714.
57. Thomas-Jones, above note 33, p. 163.

17

When community becomes a commodity

Mike Kent

Abstract: This chapter investigates how online communities are commodified. With attention to Google and Facebook, this research focuses on how and why identity is marketed, bought and sold.

Key words: online identity, online communication, commodification, gaming

The internet has accelerated the commodification of personal space. Our online research informs Google, enabling it to deliver ever more customised advertising, reinforced by our relationships and friends through Facebook. The process of courtship online has become a commercial concern. The community has become a commodity. This chapter explores how this process has emerged. It investigates the construction of fleeting digital identities and the difficulty in finding and interfacing with these online. One way to track this ephemerality is to look for these identities where virtual communities form, driven by common interest and networks. Some of these communities are brief and fleeting, built around a shared search for information. Others are more enduring, taking place on – and enabled by – online social networking sites.

This chapter begins by interrogating the nature of online identity and online communities, before following case studies of the two most visited sites on the world wide web: Google and Facebook. Both Google and Facebook employ different strategies to try to find our online digital self and use it to sell advertising to our off-screen, analogue, self. With these two examples, I explore the different approaches these corporations take as they seek to draw profit from online communities as targets of commercial advertising. The argument then turns to explore the place of online dating sites and online gaming in the ongoing process of this commodification of internet experience, and then concludes by investigating some disturbing future implications of these current approaches.

Digital identity

Sherry Turkle's famous book, *Life on the Screen: Identity in the age of the internet*,[1] was first published in 1995. The monograph captured the moment when the world wide web was still a relatively new development, particularly in terms of popular cultural awareness. The internet, while rapidly growing, had still not yet reached a 30 per cent household penetration rate in the United States (US). In this context, Turkle's work looked at the construction of identity and how the computers and internet mediated and transformed this construction. Since that time, the diversity and complexity of digital identity has grown. So, too, has the breadth and depth of its societal penetration. By mid-2010 internet penetration in the US had reached 77.3 per cent;[2] there were more than 500 million people worldwide with Facebook accounts,[3] with 43 per cent of people in the US holding an account.[4]

An individual user of the internet will have different aspects of his or her self manifest off and on screen. On screen, through the internet, the self is fragmented into many discrete digital identities that together construct the digital self. Rather than an avatar representing a single and complete digital self through cyberspace, an individual presents a variety of digital identities through different applications on the internet. In each case, these identities represent separate, politicised selves. At its most basic, this is what happens when typing 'I' in an email. The act of writing creates a projected self.

Some of these digital identities are closely aligned to an individual off screen and may be easily attached or attributed to that individual, such as when an email or instant message is sent from one person to another with which they have an existing off-screen, analogue relationship. Other digital identities are more distant and the link is less strong, such as when a web page is customised based on a user's history of visits. Still others will be quite distantly related to the off-screen self, such as when posting messages anonymously on a bulletin board, or participating in a bit torrent swarm. In these cases, much of the link between the digital identity and the individual is left behind or is substantially hidden, including notions of class, race, and even gender.

A complete digital 'self' exists only for the person that it represents. Other individuals on the screen encounter fragments of digital identities, as discrete parts of an entire identity. When others encounter this self, rather than experience it as a whole, they will come into contact with it through interfacing with discrete digital identities; digital 'selves', other than your own, are experienced at the interface of these identities.

The digital self and an off-screen individual share a number of attributes. They generally have the same bank account, both fear sanction from the state such as fines or being sent to prison, and they will share personal relationships. This makes these digital identities potentially valuable in new ways to communicate with and advertise – although given their fragmented, ethereal nature this is not a straightforward task.

Online communities

Traditional communities have many definitions and reflect a wide variety of ways in which and reasons why groups of people come together and share experiences. The idea of a community that shares a common interest, geographic location and lived experience is common to many theorists across different disciplines, although with different emphasis and focus. Online communities disrupt many of these understandings of traditional communities. This arises partly though their ability to circumvent the need for a shared physical location. Howard Rheingold wrote, in his seminal book *The Virtual Community* in 1993, '[p]eople in virtual communities do just about everything people do in real life, but we leave our bodies behind'.[5]

In addition to this geographic separation, Licklider and Taylor noted of online communities that they are 'communities not of common location, but of common interest'.[6] Virtual communities are brought together not from shared physical proximity but to places of shared interest. Licklider and Taylor wrote in 1968, before the first internet code had been developed, yet presciently predicted crucial aspects of the more modern online communities. Rheingold, writing in the 1990s, was discussing online text-based environments such as Multi-User Dungeons (MUDs) and, in particular, the WELL online community. As the internet has developed and evolved beyond a text-based environment on the PC, so too have virtual communities. They allow greater levels of identity to be projected, often unwittingly, and connections to be made. They can also exist as transitory instances, such as a shared search through

Google. However, what sets apart modern virtual communities from the experience of Rheingold and Licklider and Taylor is the increased commercial value that can potentially be attributed to such communities and how this is extracted.

Google

Google is currently the world's dominant search engine for finding information on the internet. Its service and branding extends through Google Maps and Google Earth for finding locations not on the internet. It is also the most visited website on the world wide web.[7] The company was founded in 1998 by two Stanford University graduate students. The search engine's success stems initially from its effective technique for indexing search results based on the number of links to a particular site – a measure of its popularity. Despite an initial reluctance, the site began to provide advertising with the launch of Google AdWords in October 2000.[8]

AdWords provides advertisers with a link to their own site based on search requests. While a digital identity can be defused, this mechanism is able to capture and commodify a component of digital identity when we search for a term online. Similarly Google's other major advertising product, AdSense, allows owners of different websites to host advertising through Google and receive a commission whenever a visitor follows the advertisement. This service has provided a successful funding model for many websites.

In both these instances Google is able to advertise through this commodity of our activity online. It approaches the diversity of digital identity by casting a wide net across the world wide web and capturing different parts of our digital identity as it passes through. Advertising is attracted to areas where our identities gather in this forum – to popular web pages. In this case, the commodity being sold is the attention of web surfers, linked to what is seemingly of current interest. This fleeting interaction allows for the provision of many services to those surfers 'for free', funding many of the Google products and services as well as many third party websites that are enabled and funded through returns from AdSense.

This reflects the truism in life that if something is free then you are not the person to whom the service is being sold. While each web surfer is unlikely to click on any particular advertisement, the service works on a low rate of click-throughs but from a high number of people. Just as spam takes advantage of the low cost of sending a message to many users through email and only requiring a very small proportion of recipients to follow up on the message to be successful, AdWords and AdSense take advantage of the huge number of individual views that they will receive to generate income from a low 'success rate' per view. These services are turning our interests and queries into a product that is then sold to advertisers in the hope of transforming that attention into economic transactions. In this way Google is able to bring these disparate communities of interest together, as a group, for advertisers.

Facebook

Facebook takes a different approach from Google. Rather than seeking to catch the interest of many fleeting web surfers, it seeks instead to consolidate our identities online and have them shadow, track and dialogue with our analogue identity. Facebook was founded by a student at another Ivy League university in the United States, this time an undergraduate at Harvard University in 2004. Facebook has grown beyond its original reach amongst university students in North America to – by 2010 – maintaining the accounts of more than 500 million people across the globe. Facebook has recently begun to challenge Google as the most viewed website on the world wide web.[9]

Facebook accounts can potentially provide a great service. They allow us to keep track of an extended group of people and are an easy mechanism to let our friends and family know what is happening in our lives. The site also presents a potential threat to our traditional notions of identity. The separation of experience people have in their lives between friends, family and workmates can be easily breached with unintended consequences.

Facebook contains a great deal of information about our lives. Its screens records our age, our relationship status, what we are doing, and increasingly where we are presently located in space. It also keeps track of changes in our lives. Much of the information provided is overt, such as what people type in their status update. This in itself is a great 'product' to sell to advertisers. People wanting to market a particular product or service can select very specific target criteria from the Facebook membership. Other information is more subtle and can be deduced through data mining a person's friendship network. A study by

Jernigan and Mistree[10] demonstrated how people's sexual orientation could be determined by their group of Facebook friends. How much this type of data has yet been exploited for marketing, if at all, is hard to determine.

Facebook, unlike those online social networks that predate it, makes use of people's real names and identities. It breaks down the division between online digital identity and analogue lives, creating links.[11] Importantly, Facebook also situates each individual in the context of his or her group of friends and networks, once again linking these to people's corporeal analogue identity. This direct linkage of online and analogue identities adds to the value of the community to advertisers. Rather than advertise to people who happen to be searching for a particular topic, advertising can be targeted at a particular demographic or life event. This may result in a smaller volume of traffic compared with an AdWords placement, but potentially has a greater rate of success in attracting a click through to the advertised product.

While different from the online communities of interest observed by Rheingold in 1993, Facebook allows users to join fan pages and organise politically, even to lobby for changes to Facebook.[12] This information can then be used to better refine the detail of an individual's profile and identity, to make the individual a more attractive target for marketing for Facebook to sell. Facebook has also begun to stretch its reach beyond its own closed network on the web. It now follows users to external websites, extending its 'like' function beyond the confines of the social network while, at the same time, tracking user's behaviour across a broader spectrum of the world wide web. It is also extending beyond the web, recently linking to the online video and telephony service, Skype.[13] Beyond the internet, it reaches onto mobile phones and, at the same time, draws our friends and contacts held in those devices into its database – thereby adding them, without asking, to an accounts online phonebook.[14]

Online dating

Other online environments take this commodification of the community to new levels. While both Google and Facebook are turning their users into a product that can then be on-sold to advertisers, online dating sites – while also using their membership to enable advertising – are also effectively selling the community of users to itself. People sign up and then, in many cases, pay a fee to be able to communicate with other members of the same community whose profiles they find appealing. Adding to the elegance of the economic construction, individual users try to make themselves a more attractive 'product' for other users to want to – and pay to – communicate with. People are motivated to present and customise this online identity to better support the economic interests of the sites they are already paying to access. The disturbing extension of this economic model is that it works best when members do not form continuing, long-term relationships, but rather return to 'purchase' more people in their search for romance.[15]

Online games

Another online environment where the community becomes a commodity is in online gaming. In some cases – for example, FarmVille, the most widely played online game[16] – it extends from the already popular Facebook platform, and rewards players for involving their friends on the Facebook network in the game. Other games, such as World of Warcraft, rely on their own network of players. These games will also facilitate player-to-player interaction and cooperation and, particularly in World of Warcraft, this is an essential aspect of the game if players wish to participate in much of the content. Other online games with smaller and more transitory player groups, such as Modern Warfare 2, also enable and facilitate online cooperative play. Access to this network of other players then becomes a commodity that promotes sales of the games. Increasingly these online worlds also enable more traditional advertising within the game world.[17]

Cultivating digital identity and harvesting digital community

The commercialisation of our online lives was not an easy project. Fleeting and splintered digital identities meeting in disparate communities of interest in the early pre-commercial internet were close to the predictions of Licklider and Taylor and were observed enthusiastically by Rheingold. However, different approaches have been deployed to stretch commerce onto this digital template. To capture these digital identities they needed to be found through online communities, based around common interest.

Google's initial success came from measuring the popularity of websites online, information that was derived from the online community and how it constructed and linked between different fragments of the world wide web. This information was then distilled and returned to that same community. By casting a wide net over 'communities of interest' based on similar searches for information, Google has been able to find a new market for advertising. Despite a slow rate of 'click-through' for each page impression, the sheer volume of passing traffic on the web makes this a successful strategy with the company returning nearly 23 billion dollars in advertising revenue in 2009.[18]

The number two site on the web, Facebook, takes a very different approach. Rather than trying to access many separate transitory parts of a digital identity, it tries to bring that identity together in one place and links it more strongly to a people's analogue identity – who they are 'in real life' – and the different communities of friends, family and workmates that they have in that context. This more substantial digital identity is high in value for potential advertisers. Facebook reportedly had revenue of almost 800 million dollars in 2009.[19]

While Google and Facebook represent the two most visited sites on the world wide web, other types of online community have a more integrated approach to the commercialisation of community. Online dating sites 'sell' individual members of their community to each other. Online games sell an experience to players that is derived from the presence of other players in the network and the communities they form. Similar to Facebook and dating sites, the value of these gaming sites, both to the people involved and as a commodity to be sold, is dependent on the presence of other individuals in these environments – on the construction and maintenance of online communities.

Many online games actively market this community, charging a fee for software and a subscription to participate. There are many other commercial areas of activity in the online environment, from sales of physical goods through online retailers, such as Amazon.com, to services that charge to help find a lost mobile phone. Off screen, in the analogue world, people and communities being used as a commodity for sales and advertising is nothing new. We wear Nike T-shirts as walking advertisements; we have advertising aimed at us and delivered to where we live, to what we watch on television, at live sport, or on the side of the road. Yet the commodification of the individual and his or her communities online is a more subtle and perhaps subversive process. When Facebook is harvesting our mobile phone contacts and friendship networks, the process is moving in new and potentially unwelcome directions.

Notes

1. S. Turkle, *Life on the Screen: Identity in the age of the internet* (New York: Simon & Schuster, 1995).
2. Internet World Stats, United States of America Internet and Facebook User Stats: American Internet and Facebook Statistics State by State, June 2010, *http://www.internetworldstats.com/stats26.htm*
3. M. Zuckerberg, '500 Million Stories', *The Facebook Blog*, 21 July 2010, *http://blog.facebook.com/blog.php?post=409753352130*
4. Internet World Stats, above note 2.
5. H. Rheingold, *The Virtual Community: Homesteading on the electronic frontier* (Reading, MA: Addison-Wesley, 2010), p. xvii, *http://www.rheingold.com/vc/book*
6. J.C.R. Licklider and R.W. Taylor, 'The Computer as a Communications Device', *Science and Technology*, April 1968, p. 38, *http://citeseerx.ist.psu.edu/viewdoc/download?doi=10.1.1.34.4812&rep=rep1&type=pdf*
7. B. McCarty, 'Alexa: YouTube surpasses Yahoo! as the Internet's 3rd Most Visited Site', *TNW Social Media*, 23 August 2010, *http://thenextweb.com/socialmedia/2010/08/23/alexa-shows-youtube-claiming-3-most-popular-site-over-yahoo-are-browsing-habits-changing*
8. Google, 'Google Launches Self-Service Advertising Program', Press Release, 23 October 2000, *http://www.google.com/press/pressrel/pressrelease39.html*
9. D. Ionescu, 'Google Names Facebook Most Visited Website', *PC World*, 28 March 2010, *http://www.pcworld.com/article/197431/google_names_facebook_most_visited_site.html*; M. Arlington, 'Hitwise says Facebook Most Popular U.S. Site', *TechCrunch*, 15 March 2010, *http://techcrunch.com/2010/03/15/hitwise-says-facebook-most-popular-u-s-site*
10. C. Jernigan and B.F.T. Mistree, 'Gaydar: Facebook friendships expose sexual orientation', *First Monday*, 14(10), October 2009, *http://firstmonday.org/htbin/cgiwrap/bin/ojs/index.php/fm/article/view/2611/2302*
11. This has been tried before, most notably by Friendster, but with nothing like the scale of Facebook. See D. Boyd and N. Ellison, 'Social Network Sites: Definition, history, and scholarship', *Journal of Computer-Mediated Communication*, 13(1), 2007.
12. K. Ellis and M. Kent, *Disability and New Media* (New York and London: Routledge, 2010), pp. 101–5.
13. R. Spiegel, 'Facebook and Skype Link Arms against Google', *E-Commerce Times*, 29 September 2010, *http://www.ecommercetimes.com/rsstory/70929.html*
14. S. Chapman, 'Facebook iPhone App Shares All Your Phone Numbers', *ComputerworldUK*, 6 October 2010, *http://blogs.computerworlduk.com/microchick/2010/10/facebook-iphone-app-shares-all-your-phone-numbers/index.htm*
15. Admittedly many such sites are explicitly set up with relatively short-term relationships in mind, but this will still apply to others that market themselves as a place to find lasting love.

16. T. Walker, 'Welcome to FarmVille: Population 80 million', *The Independent*, 22 February 2010, *http://www.independent.co.uk/life-style/gadgets-and-tech/features/welcome-to-farmville-population-80-million-1906260.html*
17. A. Khan, 'A Brief Look at In-game Advertising', *Social Times*, 26 May 2010, *http://www.socialtimes.com/2010/05/a-brief-look-at-in-game-advertising*
18. This represents just over $US11.50 for each person who had access to the internet at that time: Google, '2010 Financial Tables', *Google Investor Relations*, 2010, *http://investor.google.com/financial/tables.html*
19. S. Schroeder, 'Facebook 2009 Revenue Was Almost $800 Million', *Mashable Business*, 18 June 2010, *http://mashable.com/2010/06/18/facebook-800-million*

Conclusion: white men rule?

Tara Brabazon

Abstract: This conclusion completes the arc of this book, tracking the passage from community management to commodified community. With attention to the films *Catfish* and *The Social Network*, the question remains who gains from the 'flexibility' of online identity?

Key words: digitisation, democracy, social justice, content, context

> *As long as we're talking about white men competing with each other, we ... acknowledge that we live in a realistic world ... add women and blacks into the picture, though, and suddenly the scene shifts.*[1]
>
> Katie Pollitt

Digitisation is not a proxy for democracy. Digitisation is not a synonym for democracy. Neither is it an antonym. Organising and disseminating digital information can start conversation and consciousness, but such a movement of data does not substitute for conversation and consciousness. This book journeyed from Paech's community management to Kent's commodified community. The stops on the way included Second Life, YouTube, bit torrent, libraries, podcasts, dis/ability, dancing, fandom and shopping. The diversity of topics, subjects and approaches is important. Yet the studies are unified. In each chapter, there is a desire that communication and connection become more than social, and meaningful in a wider context.

Before the web becomes another shopping mall, it is important to pause and consider how a more productive, questioning, intellectually generous and interactive network can be created. To enable such a space, it is important to remember that information is not knowledge. The mitigating step between information and knowledge is media and information literacy. It is necessary to value and validate the capacity to sort, sift and shape data to transform interesting ideas into useful and useable expertise.

Maturing media

The 2010s is the decade during which a commitment to understanding information and communication systems is required. Social media are more mature and complex. Platforms are used by a wider community than just white, educated men from North America and Europe. Tunisia, Egypt and Iran activated Twitter and YouTube as engine rooms for revolution. Libya was hampered by state based controls on internet accounts. The earthquake and tsunami in Japan in March 2011 deployed YouTube and Twitter to share the horrifying images of destruction, desperation, fear and loss. These narratives of optimism and despair, change and repression provide the shape of history. Digitisation adds speed to the dissemination of these narratives and widens the audience between a street, town, city or nation.

Matching these social changes is a greater intellectual complexity in theorising these movements. The early stages of the 2010s saw an array of quality monographs published that explored the nature of this new online reality. Tim Wu discovered the relationship between information and power in *The Master Switch*, showing that every moment of technological change has supposedly heralded a revolution in thinking.[2] Sherry Turkle, in *Alone Together*, investigated how digital communication can disconnect human connections, often attended by narcissism, stating that 'I believe that in our culture of simulation the notion of authenticity is for us what sex was for the Victorians – threat and obsession, taboo and fascination'.[3] Nancy Baym probed *Personal Connections in the Digital Age*,[4] exploring new modes of relationship that disconnect from face-to-face dialogues. David Kirkpatrick logged *The Facebook Effect*, exploring the site's impact on both marketers and political campaigners.[5] Saul Levmore and Martha Nussbaum offered a provocative edited collection on *The Offensive Internet*,[6] showing the consequences of low entry barriers into the read write web, impacting on 'free' speech, censorship and privacy. Evgeny Morozov reveals *The Net Delusion*, logging the disappointments and disillusionment of radical politics in exchange for consumerism.[7] David Crystal finds new structures in internet-enabled language.[8] The Wikileaks 'scandal' triggered studies on new structures for information gathering.[9]

Through such innovative and interesting discussions of 'new media', popular cultural car alarms shrieked through the early 2010s. Surprisingly, or perhaps not, one old media – film – returned old tropes, metaphors and iconography of analogue power structures. Now that social media are used by a diversity of races, religions, ages and genders, the 'threat' to white men – via a chaotic read write web with little respect for privacy, intellectual property rights or copyright – is palpable. The films *Catfish*[10] and *The Social Network*[11] told the tales of disconnected young white men (yawn) desperate to connect with the lay-dees, flattered by attention and using Facebook as a digital dance card to fill their nights with flattery or revenge at the women who shunned and humiliated them.

Both these films occupy the odd genre space of doco/mocko/fact/fiction. The films express a desire for connection, friendship, love and intimacy. But the status of these films in and of themselves – asking whether the audience is being taken for a ride and questioning the truth of the events – is a metonymy for social media more generally. When white men use social media for commerce, revenge and chatting with women, is the resulting discussion rational, understandable, truthful, earnest and emotional? When women and disempowered communities use the same media to renegotiate the rules of social relationship, the usefulness, reliability and truthfulness of the platforms are questioned.

Catfish is the *Fatal Attraction* of social media. But the greatest crime of the crazy white woman in the 2010s was not bunny boiling, but being forty and ugly rather than twenty and beautiful. The tale follows two film-makers, Ariel Schulman and Henry Joost, as they capture the on and offline life of Nev Schulman, Ariel's brother. A photographer, Nev strikes up an online friendship with a young girl named Abby, who paints a rendering of his photographs. They connect on Facebook, and a range of family and friends build a social network of relationships – which include Abby's mother, Angela, and half-sister, Megan. An online romance begins between Megan and Nev. When a tangle of lies and inconsistencies emerges, the film-makers and Nev travel to find Angela, who constructed a web of pseudo-identities to manage the choices she made in her life. What is interesting is not that Angela lied on the internet. That is the focus of the film-makers' horror. What is more significant is why Nev assumed that a young, beautiful and talented virgin would be waiting for him on Facebook. Yet the film-makers remained horrified that an overweight middle-aged woman, desperate and trapped by marriage, would dare to create an online echo chamber for her creativity.

The Social Network, based on Ben Mezrich's *The Accidental Billionaires*,[12] is semi-biographical and semi-factual. It is a facto-fiction that tells the tale of Facebook. As Mezrich describes the narrative, it was

> geeky kids who made algorithms out of fetishes, who had nothing better to do on a Friday night than hang out in a classroom filled with crepe paper and colored posters, talking about girls they weren't actually getting.[13]

The film is as simple as this sentence conveys. While nominated for an array of awards, it is a conventional chronological history of young white men making money, validating ambition and gathering women in the process. The battles over ownership and making money became more important than the key long-term concerns about content ownership, privacy and copyright violation. While there was much discussion about the quality of the film, it was long, predictable and deployed tired geek archetypes of young white men fighting other young white men over the ownership of ideas, property and success.

The gulf between the user's lived experience, critical commentary and how old popular cultural platforms are managing the internet is stark. But the moment of celebrating or demonising digitisation is over. The internet is not a folk devil. Neither is it a deity. Instead, digitisation has offered a range of proxies for social justice and information justice. All citizens deserve high-quality information, delivered on a stable platform, in good time and in an appropriate context. Searching must not be confused with literacy. Finding content is not necessarily understanding context. Sharing is not a proxy for social change. Liking a link or re-tweeting 140 characters does not signify social change. It is the first moment in thinking about difference and thinking differently. The question is how – from this first bright moment of consciousness – ideas are created, knowledge is built and communities are formed.

Notes

1. K. Pollitt, *Reasonable Creatures* (London: Vintage, 1995), p. 83.
2. T. Wu, *The Master Switch: The rise and fall of information empires* (New York: Alfred A. Knopf, 2010).
3. S. Turkle, *Alone Together: Why we expect more from technology and less from each other* (New York: Basic Books, 2011), p. 4.

4. N. Baym, *Personal Connections in the Digital Age* (Cambridge: Polity, 2010).
5. D. Kirkpatrick, *The Facebook Effect* (New York: Simon & Schuster, 2010).
6. S. Levmore and M. Nussbaum, *The Offensive Internet* (Cambridge: Harvard University Press, 2010).
7. E. Morozov, *The Net Delusion: The dark side of internet freedom* (New York: Public Affairs, 2011).
8. D. Crystal, *Internet Linguistics* (London: Routledge, 2011).
9. D. Leigh and L. Harding, *Wikileaks: Inside Julian Assange's war on secrecy* (London: Guardian Books, 2011).
10. *Catfish* (Momentum Pictures, 2011).
11. *The Social Network* (Sony, 2011).
12. B. Mezrich, *The Accidental Billionaires* (London: Random House, 2010).
13. *Ibid.*, p. 17.

References

R. Abdulla, 'Islam, Jihad, and Terrorism in Post-9/11 Arabic Discussion Boards', *Journal of Computer-Mediated Communication,* 12(3), 2007, 1063–81

AbilityNet Web Accessibility Team, 'State of the eNation Web Accessibility Reports: Social networking sites', January 2008, *http://www.abilitynet.org.uk/docs/enation/2008SocialNetworkingSites.pdf*

'A Day in the Life of a Massey University Student', *YouTube, http://www.youtube.com/watch?v=p-TrlvsRToU*

P. Agre, 'Life after Cyberspace', *EASST*, 18(3), 1990

B. Ajana, 'Disembodiment and Cyberspace: A phenomenological approach', *Electronic Journal of Sociology* 7, 2005

L. Alcock, P. Chen, H.M. Ch'ng and S. Hobson, 'Criminal Remedies against Counterfeiting', *Journal of Brand Management*, 11(2), 2003, 138

R. Allen, 'A Night at the Monster Ball: The Lady Gaga experience', *SheWired*, 2010, *http://www.shewired.com/Article.cfm?ID=25421*

Y. Al-Saggaf, 'The Online Public Sphere in the Arab World: The war in Iraq on the Al Arabiya website', *Journal of Computer-Mediated Communication*, 12(1), 2006, 328

A. Altman, 'The Clues in Heath Ledger's Death', *Time*, 23 January 2008, *http://www.time.com/time/arts/article/0,8599,1706361,00.html*

B. Anderson, *Imagined Communities* (London: Verso, 1991)

B. Anderson, *Imagined Communities: Reflections on the origin and spread of nationalism* (London: Verso, 2006)

C. Anderson, *The Long Tail* (New York: Hyperion, 2006)

A.A. Andolsen, 'Get Smart! About Intellectual Property', *Information Management Journal*, January/February, 2006, 37

N. Andrade, M. Mowbray, A. Lima, G. Wagner and M. Ripeanu, 'Influences on Cooperation in BitTorrent Communities', Proceedings of the 2005 ACM SIGCOMM Workshop on Economics of Peer-to-Peer Systems, 22 August 2005, Philadelphia, PA, *http://people.cs.uchicago.edu/~matei/PAPERS/p2pecon.05.pdf*

A. Appadurai, *Fear of Small Numbers* (Durham: Duke University Press, 2006)

M. Arlington, 'Hitwise says Facebook Most Popular U.S. Site', *TechCrunch*, 15 March 2010, *http://techcrunch.com/2010/03/15/hitwise-says-facebook-most-popular-u-s-site*

M. Atwater-Singer and K. Sherrill, 'Social Software, Web 2.0, Library 2.0, & You: A practical guide for using technology @ your library', *Indiana Libraries*, 26(3), 2007, 48–52

A. Baggs, 'In My Language', *YouTube*, 14 January 2007, *http://www.youtube.com/watch?v=JnylM1hI2jc*

N. Baker, 'The Charms of Wikipedia', *New York Review of Books*, 55(4), 2008, *http://www.nybooks.com/articles/21131*

A. Balasescu, 'After Authors: Sign(ify)ing fashion from Paris to Tehran', *Journal of Material Culture*, 10(3), 2005, 290

N.L. Balmer, 'Fashionable IP or IP for Fashion?' *Washington and Lee Law Review*, 61(1), 2008, 277

J. Barlow, 'A Declaration of Independence of Cyberspace', 1996, *http://homes.eff.org/~barlow/Declaration-Final.html*

M. Barnard, *Fashion as Communication* (London: Routledge, 1996)

C. Barnes, *Disabling Imagery and the Media: An exploration of the principles for media representations of disabled people* (Krumlin: Ryburn Publishing, 1992), *http://www.leeds.ac.uk/disability-studies/archiveuk/Barnes/disabling%20imagery.pdf*

C. Barnes, B. Flanagan, F. Corcoran and B. O'Neill. 'Final Report: Critical Media Literacy in Ireland', Radharc Media Trust, Dublin, 2007, *http://arrow.dit.ie/cgi/viewcontent.cgi?article=1019&context=cserrep*

N. Barnes, 'Using Podcasts to Promote Government Documents Collections', *Library Hi Tech*, 25(2), 2007, 220–30

P. Bartle, 'What is Community? A Sociological Perspective', 2003, *http://www.scn.org/cmp/whatcom.txt*

A.W. Bates, 'Technology for Distance Education: A 10-year perspective', in A. Tait (ed.), *Key Issues in Open Learning – A reader: An anthology from the journal 'Open Learning' 1986–1992* (Harlow: Longman, 1993) 243

J. Baudrillard, *Jean Baudrillard, Selected Writings*, Mark Poster (ed.) (Stanford: Stanford University Press, 1988)

J. Baudrillard, *Simulacra and Simulation* (Ann Arbor: University of Michigan Press, 1994)

N. Baym, *Personal Connections in the Digital Age* (Cambridge: Polity, 2010)

J. Beilke, M. Stuve and M. Williams-Hawkins, 'Clubcasting: Educational uses of podcasting in multicultural settings', *Multicultural Education & Technology Journal*, 2(2), 2008, 107–17

Y. Belanger, *Duke iPod First Year Final Evaluation Report* (Durham: Duke University, 2005), *http://cit.duke.edu/pdf/reports/ipod_initiative_04_05.pdf*

W.L. Bennett, 'Communicating Global Activism: Strengths and vulnerabilities of networked politics', *Information, Communication and Society*, 6(2), 2003, 143–68

J. Berk, S. Olsen, J. Atkinson and J. Comerford, 'Innovation in a Podshell: Bringing information literacy into the world of podcasting', *The Electronic Library*, 25(4), 2007, 409–19

T. Berners-Lee. 'World Wide Web Consortium Launches International Program Office for Web Accessibility Initiative', 22 October 1997, *http://www.w3.org/Press/IPO-announce*

J.C. Bertot, P.T. Jaeger, C.R. McClure, C.B. Wright and E. Jensen, 'Public Libraries and the Internet 2008–2009: Issues, implications, and challenges', *First Monday*, 14(11), 2 November 2009, *http://firstmonday.org/htbin/cgiwrap/bin/ojs/index.php/fm/article/viewArticle/2700/2351*

'Best Practices for Teaching in a Video Environment', *YouTube*, *http://www.youtube.com/watch?v=u-zvPLluOgM*

N. Bhimani, in T. Brabazon, 'The Sound of Education', *Internet Archive*, June 2010, *http://www.archive.org/details/TheSoundOfEducation*

E. Bick, 'The Experience of the Skin in Early Object Relations', *International Journal of Psycho-Analysis*, 49, 1968, 558–66

T. Boellstorff, *Coming of Age in Second Life: An anthropologist explores the virtually human* (Princeton: Princeton University Press, 2009)

S. Boland and B. Dollery, 'The Value of Sovereignty-Conferred Rights in MIRAB Economies: The case of Tuvalu', Working Paper series in Economics No. 2005-9, University of New England, School of Economics, 2005, *http://www.une.edu.au/bepp/working-papers/economics/1999-2007/econ-2005-9.pdf*

D. Boyd, 'Taken Out of Context, American Teen Sociality in Networked Publics', 2008, *http://www.danah.org/papers/TakenOutOfContext.pdf*

D. Boyd and N. Ellison, 'Social Network Sites: Definition, history, and scholarship', *Journal of Computer-Mediated Communication*, 13(1), 2007

M. Boyden, *The Greatest Podcasting Tips in the World* (Stratford-upon-Avon: The Greatest in the World Book, 2007)

M. Boyle and R. Kitchen, 'New Strategy can Enrich Relations with Irish Diaspora', *The Irish Times*, 1 January 2009, *http://www.irishtimes.com/newspaper/opinion/2009/0127/1232923366914.html*

M. Boyle and R. Kitchen, 'Towards an Irish Diaspora Strategy: A position paper', National Institute for Regional and Spatial Analysis Working Paper, No. 37, National University of Ireland, Maynooth, 2008

T. Brabazon, 'BA (Google): Graduating to information literacy', IDATER online conference, Loughborough University, 2005, *https://dspace.lboro.ac.uk/dspace-jspui/bitstream/2134/2485/4/Brabazon.pdf*

T. Brabazon, 'How Imagined Are Virtual Communities?' *Mots Pluriels*, No. 18, August 2001, *http://www.arts.uwa.edu.au/MotsPluriels/MP1801tb2.html*

T. Brabazon, 'I'm not Going to be Your Monkey', *Times Higher Education*, 22 April 2009, *http://timeshighereducation.co.uk/story.asp?sectioncode=26&storycode=406259*

T. Brabazon, *Ladies who Lunge: Celebrating difficult women* (Sydney: UNSW Press, 2002)

T. Brabazon (ed.), *Liverpool of the South Seas* (Perth: University of Western Australia Press, 2005)

T. Brabazon, Podcast, *http://tarabrabazon.libsyn.com*

T. Brabazon, 'Sarah Ison talks with Tara Brabazon about Libraries,' *Internet Archive*, *http://www.archive.org/details/SarahIsonTalksWithTaraBrabazonAboutLibraries*

T. Brabazon, 'Socrates in Earpods: The ipodification of education', *Fast Capitalism*, 2(1), 2006, *http://www.uta.edu/huma/agger/fastcapitalism/2_1/brabazon.htm*

T. Brabazon, 'Teaching Learning and Writing through Popular Culture Module', Study Guide, University of Brighton, 2010

T. Brabazon, 'The Google Effect', *Libri*, vol. 56, 2006, 157–67, *http://www.librijournal.org/pdf/2006-3pp157-167.pdf*

T. Brabazon (ed.), *The Revolution will not be Downloaded* (Oxford: Chandos, 2008)

T. Brabazon, *Tracking the Jack: A retracing of the Antipodes* (Sydney: UNSW Press, 2000)

W. Briggs, 'Sea Turtles, Cell Phones and the WTO,' *Communication World*, 1 February 2000

A. Brooks, *The Battle: How the fight between free enterprise and big government will shape America's future* (New York: Basic Books, 2010)

J. Budd, *Self-Examination: The present and future of librarianship* (Westport: Beta Phi Mu Monograph Series, 2008)

M. Bull and L. Back, 'Introduction: Into sound', in M. Bull and L. Back (eds), *The Auditory Culture Reader* (Oxford: Berg, 2004) 3

A. Bundy, 'One Essential Direction: Information literacy, information technology fluency', *Journal of eLiteracy*, vol.1, 2004, *http://www.jelit.org/6/01JeLit_Paper_1.pdf*

J. Burgess and J. Green, *YouTube: Online video and participatory culture* (Cambridge, UK: Polity Press, 2009)

S. Burton, 'People Power Redux', *Time*, 157(4), 29 January 2001

F.K. Campbell, *Contours of Ableism: The production of disability and abledness* (New York: Palgrave Macmillan, 2009)

D. Carr, 'Delicately Campaigning for a Star Now Departed', *New York Times*, 5 February 2009, *http://www.nytimes.com/2009/02/06/movies/awardsseason/06carr.html*

L. Carroll, *Through the Looking Glass, and What Alice Found There*, 1871 (Milan: Taylor & Francis, 2002)

Carrotmob, *http://www.carrotmob.com*

M. Castells, *The Information Age: Economy, society and culture* (Oxford: Blackwell Publishing, 2000), Vol. 1, The Rise of the Network Society

A. Chakrabortty, 'Brain Food: Internet censorship and the Barbra Streisand effect', *The Guardian*, 20 October 2009, *http://www.guardian.co.uk/uk/2009/oct/20/brain-food-internet-censorship-barbra-streisand*

A. Chan and C. McLoughlin, 'Everyone's Learning with Podcasting: A Charles Sturt University experience', Proceedings of the 23rd Annual Ascilite Conference, 2006, *http://csusap.csu.edu.au/~achan/papers/2006_POD_ASCILITE.pdf*

S. Chapman, 'Facebook iPhone App Shares All Your Phone Numbers', *ComputerworldUK*, 6 October 2010, *http://blogs.computerworlduk.com/microchick/2010/10/facebook-iphone-app-shares-all-your-phone-numbers/index.htm*

C. Chen, 'Facebook Got More Visitors than Google Search In 2010 – Yahoo! Finance', *TechNama*, 31 December 2010, *http://www.technama.com/2010/facebook-got-more-visitors-than-google-search-in-2010-yahoo-finance*

J. Chipchase, 'Shared Phone Use', *Future Perfect*, *http://janchipchase.com/2006/12/shared-phone-use*

D. Choffnes, J. Duch, D. Malmgren, R. Guimera, F. Bustamante and L.A. Nunes Amaral, 'Strange Bedfellows: Community identification in BitTorrent', Proceedings of the 9th International Conference on Peer-to-Peer Systems, San Jose, CA, 27 April 2010, *http://www.usenix.org/event/iptps10/tech/full_papers/Choffnes.pdf*

G. Clapperton, *This is Social Media: Tweet, blog, link and post your way to business success* (Chichester: Capstone, 2009)

S. Cohen, 'Taking 2.0 to the Faculty', *C&RL News*, September 2008

C. Comegys, M. Hannula and J. Vaisanen, 'Effects of Consumer Trust and Risk on Online Purchase Decision-making: A comparison of Finnish and United States students', *International Journal of Management*, 26(2), 2009, 296

S. Conger, 'Web 2.0, Virtual Worlds and Real Ethical Issues', in P. Candace Deans (ed.), *Social Software and Web 2.0 Technology Trends* (University of Richmond, USA: Idea Group Inc., 2009)

L. Connaway and T. Dickey, 'The Digital Information Seeker: Findings from selected OCLC, RON and JISC user behaviour projects', OCLC Research, 2010, *http://www.jisc.ac.uk/publications/reports/2010/digitalinformationseekers.aspx*

Constitution of Ireland, *Bunreacht na hEíreann*, 1 July 1937, *http://www.taoiseach.gov.ie/attached_files/Pdf%20files/Constitution%20of%20Ireland.pdf*

'Conversations with History: David Harvey', *YouTube*, *http://www.youtube.com/watch?v=02eskyHJY_4&feature=related*

S. Corbett, 'Can the Cellphone Help End Global Poverty?' *New York Times*, 13 April 2008

'Cornel West Interview', *YouTube*, *http://www.youtube.com/watch?v=PMhya8SIWmY; http://www.youtube.com/watch?v=5kJpk60rFh4*

Council of the European Union and Commission of the European Communities, 'eEurope 2002: An Information Society for all', Brussels, 14 June 2002, *http://ec.europa.eu/information_society/eeurope/2002/action_plan/pdf/actionplan_en.pdf*

B. Cova, R. Kozinets and A. Shankar, *Consumer Tribes* (London: Elsevier/Butterworth-Heinemann, 2007)

'Cyber Criminals Assume Interpol Chief's Identity', *ABC News Australia Online*, 17 September 2010, *http://www.abc.net.au/news/stories/2010/09/17/3015321.htm*

F. Dall'Olmo Riley, D. Scarpi and A. Manaresi, 'Purchasing Services Online: A two-country generalization of possible influences', *Journal of Services Marketing*, 23(3), 2009, 93

J.J. Darrow and G.R. Ferrera, 'Social Networking Websites and the DMCA: A safe-harbor from copyright infringement liability or the perfect storm', *Northwestern Journal of Technology and Intellectual Property*, 6(1), 2007, 1

P. Day, C. Farenden and H. Goss, 'Maps, Networks and Stories: A Community Profiling Methodology', *Constructing and Sharing Memory: Community informatics, identity and empowerment*, Proceedings of the 3rd Prato International Community Informatics Conference; CIRN, 9–11 October 2006

M. DeAngelis, *Gay Fandom and Crossover Stardom* (Durham: Duke University Press, 2001)

S. de Beauvoir, *The Second Sex* (New York: Knopf, 1953)

M. Deflem, 'University offers Lady Gaga Sociology Course', *BBC*, 2010, *http://www.bbc.co.uk/news/education-11672679*

J. Denegri-Knott, 'Sinking the Online "Music Pirates": Foucault, power and deviance on the web', *Journal of Computer Mediated Communication*, 9(4), 2004

M. Dery, 'The Merry Pranksters and the Art of the Hoax', *New York Times*, 23 December 1990, *http://www.nytimes.com/1990/12/23/arts/the-merry-pranksters-and-the-art-of-the-hoax.html*

P. de Wit, 'Government wants Southafrica.com', 1 August 2001, *http://www.itweb.co.za*, as cited in M. Rimmer, 'Virtual Countries: Internet domain names and geographical terms', *Media International Australia Incorporating Culture and Policy.* No. 106, February 2003, 127

K. Diamandaki, 'Virtual Ethnicity and Digital Diasporas: Identity construction in cyberspace', *Global Media Journal*, 2(2), Spring 2003, *http://lass.calumet.purdue.edu/cca/gmj/OldSiteBackup/Submitted Documents/archivedpapers/Spring2003/diamondaki.htm*

A. DiFranco, 'My IQ', *Puddle Dive*, 1993

'Digital Dieting: A Keynote Presentation', *YouTube*, 2010, *http://www.youtube.com/watch?v=BU46mF89z0Q*

Disability Rights Commission, 'Talk', Disability Rights Commission Channel, *YouTube*, 26 July 2007, *http://www.youtube.com/user/DisabilityRightsComm*

Diva Boutique, *http://www.diva-boutique.com/women_welcome.aspx*

A. Douai, 'Offline Politics in the Arab Blogosphere: Trends and prospects in Morocco', in A. Russell and N. Echaibi (eds), *International Blogging: Identity, politics, and networked publics* (New York: Peter Lang, 2009) 133–51

G.S. Drori, 'Information Society as a Global Policy Agenda: What does it tell us about the age of globalization?' *International Journal of Comparative Sociology*, 48(4), 2007, 309

DSLR Video Shooters, *http://www.facebook.com/#!/DSLRVideoShooters*

L.R. Duffield, M.D. Hayes and A. Watson, 'Media and Communications Capacities in the Pacific Region', *eJournalist*, 8(1), 2008, 21–34, *http://ejournalist.com.au/v8n1/Duffield.pdf*

W. Dutton, 'The Social Informatics of the Internet: An ecology of games', in J. Berleur, M. Numinen and J. Impagliazzo (eds), *Social Informatics: An information society for all? In remembrance of Rob Kling*, IFIP International Federation for Information Processing, Vol. 223 (Boston, MA: Springer, 2006) 243–53

P. Dvorak, 'Texting Allows Multitude of Donors for Victims of Haiti Earthquake', *The Washington Post*, 15 January 2010

S. Earp, Y. Belanger and L. O'Brien, *Duke Digital Initiative End of Year Report*, (Durham: Duke University, 2006), *http://cit.duke.edu/pdf/reports/ddiEval0506_final.pdf*

Echo 360, *http://www.echo360.com*

L. Efimova and S. Hendrick, 'In Search for a Virtual Settlement: An exploration of weblog community boundaries', 2005, *https://doc.novay.nl/dsweb/Get/Document-46041/weblog-community-boundaries.pdf*

K. Ellis. 'A Quest through Chaos: My narrative of illness and recovery', *Gender Forum*, 26(2), 2009, *http://www.genderforum.org/issues/literature-and-medicine-ii/a-quest-through-chaos*

K. Ellis, *Disabling Diversity: The social construction of disability in 1990s Australian national cinema* (Saarbrücken: VDM Verlag, 2008)

K. Ellis and M. Kent, *Disability and New Media* (New York and London: Routledge, 2010)

K. Ellis and M. Kent, 'iTunes is Pretty (Useless) When You're Blind: Digital design is triggering disability when it could be a solution', *M/C Journal*, 11(3), 2008, *http://journal.media-culture.org.au/index.php/mcjournal/article/viewArticle/55*

P. Elmer-Dewitt, 'First Nation in Cyberspace', *TIME International*, 6 December 1993, No. 49, *http://www.chemie.fu-berlin.de/outerspace/internet-article.html*

L. Emberson, G. Lupyan, M. Goldstein and M. Spivey, 'Overheard Cell-phone Conversations: When less speech is more distracting', *Psychological Science*, 3 September 2010, *http://pss.sagepub.com/content/early/2010/09/03/0956797610382126*

M. Engler, 'The Limits of Internet Organizing', *Dissent Magazine*, 5 October 2010, *http://www.dissentmagazine.org/atw.php?id=278* (retrieved 15 October 2010)

B. Eno, 'What I Notice,' in J. Brockman (ed.), *Is the Internet Changing the Way You Think?* (New York: Harper Perennial, 2011)

J. Entwistle, 'The Cultural Economy of Fashion Buying', *Current Sociology*, 54(5), 2006, 711

T. Erickson and W. Kellogg, 'Social Translucence: Using minimalist visualizations of social activity to support collective interaction', in A.J. Gersie, D. Benyon, A. Munro and K. Hook (eds), *Designing Information Spaces: The social navigation approach* (London: Springer-Verlag, 2002)

Ernesto, 'BitTorrent Still Dominates Global Internet Traffic', *TorrentFreak*, 26 October 2010, *http://torrentfreak.com/bittorrent-still-dominates-global-internet-traffic-101026/?utm_source=feedburner&utm_medium=feed&utm_campaign=Feed%3A+Torrentfreak+%28Torrentfreak%29*

Ernesto, 'BitTorrent Still King of P2P Traffic', *TorrentFreak*, 18 February 2009, *http://torrentfreak.com/bittorrent-still-king-of-p2p-traffic-090218*

Ernesto, 'UK Government uses BitTorrent to Share Public Spending Data', *TorrentFreak*, 4 June 2010, *http://torrentfreak.com/uk-government-uses-bittorrent-to-share-public-spending-data-100604*

European Union Directorate, 'Factsheet on Media Literacy', General Information, Society and Media, 2010, *http://ec.europa.eu/culture/media/literacy/docs/factsheet_media_literacy.pdf*

C. Fagan, 'Globalization and Culture: Placing Ireland', *The Annals of the American Academy of Political and Social Science*, 581(1), 2002, 133–43

C. Fahs, *How to do Everything with YouTube* (New York: McGraw Hill, 2008)

J. Fernback, 'There is a There There: Notes toward a definition of cybercommunity', in S. Jones (ed.), *Doing Internet Research: Critical issues and methods for examining the net* (London: Sage Publications, 2009)

L. Ferrier, 'Vulnerable Bodies: Creative disabilities in contemporary Australian film', in I. Craven (ed.), *Australian Cinema in the 1990s* (London: Frank Cass & Co, 2011)

V. Finkelstein, 'Attitudes and Disabled People: Issues for discussion', World Rehabilitation Fund, 1980, *http://www.leeds.ac.uk/disability-studies/archiveuk/finkelstein/attitudes.pdf*

FÍS, *http://www.fis.ie*

S. Foo and J. Ng, 'Library 2.0, Libraries and Library School', Proceedings of the Library Association of Singapore Conference, Singapore, May 2008

'Food in Libraries', *http://twapperkeeper.com/hashtag/foodinlibraries*

Forbes, 'The World's 100 Most Powerful Women', 2010, *http://www.forbes.com/wealth/power-women*

D. Foster, 'Community and Identity in the Electronic Village', in David Porter (ed.), *Internet Culture* (New York: Routledge, 1996)

M. Foucault, *Discipline and Punish: The birth of the prison* (New York: Random House, 1975)

P. Freire, *Pedagogies of the Oppressed,* Myra Bergan Ramos (trans) (London: The Continuum Maiden, 2006)

D.M. Gallup, 'Moldova's .MD: The little domain that roared', in E.S. Wass (ed.), *Addressing the World: National identity and country code domain names* (Latham, MD: Rowman and Littlefield, 2003) 120–36

'Gartner Says More than 1 Billion PCs in use Worldwide and Headed to 2 Billion Units by 2014', *Gartner Newsroom*, *http://www.gartner.com/it/page.jsp?id=703807*

B. Gibson, 'Enabling an Accessible Web 2.0', Keynote presented at the 16th International World Wide Web Conference, Banff, Canada, 7–8 May 2007, *http://www.w4a.info/2007/prog/k1-gibson.pdf*

M. Gibson, 'Death and Mourning in Technologically Mediated Culture', *Health Sociology Review*, 16(5), 2007, 415–24

R. Girard, *Violence and the Sacred,* Patrick Gregory (trans) (Baltimore: Johns Hopkins University Press, 1977)

M. Gladwell, 'Small Change: Why the revolution will not be tweeted', *The New Yorker*, 4 October 2010, *http://www.newyorker.com/reporting/2010/10/04/101004fa_fact_gladwell*

E. Goffman, *Presentation of the Self in Everyday Life* (New York: Anchor Books, 1959)

E. Goffman, *Stigma: Notes on the management of spoiled identity* (New York: Prentice-Hall, 1963)

G. Goggin, 'Disability and the Ethics of Listening', *Continuum*, 23(4), 2009, 493

G. Goggin, 'Innovation and Disability: Critique of ability', *M/C Journal*, 11(3), July 2008, *http://journal.media-culture.org.au/index.php/mcjournal/article/viewArticle/56*

G. Goggin and C. Newell, *Digital Disability: The social construction of disability in new media* (Oxford: Rowman and Littlefield, 2003)

G. Goggin and C. Newell, *Disability in Australia: Exposing a social apartheid* (Sydney: UNSW Press, 2005)

G. Goggin and C. Newell, 'Fame and Disability: Christopher Reeve, super crips, and infamous celebrity', *M/C Journal*, 7(5), 2004, *http://journal.media-culture.org.au/0411/02-goggin.php*

G. Goggin and T. Noonan, 'Blogging Disability: The interface between new cultural movements and internet technology', in A. Burns and J. Jacobs (eds), *Use of Blogs* (New York: Peter Lang, 2006) 166

M. Goldberg, 'Using Mobile Phones to Spot Counterfeit Drugs', *UN Dispatch*, 7 October 2010, *http://www.undispatch.com/using-mobile-phones-to-spot-counterfeit-drugs*

S. Golder and J. Donath, 'Social Roles in Electronic Communities', Association of Internet Researchers (AoIR) Conference 'Internet Research 5.0', 19–22 September 2004, Brighton, UK

Google, '2010 Financial Tables', *Google Investor Relations*, 2010, *http://investor.google.com/financial/tables.html*

Google, 'Google Launches Self-Service Advertising Program', Press Release, 23 October 2000, *http://www.google.com/press/pressrel/pressrelease39.html*

Google, 'Staying Connected in Post-earthquake Haiti', *http://googleblog.blogspot.com/2010/01/staying-connected-in-post-earthquake.html*

Google Goggles, *http://www.google.com/mobile/goggles*

S. Gordon, 'Star Sorrow: Coping with celebrity grief', *AOL Health*, 26 July 2010, *http://www.michaeljacksonmemorialconcert.com/star-sorrow-coping-with-celebrity-grief-aol-health-blog.html*

Grameen Bank, 'Introduction', *http://www.grameen-info.org/index.php?option=com_content&task=view&id=16&Itemid=112*

Grameenphone, 'About us', *http://www.grameenphone.com/about-us*

Grameenphone, 'Every Freedom Counts – Village Phone', *http://www.grameenphone.com/index.php?id=79*

Grameenphone, 'History', *http://www.grameenphone.com/index.php?id=63*

C. Gray, 'If You Build It, Will They Come? How researchers perceive and use web 2.0', Research Information Network, 2010, *http://www.rin.ac.uk/our-work/communicating-and-disseminating-research/use-and-relevance-web-20-researchers*

J. Gray, 'The Sad Side of Cyberspace', *The Guardian*, 10 April 1995

A. Greenwald, *Nothing Feels Good: Punk rock, teenagers and Emo* (New York: St. Martin's Press, 2003)

G. Griff, 'Text the Vote', *New York Times*, 13 August 2008

J. Griffey, 'Podcast 1 2 3', *Library Journal*, 132(11), June 2007, 32

P. Hainsworth, 'Reconstruction in East Timor', *Political Insight*, 1(3), December 2010, 96–97, *http://onlinelibrary.wiley.com/doi/10.1111/j.2041-9066.2010.00041.x/full*

C. Hakim, 'Attractive Forces at Work', *Times Education Supplement*, 3 June 2010

C. Hakim, 'Erotic Capital', *European Sociological Review*, 26(5), 2010, 499–518

T. Hamm, *The New Blue Media* (New York: New Press, 2008)
C.H. Hanley 'Two Little Letters Bring Riches, and Questions, to Tiny, Trusting Nations', *AP Worldstream*, 7 April 2004
M. Harnett, *A Quick Start Guide to Podcasting* (London: Kogan Page, 2010)
K. Harrenstien, 'Automatic Captions in YouTube', *The Official Google Blog*, 19 November 2009, *http://googleblog.blogspot.com/2009/11/automatic-captions-in-youtube.html?utm_source=feedburner&utm_medium=feed&utm_campaign=Feed:+blogspot/MKuf+%28Official+Google+Blog%29*
R. Harrington and M. Weiser, *Producing Video Podcasts* (Amsterdam: Focal Press, 2008)
L. Harrison, 'US Dotcom Keeps Ownership of SouthAfrica.com', *The Register*, 12 July 2001, *http://www.theregister.co.uk/2001/07/12/us_dotcom_keeps_ownership*
A. Hartley, 'FarmVille now has 80 million Facebook users,' *TechRadar*, 2010, *http://www.techradar.com/news/gaming/farmville-now-has-80-million-facebook-users-671731*
J. Hartley, 'Uses of YouTube – Digital Literacy and the Growth of Knowledge', in J. Burgess and J. Green, *YouTube: Online video and participatory culture* (Cambridge, UK: Polity Press, 2009) 126–43
N. Hayles, *My Mother was a Computer: Digital subjects and literary texts* (Chicago: University of Chicago Press, 2005)
B. Head, 'iiNet Wins Landmark Copyright Stoush', *Itwire*, 24 February 2011, *http://www.itwire.com/it-industry-news/listed-techs/45408-iinet-wins-landmark-copyright-stoush*
'Heath Ledger', *Facebook*, *http://www.facebook.com/#!/pages/Heath-Ledger/25514023521*
'Heath Ledger – Ledger Blasts Advertising Actors', *Contact Music*, 25 August 2005, *http://www.contactmusic.com/new/xmlfeed.nsf/mndwebpages/ledger%20blasts%20advertising%20actors*
'Heath Says Sorry', *The Age*, 26 August 2005, *http://www.theage.com.au/news/people/heath-says-sorry/2005/08/26/1124563022449.html*
L. Hedrick, 'Tearing Fashion Design Protection Apart at the Seams', *Washington and Lee Law Review*, 65(1), 2008, 218
'Hélène Cixous', *YouTube*, *http://www.youtube.com/watch?v=ZKUQWv0irVw*

S.A. Hetcher, 'The Music Industries' Failed Attempts to Influence File Sharing Norms', 7 *Vanderbilt Journal of Entertainment Law and Practice* 10(11), 2004, 10–40

G. Hegel, *Phenomenology of Spirit*, A. Miller (trans) (Oxford: Clarendon Press, 1807: 1977)

J. Herrington, *Podcasting Hacks* (Sebastopol: O'Reilly Media, 2005)

D. Hevey, 'Controlling Interests', in A. Pointon and C. Davies (eds), *Framed: Interrogating disability in the media* (London: British Film Institute, 1997) 209–13

S. Hiltz, *Online Communities: A case study of the office of the future* (Norwood: Ablex Publishing, 1985)

'HM The Queen Found Guilty of Reverse Domain Name Hijacking', *Demys News Service*, 20 December 2002, *http://www.demys.net/news/2002/12/02_dec_20_queen.htm* (last accessed in 2005)

'HM The Queen Wins Domain Name Dispute', *Demys News Service*, 8 October 2002, *http://www.demys.net/news/2002/10/02_oct_08_zealand.htm* (last accessed in 2005)

J. Holt, *The Daily Show and Philosophy* (Malden: Blackwell, 2007)

J. Horwath, 'Social Tools: More than just a good time?', *Partnership: the Canadian Journal of Library and Information Practice and Research*, 2(1), 2007, 1–7

'House', Season Finale Teaser, *YouTube*, *http://www.youtube.com/watch?v=yAaZZQhuyMo*

'How to Podcast Tutorial', *http://www.how-to-podcast-tutorial.com*

'How to Use the Discussion Forum in Blackboard – RMIT University', *YouTube*, *http://www.youtube.com/watch?v=MJjLRShTpz0*

D. Hrynyshyn, 'Globalization, Nationality and Commodification: The politics of the social construction of the internet', *New Media & Society*, 10(5), 2008, 751–70

Human Rights Watch, 'Egypt: Hold police accountable for torture', 22 December 2006, *http://www.hrw.org/english/docs/2006/12/23/egypt14924.htm*

ICANN, Board Meeting, Luxembourg Approved Resolutions, *http://www.icann.org/minutes/resolutions-15jul05.htm#p2*

ICANN, Minutes of Government Advisory Council Meeting, 25 May 1999, *https://gacweb.icann.org/download/attachments/1540204/GAC_02_Berlin_Communique.pdf?version=1&modificationDate=1312231401000*

ICT Ireland, 'Smart Schools = Smart Economy', Report of the ICT in Schools Joint Advisory Group to the Minister for Education and Science, Department of Education and Science, Dublin, 2009, *http://www.into.ie/ROI/Publications/OtherPublications/OtherPublicationsDownloads/SmartSchools=SmartEconomy.pdf*

Information Gatekeepers Inc, 'Telecommunications Mergers & Acquisitions', 2006, *http://books.google.com/books?id=d8osxelUx-MC&p.=PP2&dq=youtube+telecommunications&ei=hHhBS-DNNZCclQSSsOnDAQ&cd=2#v=onepage&q=youtube%20telecommunications&f=false*

F. Inglis, *A Short History of Celebrity* (Princeton: Princeton University Press, 2010)

International Telecommunications Union, 'Ubiquitous Mobile', *ITU Statshot*, Issue 3, June 2010, *http://www.itu.int/net/pressoffice/stats/2010/06/index.aspx*

Internet World Stats, September 2010, *http://www.internetworldstats.com/stats6.htm#oceania*

Internet World Stats, United States of America Internet and Facebook User Stats: American Internet and Facebook Statistics State by State, June 2010, *http://www.internetworldstats.com/stats26.htm*

Internet World Stats: Usage and population statistics, *http://www.internetworldstats.com/euro/md.htm*

D. Ionescu, 'Google Names Facebook Most Visited Web Site', *PC World*, 28 March 2010, *http://www.pcworld.com/article/197431/google_names_facebook_most_visited_site.html*

K. Islam, *Podcasting 101 for Training and Development* (San Francisco: John Wiley & Sons, 2007)

S. Ison and T. Brabazon, 'Twitter and Librarianship', *Internet Archive*, *http://www.archive.org/details/TwitterAndLibrarianship*

M. Izal, G. Urvoy-Keller, P.A. Biersack, A. Felber, A. Al Hamra and L. Garces-Erice, 'Dissecting BitTorrent: Five months in a torrent's lifetime', Proceedings of Passive and Active Measurements (PAM), Antibes Juan-les-Pins, France, April 2004, *http://www.pam2004.org/papers/148.pdf*

L. Jackson, 'Moderation vs. Facilitation,' *Lizzie Jackson.com*, 2007, *http://lizziejackson.com/2007/08/08/moderation-vs-facilitation*

M. Jackson. 'Fluidity, Promiscuity, and Mash-Ups: New concepts for the study of mobility and communication', *Communication Monographs*, 74(3), 2007, 409

H. Jenkins, 'Complete Freedom of Movement: Video games as gendered play spaces', in J. Cassell and H. Jenkins (eds), *From Barbie to Mortal Kombat: Gender and Computer Games* (Boston: MIT Press, 1998) 262–97

H. Jenkins, *Convergence Culture: Where old and new media collide* (New York: New York University Press, 2006)

H. Jenkins, 'A Second Look at Second Life', Confessions of an Aca-Fan: The Official Weblog of Henry Jenkins, 30 January 2007, *http://henryjenkins.org/2007/01/a_second_look_at_second_life.html*

H. Jenkins, 'What happened before YouTube', in J. Burgess and J. Green, *YouTube: Online video and participatory culture* (Cambridge, UK: Polity Press, 2009) 109–25

H. Jenkins, R. Purushotma, K. Clinton, M, Weigel and A. Robinson, 'Confronting the Challenges of Participatory Culture Media Education for the 21st Century', MacArthur Foundation, 2006, p. 5, *http://digitallearning.macfound.org/atf/cf/%7B7E45C7E0-A3E0-4B89-AC9C-E807E1B0AE4E%7D/JENKINS_WHITE_PAPER.PDF*

C. Jernigan and B.F.T. Mistree, 'Gaydar: Facebook friendships expose sexual orientation', *First Monday*, 14(10), October 2009, *http://firstmonday.org/htbin/cgiwrap/bin/ojs/index.php/fm/article/view/2611/2302*

R. Jewkes and A. Murcott, 'Meanings of Community', *Social Science and Medicine*, 43(4), 1996, 555–63

JISC, 'Learning Literacies for the Digital Age', 2009, *http://www.jisc.ac.uk/publications/briefingpapers/2009/learningliteraciesbp.aspx*.

JISC, Technology and Standards Watch, 'Information Behaviour of the Researcher of the Future', CIBER briefing paper, UCL, 11 January 2008, *http://www.jisc.ac.uk/media/documents/programmes/reppres/gg_final_keynote_11012008.pdf*

Q. Jones, 'Virtual-communities, Virtual Settlements and Cyber-archaeology: A theoretical outline', *Journal of Computer Supported Cooperative Work*, 3(3), December 1997

S. Jones, *Virtual Culture: Identity and communication in cybersociety* (London: SAGE, 1997)

A. Jowitt, 'Creating Communities with Podcasting', *Computers in Libraries*, 28(4), April 2008, 54

B. Judell, 'Heath Ledger: The next James Dean?', *Culture Catch*, 5 February 2008, *http://www.culturecatch.com/film/heath_ledger_james_dean*

S. Jun and M. Ahamad, 'Incentives in BitTorrent Induce Free Riding', Proceedings of the 2005 ACM SIGCOMM Workshop on Economics of Peer-to-Peer Systems, 22 August 2005, Philadelphia, PA, *http://www.cs.sfu.ca/~fedorova/Teaching/CMPT401/Spring2008/bittorrent-free-riding.pdf*

M. Kane, 'VeriSign buys .tv web domain', *CNET News*, 7 January 2002, *http://news.cnet.com/VeriSign-buys-.tv-Web-domain/2100-1023_3-802156.html*

R. Kearney, *Strangers, Gods, and Monsters: Interpreting otherness* (London: Routledge, 2003)

M.E. Keck and K. Sikkink, *Activists beyond Borders: Advocacy networks in international politics* (Ithaca and London: Cornell University Press, 1998)

A. Kellehear, *The Unobtrusive Researcher* (Sydney: Allen and Unwin, 1993)

D. Kellner, 'Media Literacies and Critical Pedagogy in a Multicultural Society', online course materials for 253A Education, Technology and Society, UCLA, 2007, *http://www.gseis.ucla.edu/courses/ed253a/newDK/medlit.htm*

D. Kellner, 'New Technologies/New Literacies: Reconstructing education for the new millennium', *Teaching Education,* 11(3), 2000, 246

D. Kellner, 'Technological Transformation, Multiple Literacies, and the Re-visioning of Education,' *E-Learning and Digital Media,* 1(1), 2004, 9–37, *http://www.wwwords.co.uk/rss/abstract.asp?j=elea&aid=1771*

A. Khan, 'A Brief Look at In-game Advertising', *Social Times*, 26 May 2010, *http://www.socialtimes.com/2010/05/a-brief-look-at-in-game-advertising*

A. Kim, *Community Building on the Web: Secret strategies for successful online communities* (Boston: Addison-Wesley Longman Publishing Co. Inc., 2000)

D. Kirkpatrick, *The Facebook Effect* (New York: Simon & Schuster, 2010)

M. Kirkpatrick, 'Facebook's Zuckerberg Says the Age of Privacy is Over', 9 January 2010, *Read Write Web*, *http://www.readwriteweb.com/archives/facebooks_zuckerberg_says_the_age_of_privacy_is_ov.php*

B. Kirman, C. Linehan and S. Lawson, 'Exploring the Edge of Good Taste: Playful misconduct in social games', in 3rd Vienna Games Conference Future and Reality of Gaming (FROG), 25–27 September 2009, Vienna

L. Klastrup, 'Why Death Matters: Understanding gameworld experience', *Journal of Virtual Reality and Broadcasting,* 4(3), 2007

D. Kravets, '$675,000 RIAA File Sharing Verdict is "Unreasonable"', *Wired Magazine*, 5 January 2010, *http://www.wired.com/threatlevel/2010/01/riaa-verdict-is-unreasonable*

D. Kravets, 'Copyright Lawsuits Plummet in Aftermath of RIAA Campaign', *Wired Magazine*, 18 May 2010, *http://www.wired.com/threatlevel/2010/05/riaa-bump*

D. Kravets, 'Pirate Bay Retires World's Largest BitTorrent Tracker', *Wired Magazine*, 17 November 2009, *http://www.wired.com/threatlevel/2009/11/pirate-bay-shutters-tracker*

S. Lacy, *The Stories of Facebook, YouTube and MySpace* (Richmond: Crimson, 2008)

Lady Gaga, 'All is well at MEN Arena, feel free to wear your coke cans proud in hair. Security has been reprimanded for censoring Little Monster freedoms', *Twitter*, 2010, *http://www.twitter.com/ladygaga*

Lady Gaga, 'I just had to go home and suck my own hermie dick, suckka,' *Twitter*, 2009, *http://www.twitter.com/ladygaga*

Lady Gaga, 'I love you cole, just be yourself. You're perfect the way God made you', *Twitter*, 2010, *http://www.twitter.com/ladygaga*

Lady Gaga, ladygaga.net

Lady Gaga, 'Outraged ... Staff at the MEN aren't letting people into the arena with cans in their hair. So many sad Little Monsters', *Twitter*, 2010, *http://www.twitter.com/ladygaga*

LadyGagaVEVO, *YouTube*, 2011, *http://www.youtube.com/user/LadyGagaVEVO*

LadyGagaVEVO, 'Paparazzi', *YouTube*, 2009, *http://www.youtube.com/watch?v=d2smz_1L2_0*

LadyGagaVEVO, 'Pokerface', *YouTube*, 2009, *http://www.youtube.com/watch?v=bESGLojNYSo*

LadyGagaVEVO, 'Telephone', *YouTube*, 2010, *http://www.youtube.com/watch?v=EVBsypHzF3U*

J. Lanier, *You Are Not a Gadget: A manifesto* (New York: Knopf, 2010)

A. Lareau, *Unequal Childhoods: Class, race, and family life* (Berkeley: University of California Press, 2003)

R. Layton and P. Watters, 'Investigation into the Extent of Infringing Content on BitTorrent Networks', Internet Commerce Security Laboratory, University of Ballarat, April 2010, *http://www.afact.org.au/research/bt_report_final.pdf*

T. Leaver, 'FlashForward or FlashBack: Television distribution in 2010?', *Flow*, 11(5), 2010, *http://flowtv.org/2010/01/flashforward-or-flashback-television-distribution-in-2010-tama-leaver-curtin-university-of-technology*

T. Leaver, 'Watching *Battlestar Galactica* in Australia and the Tyranny of Digital Distance', *Media International Australia*, vol. 126, February 2008, 145–54, *http://www.tamaleaver.net/cv/tyranny_postprint.pdf*

Lectopia, http://www.lectopia.com.au

Lecture Capture Community, *http://www.lecturecapture.com*

'Ledger's Uncle Blames His Crimes on Grief', *News.com.au*, 5 February 2010, *http://www.news.com.au/breaking-news/ledgers-uncle-blames-his-crimes-on-grief/story-e6frfku0-1225827263474*

V. Lehdonvirta and P. Rasanen, 'How do Young People Identify with Online and Offline Peer Groups? A Comparison between UK, Spain and Japan', *Journal of Youth Studies*, 14(1), February 2011, 91–108

L. Lessig, *Remix* (London: Bloomsbury, 2008)

D.J. Leu, C.K. Kinzer, J.L. Coiro and D.W. Cammack, 'Towards a Theory of New Literacies Emerging from the Internet and Other Information and Communication Technologies', in R.B. Ruddell and N.J. Unrau (eds), *Theoretical Models and Processes of Reading* (5th edn, Newark, DE: International Reading Association, 2004) 1570

P. Levinson, 'Web of Weeds,' *Wired Magazine*, Issue 3.11, November 1995, 1, *http://www.wired.com/wired/archive/3.11/levinson.if.html*

S. Levmore and M. Nussbaum, *The Offensive Internet* (Cambridge, MA: Harvard University Press, 2010)

F. Levy, *15 Minutes of Fame: Becoming a star in the YouTube revolution* (New York: Penguin, 2008)

P.F. Li, 'Effects of Individual Difference on Choice Strategy in Goal-Directed Online Shopping', *Journal of American Academy of Business*, 15(2), 2010, 187

Library Channel, Arizona State University, *http://lib.asu.edu/librarychannel*

LibVibe, *http://libvibe.blogspot.com*

I. Liccardi et al., 'The Role of Social Networks in Students' Learning Experiences', Working Group Reports on ITiCSE (Innovation and Technology in Computer Science Education), 2007, *http://eprints.ecs.soton.ac.uk/14907/2/ITiCSE2007_WG4.pdf*

J.C.R. Licklider and R.W. Taylor, 'The Computer as a Communications Device', *Science and Technology*, April 1968, 38, *http://citeseerx.ist.psu.edu/viewdoc/download?doi=10.1.1.34.4812&rep=rep1&type=pdf*

Y. Lieberman and S. Stashevsky, 'Determinants of Online Shopping: Examination of an early-stage online market', *Canadian Journal of Administrative Sciences*, 26(4), 2009, 316

Lisadore, *https://www.lisadore.com*

S. Livingstone, E. Van Couvering and N. Thumin, 'Adult Media Literacy: A review of the research literature on behalf of Ofcom', Media@LSE, *http://stakeholders.ofcom.org.uk/binaries/research/media-literacy/aml.pdf*

T. Locher, P. Moor, S. Schmid and R. Wattenhofer, 'Free Riding in BitTorrent is Cheap', Proceedings of HotNets-V, Irvine, CA, November 2006

S. Long, 'Longshots', *Library Beat*, *http://www.librarybeat.org/longshots*

G. Lorenzo, D. Oblinger and C. Dziuban, 'How Choice, Co-creation, and Culture are Changing What it Means to be Net Savvy', ELI Paper 4, October 2006

G. Lovink, *Zero Comments: Blogging and critical internet culture* (London, New York: Routledge, 2008)

LSE Library Tour, *http://itunes.apple.com/gb/podcast/lse-library-tour/id278972091*

Z. Lukasiak, *Online Conflict in the Light of Mimetic Theory*, 2009, *http://blog.p2pfoundation.net/online-conflict-in-the-light-of-mimetic-theory/2009/11/25*

M. Lynch, *Voices of the New Arab Public: Iraq, Al-Jazeera and Middle East politics today* (New York, Columbia University Press, 2006)

R. Lynn, 'Virtual Rape is Traumatic, but is it a Crime?', *Wired*, 5 April 2007, *http://www.wired.com/culture/lifestyle/commentary/sexdrive/2007/05/sexdrive_0504*

S. Mack and M. Ratcliffe, *Podcasting Bible* (Indianapolis: Wiley, 2007)

D. MacKenzie and J. Wajcman (eds), *The Social Shaping of Technology* (London: Open University Press, 1985)

D. Macsai, 'Haiti Earthquake Disaster: Google Earth, online-map "absolutely crucial"', *Fast Company*, 14 January 2010, *http://www.fastcompany.com/blog/dan-macsai/popwise/haiti-earthquake-google-maps-Web-tech*

M. Madden, 'Podcast Downloading', 22 November 2006, *http://www.pewinternet.org/~/media//Files/Reports/2006/PIP_Podcasting_Nov06_Memo.pdf*

M. Madden and S. Jones, 'Podcast Downloading', 2008, *http://www.pewinternet.org/Reports/2008/Podcast-Downloading-2008/Data-Memo/Findings.aspx*

M. Maguire, 'East Timor's .tp', in E.S. Wass (ed.), *Addressing the World: National identity and country code domain names* (Latham, MD: Rowman and Littlefield, 2003) 17–30

P. Manils, A. Chaabane, S. Le Blond, M. Ali Kaafar, C. Castelluccia, A. Legout and W. Dabbous, 'Compromising Tor Anonymity Exploiting P2P Information Leakage', INRIA France, 12 April 2010, *http://hal.inria.fr/docs/00/47/15/56/PDF/TorBT.pdf*

A. Maslow, 'A Theory of Human Motivation', *Psychological Review*, No. 50, 1943, 370–96

M. Masnick, '"Streisand Effect" Snags Effort to Hide Documents, All Things Considered', NPR Podcast, 2008, *http://www.npr.org/templates/story/story.php?storyId=87809195*

R. Mason and F. Rennie, *Elearning: The key concepts* (New York: Routledge, 2006)

J. Maxymuk, 'Online Communities', *The Bottom Line: Managing Library Finances*, 20(1), 2007, 55

L. Maynard, '#Haiti, by way of Twitter', *Capture the Conversation*, 13 January 2010, *http://www.capturetheconversation.com/social-community/haiti-by-way-of-twitter*

B. McCarty, 'Alexa: YouTube surpasses Yahoo! as the Internet's 3rd Most Visited Site', *TNW Social Media*, 23 August 2010, *http://thenextweb.com/socialmedia/2010/08/23/alexa-shows-youtube-claiming-3-most-popular-site-over-yahoo-are-browsing-habits-changing*

A. McClard and K. Anderson, 'Focus on Facebook: Who are we anyway?', *Anthropology News*, 2008, 10, *http://www.aaanet.org/issues/anthronews/upload/49-3-McClard-and-Anderson-In-Focus.pdf*

D. McMillan and D. Chavis, 'Sense of Community: A definition and theory', *Journal of Community Psychology*, 14, 1986

Middlesex University, 'Library Subject Guides', *http://libguides.mdx.ac.uk*

Mideast Youth, 'What We're All About', 2010, *http://www.mideastyouth.com/about-us*

P. Miltenoff, J. Flanders and J. Hill, 'Podcasting for School Media Specialists: A case study from Central Minnesota', TCC 2008 Proceedings, *http://etec.hawaii.edu/proceedings/2008/Miltenoff2008.pdf*

D. Mitchell and S. Snyder, *Narrative Prosthesis: Disability and the dependencies of discourse* (Ann Arbor: University of Michigan Press, 2000)

'Mixcraft 5 Tutorials – Mixcraft 5 Windows Part 1: Launching Mixcraft and Arrangement Window', *YouTube*, *http://www.youtube.com/watch?v=CCr5WFGDQNg*

T. Mole. 'Hypertrophic Celebrity', *Media Culture*, 7(5), 2004, *http://journal.media-culture.org.au/0411/08-mole.php*

M. Moore, *Stupid White Men* (Camberwell: Penguin, 2002: 2001)

A. Moses, 'Heath Ledger's Death Triggers Net Meltdown', *Sydney Morning Herald*, 24 January 2008, *http://www.smh.com.au/news/web/net-meltdown/2008/01/24/1201025052926.html*

J. Moult, 'Woman Sacked on Facebook for Complaining about her Boss after Forgetting She Added Him as a Friend', *Daily News Online*, 14 August 2009, *http://www.dailymail.co.uk/news/article-1206491/Woman-sacked-Facebook-boss-insult-forgetting-added-friend.html*

N. Mount and C. Chambers, 'Podcasts and Practicals', in G. Salmon and P. Edirisingha (eds), *Podcasting for Learning in Universities* (Maidenhead: Open University Press, 2008) 45

M. Mowbray, *Virtual Ethnicities*, 2002, *http://www.hpl.hp.com/techreports/2002/HPL-2002-217.pdf*

L. Murray, 'Libraries "like to move it, move it"', *Reference Services Review*, 38(2), 2010, 233–49

Music News, 'Lady Gaga Helps Download Sales in UK Rise more than 50pc', *The Telegraph*, 2010, *http://www.telegraph.co.uk/culture/music/music-news/7634463/Lady-Gaga-helps-download-sales-in-UK-rise-more-than-50pc.html*

L. Nakamura, *Cybertypes: Race, ethnicity, and identity on the internet* (London: Routledge, 2002)

L. Nakamura, 'Race In/For Cyberspace: Identity tourism and racial passing on the internet', in D. Bell and B. Kennedy (eds), *Cybercultures Reader* (London: Routledge, 2000)

J. Nancy, *Listening* (New York: Fordham University Press, 2007)

National Campaign to Prevent Teen and Unplanned Pregnancy, 'Case Study: Sexinfo: A sexual health text messaging service', *http://www.thenationalcampaign.org/resources/monster/MM_CaseStudy SEXINFO.pdf*

National Center for Accessible Media (NCAM), *http://ncam.wgbh.org*

L. Negrin, 'The Meaning of Dress', *Arena Journal*, No. 7, 1996, 132–33

N. Negroponte, *Being Digital* (New York: Knopf, 1995)

Network, 'I'm as Mad as Hell', *YouTube*, *http://www.youtube.com/watch?v=dib2-HBsF08*

'New Uses for Mobile Phones Could Launch Another Wave of Development', *The Economist*, 24 September 2009

C. Newell, 'From Others to Us and Human Rights Education', in C. Newell and B. Offord (eds), *Activating Human Rights in Education: Exploration, innovation and transformation* (Deakin West: Australian College of Educators, 2008) 77–86

'Noam Chomsky – Noam vs. Michel Foucault' (Eng. subs), *YouTube*, *http://www.youtube.com/watch?v=kawGakdNoT0*

C. Nuttall, 'Virtual Country "nuked" on Net', *BBC News*, 26 January 1999, *http://news.bbc.co.uk/2/hi/science/nature/263169.stm*

Office of Technology for Education & Eberly Center for Teaching Excellence, 'Podcasting: A teaching with technology white paper', Carnegie Mellon University, 2007, *http://connect.educause.edu/files/CMU_Podcasting_Jun07.pdf*

P. O'Keefe, 'Has Anyone Called You Hitler, Stalin or Gestapo? (or How I Know I'm Doing My Job)', *ManagingCommunities.com*, 5 August 2008,*http://www.managingcommunities.com/2008/08/05/has-anyone-called-you-hitler-stalin-or-gestapo-or-how-i-know-im-doing-my-job*

P. O'Keefe, 'Creepy Banned User Guy (or Girl) is a Part of the Community Administrator's Life', *ManagingCommunities.com*, 29 March 2009, *http://www.managingcommunities.com/2009/03/29/creepy-banned-user-guy-or-girl-is-a-part-of-the-community-administrators-life*

M. Oliver, *Understanding Disability: From theory to practice* (New York: St Martin's Press, 1996)

B. O'Neil, 'Media Education in Ireland: An overview', *Irish Communications Review*, vol. 8, 2000, 57–64

OpenArabNet, 'About Us', The Initiative for an Open Arab Internet, *http://openarab.net/en/?page_id=2* (retrieved 5 October 2010)

OpenNetInitiative, 'Policing Content in the Quasi-Public Sphere', *http://opennet.net/sites/opennet.net/files/PolicingContent.pdf*

Q4Music.com, 'Lady Gaga for Q', *Q Magazine*, 2010, *http://covers.q4music.com/Item.aspx?pageNo=6150&year=2010*

V. Paech, 'A Method for the Times: A meditation on virtual ethnography faults and fortitudes', *Nebula*, No. 6.4, December 2009

V. Paech, 'Dark Matters: The inevitability of the online community exile', Dissertation, University of Brighton, 2010

C. Paglia, 'Lady Gaga and the Death of Sex', *The Sunday Times*, 2010, *http://www.thesundaytimes.co.uk/sto/public/magazine/article389697.ece*

Paris Convention for the Protection of Industrial Property, 20 March 1883, *http://www.wipo.int/treaties/en/ip/paris/trtdocs_wo020.html*

M. Park and S.J. Lennon, 'Brand Name and Promotion in Online Shopping Contexts', *Journal of Fashion Marketing and Management*, 13(2), 2009, 149

B.C. Parks and R.J. Timmons, 'Globalization, Vulnerability to Climate Change and Perceived Injustice', *Society and Natural Resources*, 19(4), April 2006, 337–55

C. Partridge, 'Needy Ugandans Develop the Mobile-phone ATM', *The Sunday Times*, 24 October 2006

S. Patarin and D. Hales, 'How to Cheat BitTorrent and Why Nobody Does', University of Bologna, Department of Computer Science, May

2005, Technical Report UBLCS-2005-12, *http://cfpm.org/~david/papers/19-eccs06.pdf*

A. Peneberg, *Viral Loop: The power of pass-it-on* (London: Hodder & Stoughton, 2009)

M. Pesce, 'Mark Pesce interviewed by Gordy Slack', Center for Theology and the Natural Sciences, 28 October 1997, *http://hyperreal.org/~mpesce/ctnsinterview.html*

M. Pesce, 'Piracy is Good? How Battlestar Galactica Killed Broadcast TV', *Mindjack*, 13 May 2005, *http://www.mindjack.com/feature/piracy051305.html*

A. Petersen, 'Celebrity Juice, not from Concentrate: Perez Hilton, gossip blogs, and the new star production', *Jump Cut*, No. 49, Spring 2007, *http://www.ejumpcut.org/archive/jc49.2007/PerezHilton/index.html*

Pirate Bay, The, *http://thepiratebay.org/legal*

Plunkett Research, 'Automobile Industry Introduction', *http://www.plunkettresearch.com/Industries/AutomobilesTrucks/AutomobileTrends/tabid/89/Default.aspx*

Podcasting Legal Guide, *http://wiki.creativecommons.org/Podcasting_Legal_Guide*

Podscope, *http://www.podscope.com*

K. Pollitt, *Reasonable Creatures* (London: Vintage, 1995)

R. Poole, 'Nationalism: The last rights?', *Arena Journal*, No. 4, 1994–95, 54

N. Poor, 'Mechanisms of an Online Public Sphere: The website slashdot', *Journal of Computer-Mediated Communication*, 10(2), 2005, *http://jcmc.indiana.edu/vol10/issue2/poor.html* (retrieved 15 April 2010)

T. Pratt, K. Holtfreter and M.D. Reisig, 'Routine Online Activity and Internet Fraud Targeting: Extending the generality of routine activity theory', *Journal of Research in Crime and Delinquency*, 47(3), 2010, 267–96

M. Prensky, 'Digital Natives, Digital Immigrants', *On the Horizon*, 9(5), 2001, 1–2, *http://www.marcprensky.com/writing/Prensky%20-%20Digital%20Natives,%20Digital%20Immigrants%20-%20Part1.pdf*

E. Probyn, *Outside Belongings* (New York: Routledge, 1996)

M. Puente. 'Dying Young is No Guarantee of Icon Status in the Internet Age', *USA Today*, 30 January 2008, *http://www.usatoday.com/life/people/2008-01-29-iconic-by-death_N.htm*

Python Software Foundation, Python Glossary (last updated March 2011), *http://docs.python.org/glossary.html*

J. Ralph and S. Olsen, 'Podcasting as an Educational Building Block in Academic Libraries', *Australian Academic & Research Libraries*, 38(4), December 2007

Rape Crisis England and Wales, 'Definition of Rape', *http://rapecrisis.org.uk/Definitionofrape2.php*

E. Raymond, 'Homesteading the Noosphere', April 1998, *The Cathedral and the Baazar*, *http://www.catb.org/~esr/writings/cathedral-bazaar/homesteading*

B. Read, 'Lectures on the Go', *Chronicle of Higher Education*, 52(10), 2005, *http://chronicle.com/weekly/v52/i10/10a03901.htm*

H. Rheingold, *Smart Mobs: The next social revolution* (Cambridge, MA: Perseus Books, 2002) / (New York: Basic Books, 2002)

H. Rheingold, *The Virtual Community: Homesteading on the electronic frontier* (Reading: MIT Press, 1993)

H. Rheingold, *The Virtual Community: Homesteading on the electronic frontier* (Cambridge, MA: MIT Press, 2000)

H. Rheingold, *The Virtual Community: Homesteading on the electronic frontier* (Reading, MA: Addison-Wesley, 2010), *http://www.rheingold.com/vc/book*

B. Rigby, *Mobilizing Generation 2.0: A practical guide to using web 2.0* (San Francisco: Jossey-Bass, 2008)

M. Rimmer, 'Virtual Countries: Internet domain names and geographical terms', *Media International Australia Incorporating Culture and Policy.* No. 106, February 2003

M. Ripeanu, M. Mowbray, N. Andrade and A. Lima, 'Gifting Technologies: A BitTorrent case study', *First Monday*, 11(11), November 2006, *http://firstmonday.org/htbin/cgiwrap/bin/ojs/index.php/fm/article/view/1412/1330*

R. Roberts, 'Podcasting for Information Literacy', World Library and Information Congress, 19–23 August 2007, Durban, South Africa

F. Rose, *West of Eden: The end of innocence at Apple Computer* (London: Arrow Books, 1989)

T. Roszak, *The Cult of Information: The folklore of computers and the true art of thinking* (New York: Pantheon Books 1986)

RSF (Reporters without Borders), 'Blogger Abdul-Moneim Mahmud Freed, but Kareem Amer Still Held', 4 June 2007, *http://en.rsf.org/egypt-blogger-abdul-moneim-mahmud-freed-04-06-2007,21995.html* (retrieved 25 October 2010)

RSF, 'Detained Human Rights Activists Allege Mistreatment at Opening of Trial', Reporters without Borders Middle East and North Africa Update, 2 November 2010, *http://en.rsf.org/bahrain-detained-human-rights-activists-02-11-2010,38730.html* (retrieved 5 November 2010)

B. Rule, 'Gemma Ward Opens up about her Life with Heath Ledger', *Sydney Herald Sun*, 30 January 2011, *http://www.news.com.au/entertainment/movies/gemma-ward-opens-up-about-her-life-with-heath-ledger/story-e6frfmvr-1225996813206#ixzz1DVnxAWcZ*

D. Rushkoff, 'Americaphobia and the Engineered Fear of Progress', paper presented at the Conference on the Internet and Society, Harvard University, 28–31 May 1996

D. Rushkoff, *Media Virus!* (New York: Ballantine Books, 1996)

S.1948, Intellectual Property and Communications Omnibus Reform Act of 1999 (Introduced in the Senate), enacted as P.L. 106-113, 19 November 1999, *http://thomas.loc.gov/cgi-bin/query/z?c106:S.1948*

E. Said, *Culture and Imperialism* (London: Chatto & Windus, 1993)

E. Said, *Orientalism* (London: Vintage Books, 1978)

N. Sakr, *Satellite Realms: Transnational television, globalization and the Middle East* (London: I.B. Tauris & Co Ltd, 2002)

G. Salmon and M. Nie, 'Doubling the Life of iPods', in G. Salmon and P. Edirisingha (eds), *Podcasting for Learning in Universities* (Maidenhead: Open University Press, 2008) 10

G. Sandoval, 'Nine Inch Nails Releases Internet Album', *CNet.com*, 3 March 2008, *http://news.cnet.com/8301-10784_3-9884180-7.html* (accessed 19 October 2010)

San Francisco Department of Public Health, *http://www.SexInfoSF.org*

S.B. Sarason, *The Psychological Sense of Community: Prospects for a community psychology* (San Francisco: Jossey-Bass, 1974)

J. Sartre, *Being and Nothingness*, H. Barnes (trans) (London: Routledge, 1943: 1996)

S. Sawyer, *Career Building through Podcasting* (New York: Rosen Publishing Group, 2008)

S. Schroeder, 'Facebook 2009 Revenue was almost $800 Million', *Mashable Business*, 18 June 2010, *http://mashable.com/2010/06/18/facebook-800-million*

B. Scruggs, 'Should Fashion Design be Copyrightable?', *Northwestern Journal of Technology and Intellectual Property*, 6(1), 2007, 129

Seattle Public Library, Events, *http://itunes.apple.com/gb/podcast/the-seattle-public-library/id191495727*

Seattle Public Library, Teens Podcast, *http://itunes.apple.com/gb/podcast/teens-podcast-from-the-seattle/id267257330*

L. Sessions, 'You Looked Better on MySpace: Deception and identity on web 2.0', *First Monday*, 14(7) (2009), *http://firstmonday.org/htbin/cgiwrap/bin/ojs/index.php/fm/article/view/2539/2242*

L. Setrakian, 'The Arab Digital Vanguard: Cyber activists reshaping the Middle East, *ABC News*, 22 September 2010, *http://blogs.abcnews.com/mideastmemo/2010/09/the-arab-digital-vanguard-cyber-activists-remaking-the-middle-east-billion-dollar-bullets-why-americ.html*

T. Shakespeare, 'Art and Lies? Representations of Disability on Film', in M. Corker and S. French (eds), *Disability Discourse* (Buckingham: Open University Press, 1999) 64–172

N. Shastry and D. Gillespie, *Podcasting for Trainers and Educators* (Boston: Pearson Education, 2008)

L. Siegel, *Against the Machine: Being human in the age of the electronic mob* (New York: Random House, 2008)

'Small and Large Acts of Resistance – Ann Sparanese', *Library Journal*, 15 March 2003, *http://www.libraryjournal.com/article/CA281662.html*

Sony, *http://www.sony.co.uk/product/cam-high-definition-on-memory-stick/nexvg10ebdi.yg*

'SouthAfrica.com Petition Launched', *Demys News Service*, 28 May 2003, *http://www.demys.net/news/2003/05/28_za.htm*

R. Spiegel, 'Facebook and Skype Link Arms against Google', *E-Commerce Times*, 29 September 2010, *http://www.ecommercetimes.com/rsstory/70929.html*

C. Springer, *James Dean Transfigured* (Texas: University of Texas Press, 2007)

A. Sreberny-Mohammadi and A. Mohammadi, *Small Media, Big Revolution: Communication, culture, and the Iranian Revolution* (University of Minnesota Press, 1994)

J. Staiger and S. Hake, *Convergence Media Culture* (New York: Routledge, 2009)

N. Stanage, 'Emigration: The next generation', *The Irish Times,* 8 January 2011

R. St Clair, 'Niue's .nu: Providing a free internet to an isolated nation', in E.S. Wass (ed.), *Addressing the World: National Identity and*

Country Code Domain Names, (Latham, MD: Rowman and Littlefield, 2003) 77–86

P.E. Steinberg and S.D. McDowell, 'Mutiny on the Bandwidth: The semiotics of statehood in the internet domain name registries of Pitcairn and Niue', *New Media & Society*, 5(1), March 2003

M.L. Stewart, 'Copying and Copyrighting Haute Couture: Democratizing fashion, 1900–1930s', *French Historical Studies*, 28(1), 2005, 103

A. Stone, *The War of Desire and Technology at the Close of the Mechanical Age* (Cambridge, MA: MIT Press, 1996)

S. Strauss, 'Twitter Co-founders Offer 5 Tips for Entrepreneurs,' *Tech Cocktail, http://techcocktail.com/twitter-co-founders-offer-5-tips-for-entrepreneurs-2010-10*

J. Suler, 'The Bad Boys of Cyberspace: Deviant behavior in online multimedia communities and strategies for managing it', in *The Psychology of Cyberspace* (1997), *http://www-usr.rider.edu/~suler/psycyber/badboys.html*

J. Suler, 'The Online Disinhibition Effect', *CyberPsychology and Behavior*, 7, 2004, 321–26

P. Szendy, *Listen: A history of our ears* (New York: Fordham University Press, 2008)

M. Sznajder and L. Roniger, *The Politics of Exile in Latin America* (Cambridge: Cambridge University Press, 2009)

S. Taggart 'Irish Eyes Smile on Dot-TP', *Wired Magazine*, 8 March 2002, *http://www.wired.com/politics/law/news/2002/03/50659*

'The Daily Show featuring Jon Stewart', *Comedy Central*, 12 January 2011

'The Right to Southafrica.com', *Sedo.com*, 13 March 2001, *http://www.sedo.com/links/showhtml.php3?Id=140&language=us*

'The University of Auckland Commercial – Dr Elana Curtis', *YouTube*, *http://www.youtube.com/watch?v=ajosnJqsQMs*

A. Thomas, *Youth Online: Identity and literacy in the digital age* (New York: Peter Lang, 2007)

A. Thomas-Jones, 'eBay: Marketing the real body in the virtual world', in T. Brabazon, (ed.), *The Revolution will not be Downloaded: Dissent in the digital age* (Oxford: Chandos, 2008) 169

C. Thompson, 'The BitTorrent Effect', *Wired Magazine*, issue 13.01, January 2005, *http://www.wired.com/wired/archive/13.01/bittorrent.html*

M. Torres, *In the Land of Mirrors: Cuban exile politics in the United States* (Ann Arbor: University of Michigan Press, 1999)

S. Turkle, *Alone Together: Why we expect more from technology and less from each other* (New York: Basic Books, 2011)

S. Turkle, *Life on the Screen: Identity in the age of the internet* (New York: Simon & Schuster, 1995)

G. Turner, *Ordinary People and the Media: The demotic turn* (Thousand Oaks: Sage, 2009)

Tuvalu Telephone Directory, *http://www.tuvaluislands.com/telecom/telecom-index.htm*

UFList, FAQ, *UFlist.org*, 2001, *http://uflist.org/why/#q47*

United Nations Conference on Trade and Development (UNCTAD), 'Information Economy Report 2010: ICTs, Enterprises and Poverty Alleviation', 2010, *http://www.unctad.org/en/docs/ier2010_embargo2010_en.pdf*

'University of Hull @ Scarborough Student Animation', *YouTube*, *http://www.youtube.com/watch?v=F1lnqqDVNKI&feature=PlayList&p=D61587798BB1F95D&index=5*

C. Urquhart, 'Why Torture is Routine in Egypt', *The Toronto Star*, 4 March 2007, *http://www.thestar.com/news/article/188036*

J. Urry, 'The System of "Automobility"' *Theory, Culture and Society,* 21(4/5), 2004, 25–39

'US Court Declines Jurisdiction over Southafrica.com Dispute', *ICANN Watch*, 25 June 2001, *http://www.icannwatch.org/article.pl?sid=01/06/25/092829&mode=thread*

E. Van Buskirk, '"Torrent Tweets" Marries BitTorrent to Twitter', *Wired Magazine*, 6 August 2010, *http://www.wired.com/epicenter/2010/08/bit-torrent-and-twitter*

K. Verlanger, 'Disability and Participatory Culture', *Beyond Broadcast: Mapping Public Media*, 9 February 2008, *http://www.beyondbroadcast.net/blog/?p=124*

T. Walker, 'Welcome to FarmVille: Population 80 million', *The Independent,* 22 February 2010, *http://www.independent.co.uk/life-style/gadgets-and-tech/features/welcome-to-farmville-population-80-million-1906260.html*

'WA Museum to Honour Heath Ledger', *ABC News*, 25 January 2011, *http://www.abc.net.au/news/stories/2011/01/25/3121011.htm*

E.S. Wass, 'Conclusion: Only time will tell', in E.S. Wass (ed.), *Addressing the World: National identity and country code domain names* (Latham, MD: Rowman and Littlefield, 2003) 147–50

R. Watling, 'Practical Media Work and the Curriculum of the Future', *The Curriculum Journal,* 12(2), July 2001, 207–24

'Web 2.0 Driving Addictive Celebrity Worship Disorder', *The Age*, 25 February 2009, *http://www.theage.com.au/world/web-20-driving-addictive-celebrity-worship-disorder-20090224-8gpc.html?page=3*

WebBoar, 'Alarabiya.net', *WebBoar Website Analysis*, *http://www.webboar.com/www/alarabiya.net*

F. Webster, *Theories of the Information Society* (London: Routledge, 2006)

D. Weinberger, *Everything is Miscellaneous* (New York: Henry Holt & Co, 2007)

S. Weinberger, 'US Government Monitoring Social Networking Sites', *AOL News Online*, 15 October 2010, *http://www.aolnews.com/nation/article/homeland-security-monitoring-social-networking-sites/19675854*

D. Weinstein, 'Celebrity as Simulacrum', *CTheory*, 28 June 1994, *http://www.ctheory.net/articles.aspx?id=244#text%201*

T. Wesley-Smith, 'Net Gains? Pacific Studies in Cyberspace', *The Contemporary Pacific*, 15(1), Spring 2003, *http://muse.jhu.edu/journals/contemporary_pacific/v015/15.1wesley-smith.html*

B. Wheeler, 'Serial Streakers, Uncovered', *Globe and Mail*, 4 July 2009, *http://artoftheprank.com/2009/07/04/jump-the-worlds-greatest-streakers*

C. White, 'Michelle Williams will not take Daughter Matilda to see Heath Ledger's Family this Christmas', 22 December 2010, *Perth Now*, *http://www.perthnow.com.au/entertainment/michelle-williams-will-not-take-daughter-matilda-to-see-heath-ledgers-family-this-christmas/story-e6frg30c-1225974830404*

R. White, 'Special Feature on Brokeback Mountain: Introduction', *Film Quarterly*, 60(3), Spring 2007, 20

S. Whitford, 'SA Negotiates for Southafrica.com', *IT Web: The Technology News Site*, 6 May 2003, *http://www.itweb.co.za/sections/internet/2003/0305061036.asp?O=S&cirestriction=southafrica.com*

D. Whitney, 'Search Engines Lead Way to Video', *Television Week*, 27(2), 2008, 14.

M. Williams, 'Virtually Criminal: Discourse, deviance and anxiety within virtual communities', *International Review of Law, Computers & Technology*, 14(1), 2000, 95–104

R. Williams, *The Long Revolution* (London: Penguin 1965)

S. Williams, 'New Tools for Online Information Literacy Instruction', *The Reference Librarian*, 51(2), April 2010, 148–62

World Fact Book, Central Intelligence Agency, 2011, *https://www.cia.gov/library/publications/the-world-factbook/geos/tv.html*

World Intellectual Property Organization, 'The Recognition of Rights and the Use of Names in the Internet Domain Name System: Report of the Second WIPO Internet Domain Name Process' 3 September 2001, *http://www.wipo.int/amc/en/processes/process2/report/html/report.html*

T. Wu, *The Master Switch: The rise and fall of information empires* (New York: Alfred A. Knopf, 2010)

N. Yee and J.N. Bailenson, 'The Proteus Effect: The effect of transformed self-representation on behavior', *Human Communication Research*, No.33, 2007, 271–90

R.J.C. Young, *Postcolonialism: An historical introduction* (Oxford: Blackwell, 2001)

M. Zajicek, 'Web 2.0: Hype or Happiness?', Keynote presented at the 16th International World Wide Web Conference: Banff, Canada, 7–8 May 2007, *http://www.w4a.info/2007/prog/k2-zajicek.pdf*

M. Zeidman, 'Anne Hathaway Discusses Oscars, Heath Ledger and Life', *Hollywood Today*, 22 February 2009, *http://www.hollywoodtoday.net/2009/02/22/anne-hathaway-discusses-oscars-heath-ledger-and-life*

C. Zhang, P. Dhungel, D. Wu, Z. Liu and K.W. Ross, 'BitTorrent Darknets', Proceedings of IEEE Conference on Computer Communications (INFOCOM'10) San Diego, CA, March 2010

'Zizek Receives a Phonecall From God', *YouTube*, *http://www.youtube.com/watch?v=sKvcN9CVFec&feature=related*

M. Zuckerberg, '500 Million Stories', *Facebook*, 21 July 2010, *http://blog.facebook.com/blog.php?post=409753352130*

Index

Zeitfracht Medien GmbH
Ferdinand-Jühlke-Straße 7
99095 Erfurt, Deutschland
produktsicherheit@kolibri360.de